FINAL MEMORIES
of
an Old Country Priest

Volume III

D1452880

Memories of
an Old Country Priest

FINAL MEMORIES
of
an Old Country Priest

Volume III

Monsignor
Francis J. Weber

Saint Francis Historical Society
Mission Hills, California
Anno Domini MMXVIII
Second Printing 2022

Table of Contents

Chapter 6
Funeral Homilies

Chapter 7
Selected Memorials

Chapter 8

Chapter 9
Miniature Books
(Written, Edited and/or Published)

Chapter 10

Miscellaneous Articles from the Past

Chapter 11

Obiter Dicta

Chapter 12

Chapter 13

❧ ❧

APPENDIX I

❧ ❧

APPENDIX II

❧ ❧

APPENDIX III

❧ ❧

APPENDIX IV

❧ ❧

APPENDIX V

❧ ❧

APPENDIX VI

Preface

I had an elderly grand uncle who composed his own distinctive vocabulary. He might have begun this book in very colorful language, maybe something like this: "Who would have thunk that little Frankie Weber from Valley Mills, Indiana, would live long enough to justify a three-volume autobiography? But he did and here it is."

The Webers are not long-lived. I have now lasted longer here on planet Earth than any other members of the family, at least for the previous five generations. However, faced by statistics and mindful that "the clock of life is wound but once," I feel confident that this installment of memories will be the last.

Looking back through the tomes of American ecclesial history, I see no sacerdotal diaries or memoirs stretching beyond a single volume. Not even the prolific Father Andrew Greeley surpassed that accomplishment.

Two chapters are devoted to homilies and several miscellaneous articles that appeared in hard-to-locate journals from the past.

Maybe it's true, as some have observed, that "the old country priest never had a single unpublished thought." But that's not the worst thing ever said about this writer. Perhaps I should just pleaded guilty and move on!

For the moment I have omitted a contemplated chapter on the current Archbishop of Los Angeles. And that's fair enough given my present status as "retired." Anyway, he rarely answers letters which is a radical departure from his predecessors. But all in all, I find him a very pleasant man who has treated this old country priest with utmost kindness.

Also omitted in this last of my trinity of memories is a chapter of questions and answers. Increasingly, I have noticed that people care less and less what I say or write and more and more on what I do or don't do. And that makes good sense to me. So I will leave the Q and A this time to Abby and her cohorts. (Did I ever mention that Louella Parsons was a parishioner when I was stationed in West Hollywood?)

Finally for those who wonder how this volume will be accepted by my counterparts in the historical field, don't bother looking. My instincts tell me not to send this book to reviewers.

To my readers and/or friends, may we all meet in paradise where we will be able to communicate in better ways! By then what earthly differences will it all make?

Msgr. Francis J. Weber

a.k.a.

The Old Country Priest

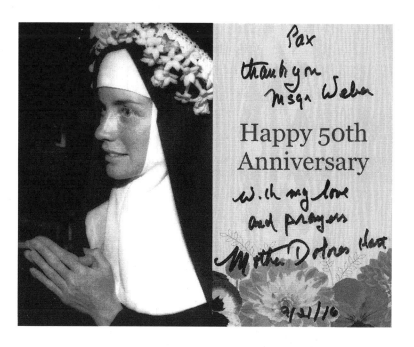

1

San Fernando Mission Chronicle **(2010 Onwards)**

Since early in 1981, we have sent out monthly letters to those who attend Sunday Mass at the seventeenth of the California missions. Enclosed in each letter is a "pinkie" or envelope marked "Restoration Fund."

In this chapter we have selected excerpts from those monthly letters, which highlighted the various activities, projects, alterations or additions to the Old Mission.

* * * * * *

On May 30, 2009, the United States Postal Service issued a 44¢ commemorative stamp to honor Bob Hope, who is buried here in the cemetery of San Fernando Mission. The postage stamp was unveiled and released on the retired aircraft carrier *Midway*. On hand were his children, Linda and Kelly. Interestingly, on the previous Wednesday, Dolores Hope celebrated her hundredth birthday in the Chapel of Our Lady in Saint Charles Borromeo Church in North Hollywood. It was my privilege to present her with a giant birthday card that many of the good people here at the Old Mission signed.

Bob's humungous collection of jokes and related materials was given some years ago to the Library of Congress. Happily the officials there have opened it to researchers. It's amazing how many people come to the Old Mission to visit the Bob Hope Memorial Garden. Interestingly, only people over twenty-three years of age remember Bob – but that number is legionary at present. This is just one of the many reasons why San Fernando is the most interesting and relevant in the chain of missionary foundations established along California's *El Camino Real*.

In mid-September 2011, we buried Dolores next to her late husband in the Hope Memorial Garden. As you know, Mrs. Hope was a good friend of the Old Mission. You will recall she graciously provided the ramp that makes it possible to access the church from the walkway.

In Loving Memory of

Dolores DeFina Hope

May 27, 1909 - September 19, 2011

PRAYER OF ST. FRANCIS OF ASSISI

Lord, make me an instrument of your peace.
Where there is hatred, let me sow love.
Where there is injury, pardon.
Where there is doubt, faith.
Where there is despair, hope.
Where there is darkness, light.
Where there is sadness, joy.

O Divine Master,
grant that I may not so much seek
to be consoled, as to console;
to be understood, as to understand;
to be loved, as to love.
For it is in giving that we receive.
It is in pardoning that we are pardoned,
and it is in dying that we are born to Eternal Life.

Amen.

In any event, please pray for her and, when you get a chance, take a glimpse at the exhibit we have on the Hopes in the building adjacent to the church. We now have a new and expanded exhibit on the Hopes. Dr. Richard Doyle has given us a number of pertinent items, which recall the great humanitarian; Linda Hope has also provided funds for the new cabinetry.

One of our Plant Maps was recently damaged and had to be replaced. You may recall that Bill Hannon erected those signs about twenty years ago. Happily it is now up and "running" again.

* * * * * *

In mid-2010, Archbishop José Gomez came to dedicate the new mausoleum in our adjoining cemetery. You must drive over to see it – a really attractive addition to the *campo santo*. And there are some condos left if you like the view.

* * * * * *

On Wednesday March 14, 2012, we celebrated a funeral Mass for our beloved **Peter Buffo** here at the Old Mission. Over seventy people gathered to pay their final tribute to "Little Peter" who served daily Mass here for over fifty years.

Peter's sister Mary, daughter Brandy and a host of well-wishers joined *Las Damas Archivistas* and representatives from SAV-ON to honor this good and faithful client of San Fernando Mission.

Among other things, we recalled Peter's service in the Air Force where he fought for his country in the Vietnam War. Peter was stationed on a fuel tanker where he participated in fueling airborne fighter planes.

On Sundays Peter was here to open the Church and Museum. He became somewhat of a legend and was always in demand for leading tours. He now watches over the mission from his place of honor in the cemetery, the only person interred there in the last century.

* * * * * *

Someone asked whether dogs have a place in heaven. Theologians haven't expanded on that topic as yet. However, if heaven is a place of total happiness, how could dogs be excluded?

Late in November 2006, Brewster, my Sheltie sheepdog, died after a long illness. I have often been asked why so many shelties have shared my life. Well, here's the official story. The Shetland Islands, which lie north of Scotland and east of Norway, are home to the Shetland Sheepdog. Due to the poor condition of the land, all the livestock there is small. An example is the Shetland Pony. The islanders began to breed small agile dogs, called "loonies," to keep livestock out of their precious crops.

Around 1890, British dog fanciers noted that loonies were becoming rare and decided to preserve these dogs. Today Shetland Sheepdogs range in size from thirteen to twenty inches at the shoulder. Although the American Kennel Club standards only allow thirteen- to sixteen-inch-high dogs to be entered in shows, many quality dogs are larger than this. Shelties are found in many colors, including Sable, Black, Blue

Merle and Tricolor. Although they have thick coats, Shelties do not do well left out in the weather for extended periods.

They make affectionate and intelligent pets and are good with children. There are two challenges to living with a Sheltie. The first is that the dogs need a lot of grooming, at least one brushing weekly and daily brushing during the shedding season. Second, they are notorious barkers.

People often ask me about "Michael, the Archangel" the little dog who helped guard and otherwise protect the Old Mission for so many years. Michael was among that small but select cadre of Shetland Sheepdogs that have watched over the California missions since 1769. According to such early commentaries as Richard Henry Dana, Michael's ancestors were imported to the Pacific Slope by the Spaniards and traders.

Canines served a very important role in early California. Especially was that true of sheepdogs because there were no fences and few natural barriers to segregate the domestic cattle on the vast terrain of the mission ranches. Shetland sheepdogs were well suited for the task of keeping the herds in their assigned pastures. Few of the missions were without their "toy collies." Mentioned frequently in the annals, "Shelties," as they are popularly known in canine circles, are an even-tempered breed. There appears to be a telepathy-like and unbreakable bond between the dogs and their masters. Michael served at San Fernando Mission for some years and also served as senior guard dog and favored mascot for all other members of the animal kingdom attached to California's seventeenth mission. Like others of his kin, Michael was innately bashful. When someone touring the Old Mission recognized him, he generally scampered off and hid with the cats behind the boxwood.

Some years ago, one of the little dog's fans from Spain had a specially made tile set in place on the mission grounds. It portrayed a bust, above the words, *"Cuidado con El Perro."* Likely there will always be a Sheltie at San Fernando Mission and probably at many other missions as well. The vast herds of cattle are gone now, but there is still a need for the distinctive love, friendship and loyalty imprinted on the California landscape by Shetland Sheepdogs.

* * * * * *

Every year, over 35,000 grown-ups and youngsters visit our mission as tourists, pilgrims, scholars and friends and each one carries away his or her remembrance of a holy place, historic shrine, revered sanctuary or house of worship. Inasmuch as everything here is old and fragile, we do have a lot of "maintenance" to do on our exhibits, grounds and buildings.

Things here at the Old Mission are moving along quite well, despite the usual anxieties and challenges that befall us all. Because of their age, our pipes are leaking, our electric lines are shorting and our very existence is often compromised. Rare is the week that we don't host a plumber, electrician or carpenter. But, it's all great fun and we daren't complain for fear that things might get worse.

The seasonal crowds from the Los Angeles Unified School District and private schools are coming at their usual rate. And we are grateful to the Mission Guides who are so ready to explain our background and heritage. And *Las Damas Archivistas* in the Archival Center come twice weekly to provide tours for those fortunate enough to visit on Monday and Thursday afternoons.

* * * * * *

In the interest of proper liturgical decorum, we occasionally need to reiterate some of the procedures followed here at San Fernando Mission. All of these are part of the official directives provided by the American Conference of Catholic Bishops.

Whether it be for the excellence of the homily, the smoothness of the liturgy or the quality of the music, applause after Mass is NOT appropriate. The Liturgy is not a performance.

The holding of hands with a child, parent or friend during the recitation or singing of the Our Father is NOT an approved gesture.

At the Kiss of Peace, only one's immediate neighbor should be greeted. Especially to be avoided is crossing the aisle to greet an acquaintance. A smile, handshake and/or the words "Peace with you" is an appropriate greeting.

It is the recipient's choice to either kneel or stand to receive Holy Communion. Here at the Old Mission, standing is the *preferred* posture; the proper response to "Body of Christ" before receiving Holy Communion is "Amen" and it should be audible.

At the reception of Holy Communion, those who wish to receive in the hand must NOT have anything else in their clutch, whether it be a baby, rosary, handkerchief, prayer book or whatever.

Non-Catholics who approach the railing at the time of Holy Communion are most welcome. They are invited to fold their hands over their breast for a blessing. This directive also applies to youngsters who have not made their first Holy Communion.

And, please, do not visit with friends before or after Mass *inside* the church. Many people find that practice an obstacle to their private prayer.

There is no provision for cell phones in the liturgical directives. Here at the Old Mission, we have a policy that if a cell phone goes off during a service, the offender is exhorted to double his or her offering that day.

Finally, clothing at Holy Mass should be appropriate for the solemnity of the occasion. For example, short trousers for men and profound cleavage for women violate good taste. San Fernando Mission has adequate heat in the winter and cool air in the summer to allow for maximum comfort.

Maybe you haven't noticed, but the ramp into San Fernando Mission's historical cemetery has been re-structured. This change was made

to match the newly redesigned entombment area directly west of Alemany High School. This surely is a most attractive part of the cemetery.
Other changes have been completed recently here at the Old Mission,
including a new entrance into the Church through the sacristy. A number of new signs also have been added to assist visitors with easier access to the many public areas of our property.

* * * * * *

You might recall that shortly after Vatican Council II, the Holy See
asked that thereafter the Sacrament of Baptism be conferred during
Mass inside the sanctuary. We've been slow to make this change only
because of finances. Now we have a new font, designed and imple-
mented by King Richard's Liturgical Arts. With the gracious generosity of the Daniel Murphy Foundation we have had the new font
designed to match the other artwork of San Fernando Mission. This
is the latest project we have initiated to further beautify the chapel at
San Fernando Mission.

Baptismal Font

We have installed a beautiful glass rendition of the Last Supper in the Madonna Room of the Convento. It is a miniature reproduction of the one at Forest Lawn, which dates back to the 1920s.

In January of 2007, we discontinued our monthly Tridentine Mass. And in December of 2007, we did away with the Midnight Mass because of the sparse crowds. Many people do not feel safe going out in the evening anymore.

Convento

People noticed that as they walk through the *convento* building there are three new exhibit cases designed and built by Don Towell. One has an historic chair on display, the one used by Pope Saint John Paul II here at San Fernando Mission in 1987. There is also a wicker chair given to the late Archbishop John J. Cantwell by John Steven McGroarty, poet laureate of California. Finally there is the official *sedes* that belonged to the proto Bishop of *Ambas Californias*, the Right Reverend Francisco Garcia y Moreno, 1840–1846. These are items that need extra "protection." They are neatly and safely exhibited for our thousands of visitors.

In January 2013 we were able to open the wine cellar in the *convento* building. Ours is the only wine cellar still intact in all the missions. It measures 18'6" by 46' in size and is 8 feet in height from the floor to the huge handrail beams. Wine was stored in the cool, dark and dry area in wooden casks.

Closed now for some years, the brick area wall was reinforced with ten square yards of poured concrete. The lighting was enhanced with 225 watts of lights. A new handrail was installed for the safety of visitors. A visitor to San Fernando in 1853 noted that the grape cultivated here was very pleasant red wine, similar to claret. "Mission grape" was a large reddish-black berry full of tasty juice. Before 1833 it was the only variety of grape produced in California although wines were surely procured from other wild fruits as soon as the natives mastered the techniques of fermentation and distillation. The fertile soil and temperate climate at San Fernando accounted for the quantities of wine processed at the mission. In some years as many as 2,000 gallons were yielded, some of which were exported to Europe.

* * * * * *

A rocking chair dating back to the early 1860s has found its way back to San Fernando Mission where it once adorned the lobby of the Butterfield Stage Coach company office. It was removed (alienated or sold) and eventually was discovered at the San Fernando Swap Meet. Carlos Augusto Chiri purchased it for $150 and then spent some months restoring it. Late in October of 2011 he offered it back to the Old Mission. Isn't it interesting how things gravitate back to their original owners?

* * * * * *

We have been asked what motivated the wrought iron fence work on the front porch of the *convento* building. Throughout 2014, an uninvited guest (we used to call them "bums") had been sleeping on the porch. He would scale the gates and crawl over the barricades. Repeatedly we called the police to have him evicted! But he always managed to return.

In addition to leaving behind trash, he recently began starting small fires to warm himself during the night hours. Several times the fires burned beyond his control. To comply with the law, we had "no trespassing signs" posted, some of which he used as kindling. Not being able to afford a night watchman, we had to resort to a fencing project. Though not overly attractive, it was modeled after contemporary barriers. The *convento* building is not fire resistant and our insurance carrier strongly advised we take precautionary measures. So that answers the basic question. The project was quite expensive.

People are glad to know that the painting of the assumption for the Virgin Mary was restored and reframed. Here is a copy of the report from the Conservation people.

"This is an oil on canvas painting. The scene was previously repaired and is glued onto a 1/4" thick masonite panel. There is a thick layer of shiny, yellow deteriorated varnish with large brown drip marks running vertically down the painting. There are several areas of over-paint throughout. Conservation of the painting was carried out in two phases.

PHASE 1: The deteriorated varnish was removed using acetone and then rinsed with naphtha. Some old repairs were removed with acetone during varnish removal. Additional cleaning was done with conservation detergents. Several areas of the painting appeared to have been over cleaned resulting in thin areas of paint.

Testing was done on the previous lining method used. It was determined that the painting could not safely be removed from the masonite panel without damage to the painting. The painting appears fairly flat and is not loose from the panel. An extremely hard filler was used to fill all tears and holes. These also were not removable except by scrapping with a surgical scalpel. Areas on and around the old fills appeared to have been sanded causing further damage to the paint surface. Old fills were leveled where possible and then textured to match original canvas weave. The painting was then varnished with a brush coating of B-72 acrylic varnish.

PHASE 2: The majority of work completed in Phase 2 was the recreation of missing and damaged paint. All additional losses were filled with Modostuc Italian filler, textured to match original canvas weave and then sealed with AYAA varnish. In-painting of all losses and thin areas was then completed using Maimeri and Golden conservation paints. A final protective coat of Larapbl Satin finish acrylic varnish was brushed onto the surface."

We had a grant from the Dan Murphy Foundation that covered about half the overall cost.

In order to keep our position as the premier member of the California missions, we need to constantly keep upgrading our exhibits here at the Old Mission. The latest of these innovations is a selection of postcards (1905–2005) issued over the years about "the Mission in the Valley". Dave Beaumont has given the Old Mission a collection of postcards, which is now exhibited in the central foyer of the *convento*.

Visitors may have noticed that we have a new painting in the *Estenega* Room, one depicting Sir Daniel Donohue, whose foundation built and gave the archdiocese its Archival Center in 1980–81. There are two reasons why the painting was hung in that room. Beyond being the only place that would accommodate the massive painting, it is related in theme to the three manikins already on exhibit there. The painting itself was commissioned and paid for by Daniel's friends at Saint John's Retirement facility in July of 2000. Executed by Mark Radloff Beniford, the painting depicts its subject in the uniform of a Gentleman-in-Waiting to the Holy Father, a title conferred by Pope Paul VI. It was entrusted to San Fernando Mission by the Dan Murphy Foundation of Los Angeles. In recent years San Fernando Mission has acquired numerous paintings, mostly artistic renditions of sacred scenes. Surely we are pleased to exhibit so many works of art. San Fernando Mission continues to be the "showpiece" of *El Camino Real.*

* * * * * *

We are always looking for historic treasures with which to enrich our historical holdings. Late in 2014, we were blessed with an historic painting by W.A. Coulter of San Carlos Borromeo Mission in Carmel, which now hangs in the *convento*. It was presented by the legendary Southern California bookseller, Glen Dawson, who, at 101, was the oldest resident of the Villa Gardens in Pasadena. The painting, executed in 1887, was commissioned by Benjamin Cummings Truman (1835–1915), onetime secretary to President Andrew Johnson. It was acquired by Mr. Dawson in 1970 from the estate of Truman's daughter, Augusta Mallard.

When the new archival facility for the archdiocese was completed in 1981, Cardinal Manning asked if I would come back to Mission Hills to serve as director of San Fernando Mission. As an incentive for my giving up the pastorate of San Buenaventura Mission, the cardinal offered to advance San Fernando Mission to the status of a canonical parish. However, after considerable thought and prayers, I concluded that this area didn't really need another parish. Nor did I think the neighboring pastors would welcome such a move.

* * * * * *

A "forest" is defined in one dictionary as "a tract of land covered with a natural growth of at least a hundred trees and assorted underbrush". Based on that designation, we can describe San Fernando Mission as being located in a "forest" within the city of Los Angeles. When the trimmers were here last May, they serviced no fewer than 119 trees within the five square acres comprising San Fernando, Rey de España Mission. Among the many trees currently on the property are several kinds of Pine trees, Jacaranda, Juniper, Oak, Alder, Elm, Bottle Bush, Eucalyptus, Crepe Myrtle, Yucca, Floss Silk, Locust, Magnolia, Carrott Wood and several others. Then there are the fruit trees: Olive, Orange, Lime, Avocado, Mulberry, Fig and Plum.

* * * * * *

Some years ago, we circulated a questionnaire to visitors asking what they most liked about their tour of San Fernando Mission. The youngsters were fairly uniform in selecting the peacocks, especially those who came from the inner city and had never experienced such elegant and colorful birds. Now their focus has changed. Most like the *Teatro de Fray Junípero Serra* where they can choose one of three films on the missions and related topics.

For their part, the grown-ups are impressed by the extensive instructive and attractive displays, which touch practically all the aspects of missionary life in Provincial California. And since the opening of the Bob Hope Memorial Garden, a large number of tourists, especially veterans, are fascinated by the Hope Sarcophagus. Increasingly, people are drawn to our Gift Shop and the many boutique items available there. And our wide selection of books is outstanding.

* * * * * *

We have over 35,000 people a year coming to the old Mission, most of them students from the Los Angeles Unified School District and other public and private institutions. We mounted a special exhibit to commemorate the tri-centennial of the birth of Fray Junípero Serra.

San Fernando Mission hosts Junípero Serra exhibit

Several dozen items related to Blessed Junípero Serra, founder of the California Missions, are on display at Mission San Fernando.

■A special exhibit commemorating the tricentennial of Blessed Junípero Serra will be featured at Mission San Fernando, Rey de España, in Mission Hills for the rest of the year.

Among the several dozen items on display are a U.S. stamp bearing the likeness of Serra (1984), a copy of Palou's "Relacion Historia" (1787), a chalice and altar stone used by Father Serra and other items associated with the founder of the California Missions.

The first nine of the California Missions established along California's El Camino Real were founded by Father Serra, who was beatified by Pope John Paul II in 1985.

In a recent poll, Californians voted October as their "favorite" month of the year. Surely it is a celebratory time here at the Old Mission – as the flowers begin changing colors and preparing for wintertime. You'll probably notice that we have updated the walkways with a new rubbery substance separating the tiles from the paved concrete. Would that city officials take such care of the public sidewalks and streets. A lady told me recently that she suffered a broken axle from a pothole on Mission Boulevard.

As a young pastor at San Buenaventura, I early learned that maintenance is the cheapest long-term challenge even for historic and aged buildings. In that regard we have recently had our roofing tiles repaired where needed, the drainage system was cleaned and our night-lights re-anchored.

* * * * * *

Tucked away in the West Garden is a gently flowing stream that winds its way through the trees and undergrowth. Running from just outside the rear door of the church to the Archival Center, it follows a concrete bed poured dozens of years ago. We recently had to shut it down when we found that the bed was badly cracked. We re-lined the bed to keep the water from evaporating and overflowing its banks.

* * * * * *

Rarely does a month pass that we don't refurbish, repair, replace or acquire something to better relate the Old Mission to modern times. There are even machines offering cold drinks to our visitors. The three machines are maintained and stocked by a company which shares its profits with San Fernando Mission. Unhappily, people treat those machines poorly – yelling at, kicking and jerking them whenever the service is not up to par. That's why it's best for us to farm out the whole operation. The new machines offer a wider assortment including Arrowhead and Dasani water, Gatorade and Monster energy drinks.

The 25,000 school urchins who pass through our portals every year are especially pleased to see their ever-friendly and tasteful drinks.

* * * * * *

Our exhibits here at the Old Mission are always being updated and or expanded. Visitors are impressed that there's something new each time they tour the facilities. Among the recent examples is an historic organ which is displayed in the *gran sala* of the *convento* building.

The *Daily News* noticed this item and did a small article in a recent edition.

Century-old organ on Display at mission.

A historical Mason and Hamlin organ is now on display at the San Fernando Mission.

Still in its original oak cabinet, the century-old instrument, also called harmonium, was restored and donated to the Mission by Michael Pierceall of Pasadena. The organ was used by Dominican nuns at the San Jose Mission starting in 1916, and passed through several hands before landing at its current site in the Gran Sala of San Fernando's Old Mission.

"Actually, it does play," noted Monsignor Francis Weber, SFM's retired director. "But it's 100 years old, so it's not going to be used for church services anymore. We have it on exhibit because of its historic connotation."

And no, you won't be able to bang out a rhapsody on it; a glass case protects the organ from would-be musicians.

"The case is really nice, too," Weber assures visitors.

Speaking of organs:

Pre-owned Organ for Serra Chapel

About twenty years ago, at the intervention of the late Sister Miriam Joseph Larkin, C.S.J., the Serra Chapel at San Fernando Mission became the recipient of an antiquated but still usable Thomas Electric Organ.

Edward G. Thomas founded the Thomas Organ Company in 1875. The first instruments were pipe organs and, later, reed organs. In 1956, the company developed an electronic organ from its headquarters in Sepulveda, California.

Those early models used a shared-generator system, which utilized one generator for every two adjacent notes. Soon, this clumsy system was abandoned and Thomas went to master oscillators. Two manual and pedal models with a large number of stop dials were introduced and the dials eventually gave way to conventional stops with a minimum for less important functions.

Thomas built a house organ, for which Avon became his largest market. Then came the transistor organ, a version of which was adopted by Lawrence Welk whose musicians used a version with two 44-note manual and 25 short pedals.

In 1979, the Thomas Organ Company was among the first of the giant organ companies to go out of business. Gradually it became impossible to acquire replacements.

The organ in the Serra Chapel functioned until early in 2009, when its speaker system burned out. A closer inspection revealed that most of the felt on the keys was no longer serviceable. We began looking around for another organ.

Happily Robert Tall, who installed the giant Rodgers organ in the church, was able to acquire an almost mint Rodgers 700 organ from an estate in Palm Springs. It was installed in the Serra Chapel on April 17.

The Rodgers Organ Company was established in 1958. Shortly thereafter, Rodgers introduced the first single-contact system on any organ and four years later launched reed switch pedal keying. The first completely transistorial organ, which eliminated vacuum tubes, also appeared in 1962 and was the first solid-state organ in history.

The Rodgers Trillium 700 was designed as all-digital and included features of the larger models. These Allegiant models were developed for home, chapel and casino use.

There is an "owner's manual" for anyone who might like to drop by and read more about our new pre-owned Rodgers 700 Series.

* * * * * *

The big news hereabouts is the painting of the ceilings in the *convento* building white. Our late friend, Dr. Norman Neuerburg, always wanted the ceilings restored to their original coloration. And you will notice how much brighter the rooms are now. Would you believe that the workers used 130 gallons of paint!

* * * * * *

Someone recently asked if we have a "security problem" here at the Old Mission. Yes! In the late afternoon of August 15, someone tried to steal *El Santo Nino de Atoche* from its perch in the *Teatro* of the *convento*. Happily it was securely anchored and could not be removed from its enclosure. Now it has been cleaned, repaired and restored to its place of honor. Occasionally, we have incidents along similar lines. The best insurance against such incursions is careful exhibiting. In this case we had the statue back on exhibit the next morning, thanks to the support provided by the pinkies.

* * * * * *

Few people remember that San Fernando Catholic High School (now Alemany High School) began in the buildings of San Fernando Mission in 1950. What is now the Serra Chapel, Cantwell Hall and the present Gift Shop were classrooms for the chemistry and physics laboratories.

Cauldron

According to a story in the *Sacramento Bee* for September 22, 2016, this 650-pound historic cauldron was removed from San Fernando Mission in the 1800s by Jesus Santa Maria, the first settler of Topanga Canyon. It was utilized at the family *rancho* for over a century, before being returned to Mission Hills in 2016.

In the Spring of 2017, we decided to update the displays in the Workshop area. The weaving display was reconfigured to hold a number of food preparation items as well as the cauldron, as the latter was beginning to show wear from being outside.

We also commissioned the construction of two new cases to hold a set of unique antique fans that were crafted in Europe and brought to the United States by Anita Watson in the 1920s.

Marian Presence at San Fernando Mission

The Madonna Room at San Fernando, Rey de España Mission, contains one of the largest and most diverse portrayals of the Blessed Virgin Mary in the United States and probably in the world. According to annual surveys among our tourists, the exhibit is the most popular of all the historical displays available at the seventeen missions along California's *El Camino Real*. Located in what was known as a *carcel*, or prison, in provincial times, the Madonna Collection emphasizes why Mary is and remains the centerfold of Catholic devotion to the Lord.

Upon entering the Madonna Room, visitors are captivated by a back-lit miniature reproduction of Rosa Caselli Moretti's portrayal of the Last Supper, which was commissioned by Hubert Eaton for Forest Lawn Memorial Park in Glendale. The original stain glass window, dating from 1931, is regarded as one of the most colorful and artistic masterpieces in the United States.

Marian devotion is intricately linked to all of the missionary estab-lishments along *El Camino Real*. The earliest works of art in California were statues and paintings of Mary, some of which are still in place at one or another of the historic foundations. From 1492 onward, Marian devotion has been expressed in the *New World* in a remarkably diverse manner. Even today in Mexico, for example, almost every village has its own Madonna tailored to local customs, needs and expressions.

The depictions of Mary at Mission Hills are an amalgam of three major collections gathered over the years by Lula Anna Shipstad (44 statues), Jean Hill (43 statues) and Anita Watson (11 statues and 33 plaques). The Shipstad name has been associated with one of the most exquisite and artistic Madonna collections ever assembled. Her unique collection was presented to the Old Mission by the late Msgr. Laurence O'Leary, the pastor of Saint Martin of Tours parish in Westwood.

Twenty-four of the Shipstad Madonnas were designed by the late Clarise Harvey, a longtime resident of Encino. Though not a Catholic, Ms. Harvey's interest in symbolism and detail makes her renditions both accurate and beautiful. Each of the Madonnas represent local themes. With the exception of Our Lady of Chavez Ravine and the Madonna of Baseball, all the statues are one of a kind.

The charming statue of Our Lady of Japan has a cherry blossom halo and an obi with two folds at the back, recalling Mary's ancestry in the royal house of King David. The African Madonna and Child stands apart from the others inasmuch as it is the only one made of terra cotta.

The statue of Our Lady of China is portrayed in authentic and festive garments. Among the most colorful statues is the Belgian Madonna, Our Lady of Leopoldville, which depicts Mary carrying a basket, with the infant Jesus safely tucked away in the fold of her broad sash.

The portrayal of the Immaculate Heart of Mary has Our Lady seated with the infant in her lap. Twelve jewels and an equal number of peaks, representing the apostles, form the halo. The statue of Our Lady of the Prairies features the notion of thanksgiving. This depiction has a captivating simplicity that eloquently expresses the American spirit of gratitude. Mary holds a sheaf of grains and, at her feet other symbols of harvest time are depicted.

Under the patronage of Our Lady of Ethiopia, the Blessed Lady is pictured with outstretched arms, one representing God the Father and the other portraying God the Son, while the dove is the Holy Spirit.

Interest in the missionary work of the Catholic Church is evident in the portrayal of Mary, Queen of the Apostles. The Blessed Mother is holding the Infant Jesus against a backdrop of latticework, attended on each side by an apostle. The evangelical theme is further evident in the statue of Our Lady, Queen of the Missions. The cross-topped world rests in Mary's hands and, at her feet, are replicas of the various missionary areas of Japan's Fujiyama and America's desert cactus. Symbolically, Mary is crushing the head of the serpent.

The most historic item in the Madonna Room is an original depiction on tin of Our Lady, Refuge of Sinners, brought to California by Bishop Francisco Garcia Diego y Moreno in 1840. It was this proto Bishop of *Ambas Californias* who proclaimed Mary, the *Refugio,* as Patroness of the Californias. Probably the most intricate rendition in the collection is a mother-of-pearl nativity scene from the estate of the late Msgr. Robert Brennan.

The *Pieta* is an exact reproduction of the masterful work executed by Michelangelo Buonarroti and presently exhibited in Saint Peter's Basilica, Vatican City. Sculpted from a single piece of Carrara marble in 1605, this artistic rendition portrays the body of Christ taken from the cross and reposing in the lap of Our Lady. The original work, the only one ever signed by Michelangelo, was commissioned by Jean Cardinal de Villiers, the ambassador of the French King, Charles VII.

The famous artist Eugenio Pattarino (1885–1971) is represented with seven masterpieces, which are among the world's most sought-after renditions of Our Lady. Undoubtedly, the most spectacular rendition is a cloisonné reproduction of Murillo's Assumption.

The walls of the Madonna Room are adorned with fourteen paintings of Mary, including one of Our Lady of Guadalupe, which has been at San Fernando Mission since the 1790s. Hanging on the eastern wall is a hand-fabricated, framed cutout of the *Hail Mary* in its entirety. Dating from the late nineteenth century, it likely originated in Austria. The adjoining petit point portrayal of *The Madonna of the Chair* is a copy of the famous painting by Raphael in the Pitti Palace in Florence.

Among the works by local artists are three kiln depictions of Mary cast by Betsy Brown in the late 1950s. Also included are several renditions by the internationally acclaimed California artists Edith and Isabel Piczek.

The elaborate rosary is an oversized version originally manufactured from alabaster as an adornment for a large statue. Over the years the rosary was separated from its original setting. There are numerous panels or plaques, most of them originating in Europe in the early years of the last century. Outstanding is a hand-executed wooden Madonna with the face of Mary and the Infant carved in ivory.

Apart from the actual Madonnas, the more interesting is the "hand," which is all that remains of a sixteenth-century ivory statue of the Blessed Mother, acquired by Howard Sanshack in the 1950s. It was previously owned by a Mr. Spencer who found it in a cave in Northern Arizona. Another coveted treasure in the collection is part of the Veil of the Blessed Mother, which forms the central focus in one of the displays. It is exhibited in a wooden container reminiscent of seventeenth-century reliquaries.

By all the recognized standards, Mary alone qualifies as the most important, influential and recognizable person in our very busy sophisticated and modern society. Having appeared more often on the cover of *Time* magazine than any other person, she also has motivated more books, movies and television programs than any other single person in history. Her presence at San Fernando Mission is manifested in no fewer than 270 statues, 14 framed portrayals, 60 new postage stamps and numerous other related treasures.

Inlaid in one of the *convento* walls is a Viaticum Communion Set which features a stationary portrayal of the Holy Family with an insertion of the last Supper from the 1880s.

The Serra Chapel

One of the most devotional chapels in the Archdiocese of Los Angeles is that bearing the patronage of Saint Junípero Serra at San Fernando Mission. Dedicated by Timothy Cardinal Manning on March 2, 1984, the chapel is the first dedicated to the founder of the California missions.

Located in the eastern-most wing of the mission quadrangle, the chapel is used for daily Masses and for smaller weddings and funerals. It is a favorite of couples renewing their marriage vows.

Though there is no tradition that the area served as a chapel in mission times, the room now houses numerous items closely associated with or related to the provincial era of California's history.

The Serra theme is evident throughout the chapel. For example, the almost life-size statue of Fray Junípero Serra is patterned after the one sculpted in bronze by Douglas Tilden in 1907 for San Francisco's Golden Gate Park. It was fashioned from lindenwood in the Studio of Vizenzo Demetz Figlio in Ortisei, Italy.

The massive wooden case housing the relic of Saint Junípero Serra was built at Carmel by Richard Joseph Menn. It was originally designed for the Cathedral at Palma de Mallorca, where Serra preached several times prior to leaving for the New World. A large bronze plaque, mounted on the south wall, commemorated the 200th anniversary of Saint Junípero Serra's demise. Serra International presented it to The Old Mission in 1984.

A massive enlargement of the 44-cent postage stamp issued in 1985 to honor Fray Junípero Serra dominates the area above the windows along the southern wall of the chapel. A gift of the U.S. Postal Service, the commemorative reproduction portrays the Franciscan *Presidente* against the outline of the Southern California coastline and the Baja California peninsula.

The oak Presidential chair belonged to Fred A. Meier and for many years was part of the furnishings in a home at Lake Arrowhead. It features the carved image of a medieval monk, along with hand-embellished filigree on its arms and feet.

The beautiful porcelain vases at either side of the altar were once in the Pompeian Room of the Doheny mansion at #8 Chester Place in Los Angeles. The handsomely fashioned, gold-leafed wooden platforms are from the Estelle Doheny Collection at Camarillo.

Dominating the chapel, behind and above the main altar, is a hand-carved crucifixion scene fashioned from a single piece of bark. It portrays the dying Christ being administered to by angels.

For many years, the rug in front of the altar was located in the sanctuary of the main church. It was a donation from Mark Harrington (1882–1971), who was responsible for much of the restoration work at San Fernando.

The three chandeliers, produced by Harry Downie at his workshop in Carmel, were designed and hung in the main church of the Old Mission by Mark Harrington in the 1940s. They were replaced by electrified reproductions in 1984. The wooden chairs were commissioned in 1940 for the Prayer Hall at Saint John's Seminary, Camarillo. They were entrusted to the Old Mission by Msgr. Eugene Frilot, a former administrator.

An old wooden faldstool, now used by acolytes at daily Mass, belonged to the late Archbishop Joseph T. McGucken (1902–1983) and comes from the chapel of his residence on Broadway in San Francisco.

Situated at the rear of the chapel is a kneeler, or *prie-dieu*, acquired from the estate of Father Peter Gabriel Foster (1933–1984). It earlier belonged to Msgr. John J. Cawley (1882–1953), longtime Vicar General for the Archdiocese of Los Angeles.

The artwork embellishing the chapel walls was hand-painted. It is adapted from an Indian design used in the main church of the Old Mission. It was executed in 1983 by Dr. Norman Neuerburg, assisted by Helen Moran, Marcella Hickey, Ruth Eide and Clarese Kroll.

A massive clock, manufactured by the Herschede Hall Clock Company of Cincinnati, Ohio, in 1915, belonged to the late Archbishop John J. Cantwell (1874–1947). It was located at the foot of the stairwell in the archiepiscopal residence in Fremont Place until 1947, when it was moved to Beverly Hills. In 1984, it was given to the San Fernando Mission by Eileen Cantwell.

For many years, the modern rendition of San Carlos Borromeo occupied a place of prominence at the Borromeo Guild, the archdiocesan bookstore that operated between 1943 and 1987. It was fabricated in Milan.

The statue of Saint Joseph and the Infant Jesus was bequeathed to the Old Mission by the late Msgr. John J. Devlin (1898–1977). For many years it was enshrined in a niche at the rectory of Saint Victor's Church in West Hollywood.

Above the statue is a plated bronze relief of Our Lady and Child attended by various apostles. The attractively matted icon is displayed on red felt in a specially made shadow box.

The polychrome statue of the Madonna hanging on the south wall of the chapel was carved sometime between 1630 and 1650. Acquired from the estate of Msgr. Martin Cody Keating (1893–1971), it was restored by Fred Rolla in 1975.

The rendition of Our Lady, Refuge of Sinners painted on tin, a gift from Richard Joseph Menn, was one of several dozen brought to Alta California by the area's proto bishop, the Right Reverend Francisco Garcia Diego y Moreno (1785–1846) in the 1840s. Saint Francis of Assisi, whose followers introduced Christianity to the Pacific Slope, is portrayed in a rectangular wooden relief that came from San Juan Bautista Mission in the mid-1980s.

The double tile rendition of Our Lady of Guadalupe, displayed in a wooden frame embellished with inlaid chunks of ivory, was a gift of Archbishop Francisco Orozco of Guadalajara (1864–1936) to Marie Walsh Harrington, founder of *Las Damas Archivistas*. There is also a framed memento of the Holy Land with sixteen chips of rock from the major Jewish and Christian shrines of Israel. It was presented by the Latin Patriarch of Jerusalem to the late Timothy Cardinal Manning on November 8, 1986.

The richly ornamented tile depiction of *Nuestra Señora de Montserrat* was acquired at the famed Spanish Marian shrine near Barcelona. It commemorates a pilgrimage to Saint Junípero Serra's birthplace at Petra de Mallorca in 1984.

The handsome display case housing relics of the saints has long been associated with San Fernando Mission. Among the relics exhibited for veneration are those of Saints Thomas, Bartholomew, Matthew, James, Andrew, Thaddeus, Philip, James the less, Alphonsus, John Bosco, Victor, Philomena and Theresa. Also enshrined is a relic of the True Cross.

The sanctuary lamp, a modern bronze reproduction of a wooden fixture in Westminster Abbey, was a gift of Henriette Setterfield of San Buenaventura Mission. Its flickering light indicates the presence of the Blessed Sacrament.

The Ezcaray Altar Pieces

at

San Fernando Mission

Msgr. Francis J. Weber

1991

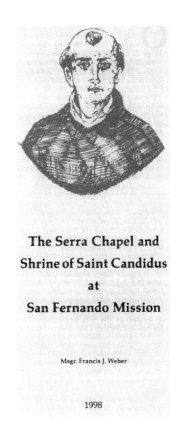

The Serra Chapel and Shrine of Saint Candidus

at

San Fernando Mission

Msgr. Francis J. Weber

1998

St. Candidus

According to Alban Butler, Candidus was a member of the Theban Legion, a group of Christian soldiers recruited by Maximian Herculius in Upper Egypt for the purpose of putting down a recalcitrant tribe of the Gauls called Bagaudae.

When Maximian ordered all his soldiers to join in offering sacrifice to the pagan gods for the success of their expedition, the members of the Theban Legion refused to take part in the rites.

Candidus, known as the *senator militum,* was among the leaders of the Theban Legion who led the opposition to Maximian, noting that "we are your soldiers, but we are also servants of the true God. We cannot renounce Him who is our Creator and Master, and also yours, even though you reject Him."

Maximian, seeing no hope of overcoming their constancy, ordered that the entire legion be put to death. This all occurred near Agaunum (c. 287 A.D.). September 22nd is the day that Candidus and his companions are commemorated in the Roman Martyrology.

Saint Eucherius, the bishop of Lyons during the first half of the fifth century, is the source for the story about Candidus. Although certain aspects of the account are ambiguous, it seems clear that his martyrdom is an historical fact.

For many centuries, the principal relics of Candidus and his companions of the Theban Legion were preserved in a sixth-century reliquary at the Abbey founded by Saint Theodore of Octodurum.

Prior to the third century, Candidus was a name without Christian significance and one probably derived from pagan ancestors. That Candidus was fairly well known by the ninth century is attested to by at least two prominent clerics who took his name, Candidus of Fulda (d. 845) and Candidus, the Anglo-Saxon disciple and confidant of Alcuin.

Very little is known about the peregrination of the relics of Saint Candidus, which were enshrined in the Serra Chapel at San Fernando Mission in the final weeks of 1992. The presumption is that shortly after they were encased within a waxen portrayal of the saint, the relics were brought from Rome by Bishop Thaddeus Amat, probably in January 1868.

In any event, upon his return from the Eternal City, Bishop Amat entrusted the relics to the care of the Lazarist Fathers, who then conducted Saint Vincent's College in Los Angeles. It was probably at that time that the bishop removed a portion of a bone from the reliquary. Since the 1860s, over 90 percent of the altar stones used in Southern California contain relics of Saint Candidus.

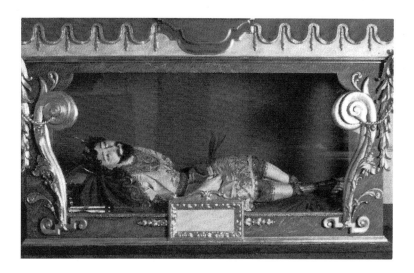

Shortly after the new church of Saint Vincent de Paul was dedicated by Bishop Francis Mora, on February 20, 1887, the relics were moved from the college chapel to the new edifice at the northeast corner of Grand Avenue and Washington Boulevard.

In 1892, new altars were installed in the church and the relics of Saint Candidus were placed beneath the shrine of the Sacred Heart, at the far end of the Gospel side of the sanctuary. The relics remained in place for the next thirty-eight years, until 1925, when the present Saint Vincent's Church was opened at West Adams Boulevard and Figueroa Street.

Father Terence O'Donnell, C.M., a former pastor of Saint Vincent's parish, explained that when the relics were moved from the old to the new Saint Vincent church in 1925, the documentation (along with one of the parochial Baptismal registers) was stored in a wastepaper basket. An overly zealous custodian threw the basket and its contents into the trash.

For some unknown reason, there were no provisions made in the Spanish Renaissance church for the relics of Saint Candidus, although portions of his relics were placed in the altars of the Miraculous Medal and Saint Joseph for their consecration in 1930.

The wooden sarcophagus was placed atop the vesting cabinets of the eastern-most sacristy and there they remained until the mid-1980s when they were consigned to a storage area in the church's cavernous basement.

In September 1991, the massive sarcophagus and its contents were moved to San Fernando Mission. The waxen figure of Candidus was sent to the South Coast Fine Arts Preservation Center for cleaning and the wooden case to Carmel, where it became the model of a wholly new altar-shrine built by Richard Menn.

The shrine's tabernacle is part of the Escaray collection acquired by the archdiocese in 1944. Hand-finished wooden candlesticks were the gift of the late Msgr. John Cosgrove.

Without any question, the Serra Chapel, with its altar-shrine of Saint Candidus, is unique along the Pacific Slope. Its beauty, history and tradition combine to produce one of the truly outstanding houses of worship in the Western United States.

I Said A
Prayer For
You Today At
Mission San
Fernando

I said a prayer for you today and I know God must have heard.

I felt the answer in my heart although He spoke no word.

I didn't ask for wealth or fame; I knew you wouldn't mind.

I asked Him to send treasures of a far more lasting kind.

I asked that He'd be near you at the start of each new day;

to grant you health and blessings and friends to share your way.

I asked for happiness for you in all things great and small,

but it was for His loving care I prayed for most of all.

© Southwest Church   -Margaret Gould   MC18

2

Archival Center Chronicle

‮ও ও‬

I t has long been recognized that responsible preservation of documents is absolutely essential for authentic history. For it to be above evasion or dispute, history must be grounded on documents, not on opinion or hearsay. The basic function of the Archival Center is to collect, preserve, study and interpret pertinent documents, diaries, manuscripts, brochures, photographs and other assorted historical heritage. Although the term "Catholic" is not meant here to be restrictive, it is only logical to limit our goals within reasonable parameters.

The Friends of the Archival Center have two major objectives – purchasing, repairing and preserving items not provided in the Center's budget and expanding our Endowment Fund, which will one day make the institution totally self-supporting.

Our quarterly newsletter, *El Camino Real*, is mailed to the Friends of the Archival Center, outlining many other activities of the Archival Center. Since the newsletter's inauguration, there have been 142 issues sent to our supporters. (That's 852 pages.)

Searching through the copies of the *Quarterly Newsletter for the Archival Center*, 2010 to present, one can string together a fair, if not complete, list of acquisitions and significant events catalogued by the Archival Center in that brief period.

* * * * * *

For over forty years *Las Damas Archivistas* have conducted tours of the Historical Museum in the Archival Center on Mondays and Thursdays between 1 p.m. and 3 p.m. It's amazing how varied and interesting our visitors are. In the course of an average year, people from almost every state and many nations visit our facilities.

Recently, for example, there was a couple from Alaska, followed by three students from Hawaii. What fun it is to listen to the accounts of their reflections "about the mainland." The ladies are always looking for new members of *Las Damas Archivistas*. From their feedback, the time with visitors is well spent.

* * * * * *

The grand opening of the William H. Hannon Library at Loyola Marymount University took place on August 30, 2009. Located on the bluffs overlooking Los Angeles, the modern building incorporates scholarly tradition and the latest technology; moving students forward with the tools they need to achieve academic excellence. Bill Hannon was a dear friend of the Archival Center whom we hold in the highest esteem.

Mr. William H. Hannon

While moving things about in our storage facility, we came across a long-retired box of records that contained two gems. Both were migrated to CD and are available now to researchers.

The first is the audio recording of proceedings held at the Biltmore Hotel on November 26, 1948, to welcome Archbishop J. Francis A. McIntyre to the City of Los Angeles. Hosted by the Rotary Club, it contains an address by the archbishop regarding the evils of Communism.

The second is a civic program honoring Joseph Scott from 1951, organized as a tribute in celebration of his 84th birthday. Issued as a keepsake, it is comprised of five long-playing records. Fortunately, the casing with its liner notes had survived the intervening fifty-eight years, and the audio remained crystal clear. The liner notes show the following speakers were in attendance:

A Civic Tribute to Joseph Scott
Los Angeles Biltmore Hotel, August 13, 1951.

*

Lt. Gov. Goodwin Knight
Welcome on behalf of the State of California
County Supervisor Roger W. Jessup
Welcome on behalf of the County Board of Supervisors
Mayor Fletcher Bowron
Welcome on behalf of the City of Los Angeles

*

Justice Emmet L. Wilson
Judge of the District Court of Appeal:
Speech: Joe Scott, the Educator

Homer D. Crotty
President of the State Bar of California:
Speech: Joe Scott, the Lawyer
Rabbi Edgar F. Magnin
Wilshire Boulevard Temple:
Speech: Joe Scott, Opponent of Intolerance

Judge Paul McCormack
Judge of the U.S. District Court for Southern California:
Speech: Joe Scott, the Patriot

Archbishop James Francis McIntyre
Archdiocese of Los Angeles
Speech: Joe Scott, Disciple of Christ

*

Joe Scott
Words of Appreciation
Speech: Atheism in Educational Institutions

*

Closing comments regarding the career and burial of Senator Stephan
A. White

*

Benediction
Msgr. George Scott – St. Mary, Star of the Sea Church

* * * * * *

America's First Postage Stamp

Prior to the 1840s, patrons who wished to prepay the postal rate had
to travel to the post office during business hours. On July 1, 1847, the
United States issued its first postage stamps – a convenience for private
citizens and business alike.

Benjamin Franklin, the first Postmaster General of the United States,
was selected to grace the 5¢ stamp. Printed in rich red brown ink the
5¢ denomination paid the rate for letters sent to destinations within a
300-mile radius.

The 1847 law that created the first adhesive U.S. postage stamp didn't
make its use mandatory, and many continued to send letters based on
an estimate – only one in fifty letters sent before that time bore a stamp.

* * * * * *

One More for Serra

In my office are eight shelves of books, pamphlets and brochures
which I have long referred to as "a complete collection of writings by,
on or about Fray Junípero Serra." Or so I thought, until Ken Karmiole
came along to tell me of a book about Serra that had never entered our
radar zone.

After offering me a copy of Daniel Magee's *An Original Leaf from Francisco Palou's Life of the Venerable Father Junípero Serra* (1787), Ken casually mentioned that there was another leaf book with a page from Palou that predated the Magee book by twenty-eight years! And he had one for sale from the late John Class.

Entitled *The Miracle of the Anchor,* the seven-page opuscula tells about the long-delayed ship, the *San Antonio,* in 1770, its eventual arrival in San Diego and how "the want of an anchor saved California for Spain."

The book is signed by Douglas S. Watson "as a Christmas greeting" from San Francisco in 1930. A penciled note states that "only 43 copies were printed." No printer is indicated, but the copy bears the bookplate of Robert Strong of the Grabhorn Press. Measuring 10 × 7 inches, the book is bound in green wrappers, stitched with a white label printed and decorated in black on front.

Further research determined that *The Miracle of the Anchor* was indeed printed by the Grabhorn Press. It is described by Elinor R. Heller and David Magee in their *Bibliography of the Grabhorn Press* in 1940. Never say "complete"!

* * * * * *

From the Vaults

Another foray into our storage facility brought to light two more items – this time with ties to the mission. The first is an audio recording from November 4, 1974, recorded on reel-to-reel tape. Marked *Mission Chapel Dedication,* we were pleasantly surprised to find it contained the complete ceremony for the rededication of San Fernando Mission's Chapel after its restoration from the 1971 Sylmar earthquake. Timothy Cardinal Manning presided and spoke on the significance of the missions, San Fernando's origins and the re-building task. Geraldine Biggs McGrath and the mission choir were on hand to provide the music for the ceremony.

The other find was a copy *of Regina Angelorum* from 1964, one of the records recorded by Our Lady Queen of Angels Seminary Choir and Glee Club.

Rev. James Hanson, the administrator of the Mission, was director of the seminary choir in the 1960s. On two occasions he was able to arrange for the choir to be recorded professionally. Interestingly, it was recorded live in the Mission Chapel, and the choir members signed the cover. The cover shows a view of the mission's east garden that many of our Friends may have never seen. Comprised of classical pieces, Christmas carols, barbershop staples and American spirituals, it was in very good shape when we discovered it.

Both recordings have been digitally remastered and transferred to CD to preserve their content. Because the dedication recording contains a Manning sermon for which no hard copy exists, we are looking into having it transcribed.

* * * * * *

Glen Dawson has presented a letter from Lucille Miller, the secretary for Carrie Estelle Doheny, which is dated March 19, 1974, and mailed from her home in San Buenaventura, California.

March 19, 1974

Dear Glen:

Thank you for replying to my letter so promptly.

Ward also asked me about the specially printed prayers he did for Mrs. Doheny. I do not know of any copy anywhere.

After Mrs. D. died we were given three months to clear out that enormous house and the accumulations of over half a century. Everything was thrown out helter-skelter with no thought of what we perhaps should preserve. The prayer leaflets were the last things we would have thought of.

Concerning the photographs: I gave to U.S.C. all the photos of Number Eight in its various transformations from 1900 to about 1950; the yacht; the Beverly Hills Ranch and other properties. The photos at the library are personal – Mr. and Mrs. Doheny. When you come to the library I would like to meet you there and look over the photos with you. I might be of some help. In the old billiard room at Number Eight there was hanging on the wall, a very long panoramic view of the *Cerra Azul* field. Just the field, no people. You might be interested in that. I also remember seeing a photo of an oil well and men standing around it completely soaked with oil from head to feet. Where that would be I don't know – maybe USC. I think that Pat Doheny may have some photos of Mr. D and Ned taken in the field, I am not sure but you could ask him.

I talked to Ellen on the phone this morning and she is busy, busy. Looking forward to her trip to Greece next month. Hope to see you one of these days.

* * * * * *

We are grateful to Richard Grant and the board members of the Dan Murphy Foundation, which gave us a grant of $15,000 to digitize a large collection of films that belonged to the late Archbishop John J. Cantwell. Here is the outline provided by Kevin Feeney when we asked for the grant.

The Cantwell Films

While there are numerous photos of the late Archbishop John J. Cantwell available, there is virtually no motion picture film of him in existence.

The Archival Center, however, is in possession of approximately 5,500 feet of 8 mm black and white film taken by Archbishop Cantwell and his sister during their travels abroad in the early part of the last century.

The film logs, which are very sketchy, indicate trips were taken to Britain, France, large portions of Europe, to Egypt and to Africa. Brief notes on the storage boxes, presumably in the archbishop's or his sister's hand, indicate that the films date from 1920 through 1941. A cursory review of the ends of the rolls shows the archbishop and his sister as tourists in numerous locales. The roll marked Egypt shows the archbishop and his sister atop camels.

The films are brittle, and as they were not secured in their canisters, 10–20 feet of the outer leads have curled in upon themselves into tight cylinders. In addition, given their age, the machinery upon which to view them is unavailable outside of professional labs.

The Archival Center would like to preserve these images and migrate the film to archival-quality DVD disks. In the process, the film would be re-hydrated to address the curling issue, and cleaned to insure that the best possible image could be retrieved. To do so requires a specialized lab. We have already ascertained that the equipment to convert the images is available and have secured a quote for the work in the amount of $15,125.00.

(Following the successful completion of this project and the return of the refurbished films, we were pleasantly surprised to find it included an unmarked recording of a reception hosted by Mr. & Mrs. Edward Doheny in honor of the 1939 visit to Los Angeles of the Notre Dame Football Team. Knute Rockne is prominently featured in the surviving images, along with a host of dignitaries invited to lunch at the Doheny mansion.)

* * * * * *

During a pastoral visit to Rome, Archbishop Jose Gomez presented the Spanish edition of our book on the California missions to Pope Francis.

Archbishop Gomez presents History of the California Missions *to Pope Francis.*

Doyce Blackman Nunis–2011

Dr. Doyce Blackman Nunis, 86, recipient of the *Benemerenti* Medal from Pope Paul VI and the Knighthood of St. Gregory from Pope John Paul II, died on January 29th after abdominal surgery. He was the founding president of The Friends of the Archival Center.

Doyce Blackman Nunis, born at Cedartown, Georgia, on May 30, 1924, member of Our Mother of Good Counsel Parish in Hollywood (attended weekly Mass at the nearby Lithuanian Church because of his teaching schedule), was the author of more than forty books on the American West.

He established the Oral History Program at UCLA and later spent the majority of his professional career as full Professor at the University of Southern California.

After his conversion to the faith, in the 1950s, he became active in promoting the history of the Catholic Church in California. He served as President for the Friends of the Santa Barbara Mission Archives since 1972 and was the Founding President for the Friends of the Archival Center for the Archdiocese of Los Angeles. He was a Guggenheim Fellow.

Doyce Blackman Nunis

In addition to his scores of historical articles in learned journals, several of them about the California missions, Dr. Nunis served as editor of the prestigious *Southern California Quarterly* for thirty years and during that time published several dozen essays about the Catholic Church in the west.

A fervent Catholic, he was a spokesman for the Serra Bicentennial Commission and was well known in the local community for his support of efforts to promote the recording of local ecclesial history.

* * * * * *

Cardinal Roger Mahony has entrusted to the Archival Center a pectoral cross from Ken Hill of Santa Barbara. Here is part of the letter to the cardinal from Mr. Hill:

> The wood that this cross was made from comes from Madagascar. It is precious rosewood. I brought back several pieces the last time I was in South Africa. This particular type of rosewood is extremely hard and almost impossible to cut with a band saw. I had it custom cut on a laser machine at Trappist Caskets. That laser machine cost over $60,000. This wood really symbolized the character of the person that it is being given to.
>
> The inlaid cross was given to me about 50 years ago by a very sweet nun at my mother's funeral. She died when I was 9 years old. Originally, it was pewter. I had it plated with 14k gold, to represent my respect for you.
>
> The stone is amethyst; which is actually your birthstone, which I also got from the South African diamond mines. I had it mounted in 14K gold and secured on the top with a hole in the back.

Cardinal, I know you probably receive many gifts, but hopefully this one will represent how much I respect you and all the good work you have done for so many years. Obviously it is not one that you would wear daily, but hopefully, on special occasions, you will wear it and think of this person who has so much respect for you! It comes to you blessed by my dear friend, a Trappist monk, 104 years old!

If you ever find that it is not something that you will use or the time will come when you have no need for it any longer, I would only ask that it be worn one time and that it would find its way back home.

* * * * * *

The late Peter Buffo left his stamp collection to the Archival Center. Included therein is a page of mint U.S. stamps issued for the bicentennial of Fray Junípero Serra; another for the United States in Peace, an album for Vatican City stamps, the *Comprehensive World Wide Stamps Album* and several "first day" covers.

Lloyd Nielson, one of our friends, sent us a lovely memento of early pre-fire San Francisco. We had it framed and it now hangs in the

archivist's office. The following reproduction is the description that accompanied its original sale:

Rare pre-earthquake "book" of views. Folded, a 3 1/8 octagon. Opened,
it assumes the shape of a bowl, 7½" wide and about 2¼" deep. The center
of the bowl is adorned with a 1¾" brightly hand-colored picture of a floral
bouquet. Surrounding the picture on the sides of the bowl are the following
views: From California and Powell St; California St; Merchant's Exchange;
Bank of California; U.S. Branch Mint; Woodward's Gardens; Golden Gate;
Market Street. Each view is round with an inner red line border and an
outer twisted rope border which is rightly gilt. A third outer border outlines
the shape of each panel. The silver print views are each 1 5/8" in diameter.

The Golden Gate view does not show the bridge, which was con-
structed in the 1930s. There are horse-drawn streetcars in several of the
views; the garments worn by people in the streets suggest the 1870–1880
era. The view of Woodward's Gardens seems to date the entire piece at
about 1885, since the gardens fell into disuse and were closed in 1891.
The United States Mint as shown was built in 1874. There are no electric
or telegraph wires visible in any of the views, and the automobile had
not made its appearance. Extremely rare and in nice condition. There
is some rubbing along the outer edges but the views are in excellent

condition. There is no general title label or any identification of the document's origin.

* * * * * *

The Archival Center has recently acquired a series of five one-hour videos on *The Faithful Revolution; Vatican II,* produced in the 1990s by Richard C. Leach. It was created as a labor of love, to provide a documentary record of some of the most significant events of the Second Vatican Council. It includes testimonies by many people who were fortunate enough to be present, either as participants or observers, at this event of such importance to the Catholic Church. Today, theologians and religious educators acclaim it as a timeless treasure.

The Faithful Revolution: Vatican II documentary is of the highest quality and was filmed at various locations throughout the world. The Vatican Council had tremendous impact on the Catholic Church, and must be studied by each succeeding generation.

Pope Saint John Paul II claimed that Vatican Council II was one of the greatest religious and cultural events of the twentieth century. Many people agree with that assessment. For that reason, it is an event that deserves to be discussed and better understood both by those people who can recall it from memory and by others who have only selective secondhand information. Surprisingly, many Catholics today have little understanding of Vatican Council II.

Nina Galpren recently presented to the Historical Mission of the Archival Center a complete and framed collection of all the metallic mementos issued for the 1984 Olympics held in Los Angeles. Experts have advised us that there are relatively few complete collections of these important keepsakes of the Los Angeles Olympics.

A special exhibit commemorating the tricentennial of Saint Junípero Serra was featured at Mission San Fernando, Rey de España, in Mission Hills for 2015.

Among the several dozen items on display are a U.S. stamp bearing the likeness of Serra (1984), a copy of Palou's *Relacion Historica* (1787), a chalice and altar stone used by Fray Junípero Serra and other items associated with the founder of the California missions.

The first nine of the California missions, established along California's *El Camino Real*, were founded by Serra, who was canonized by Pope Francis in 2015.

Press Release – Archival Center Archdiocese of Los Angeles

The Archival Center for the Archdiocese of Los Angeles has been given a full-size, hand carved reproduction of the presidential desk used in the Oval Office of the White House.

This historic desk is a replica of the one created from the timbers of the *British H.M.S. Resolute*, given to U.S. President Rutherford Hayes in 1880 by Queen Victoria and used by most American heads of State.

A presidential 6-feet in width, this solid mahogany masterwork features hand carvings that include an American eagle on little John-John Kennedy's opening panel and an enviable, antique brown leather top with gold tooling.

This extradordianry Victorian replica boasts letter and file drawers hidden behind doors with metal pulls along with three shallow drawers to hold the presidential pen.

This stunning work almost unparalled among pieces that carry a rich American history, was given in memory of the late Ernest and Helen Chagon of San Buenaventura.

Archival Convention – 1998

This address was written for Roger Cardinal Mahony, who delivered it on July 26, 1998, at the Association for Catholic Archivists at Saint Mary's Seminary, Mundelein, Illinois.

The late John Tracy Ellis once identified the four evangelists as the first archivists. They gathered and preserved God's covenant with His people so that those of succeeding generations could know about His word and implement it into their lives. Today's Gospel according to Luke is then a part of that great archival treasure-trove which continues to nourish and sustain the followers of Christ.

In addition to presenting that perfect prayer of the Lord Himself, Luke also reminds us about the super abundance of God's bounty available to His people. He asks only that we express our needs:

Ask and you shall receive,
Seek and you will find
Knock and it will be opened to you.

I am humbled and pleased to have been asked to serve as the Episcopal Moderator for the Association of Catholic Diocesan Archivists. Knowing how concerned Cardinal Bernardine was for you and your work, I pledge to you my own services in whatever manner they can be of assistance.

Coming from an area where my predecessors have provided well for their archives, I am fully in accord with the need for preserving and caring for the records of the Church's accomplishments. In a sense, archivists carry on, in our own time, what Luke did for his – and that is indeed a most important part of my ministry and yours.

We are extremely pleased that Archbishop Francesco Marchisano could be with us. I would exhort all of you to read and study, digest and implement his letter on the Pastoral Function of Church Archives. And I do so because in this era of widespread confusion, the Church desperately needs to accurately and completely record and make known its activities as the outreach of the Holy Spirit.

Just recently, the Holy Father authorized the opening of that part of the Church's archives pertaining to the Inquisition. John Paul II is confident that an open policy in that regard will portray the Church in a light favorable to even its severest critics. We must endeavor to mirror the pontiff's sentiments in our own area.

En route to Mundelein today, I reread Archbishop Marchisano's letter and I was especially struck by his remarks that "Archives are places of Church memory which must be preserved, transmitted, renewed and appreciated because they represent the most direct connection with the heritage of the Church community. The prospects for relaunching them are favorable, due to the sensitivity which has developed in many particular churches for the cultural heritage and, in particular, for the memory of local events. Initiatives in this regard have been many and significant not only within the Church but also in the civil community."

The National Conference of Catholic Bishops entrusts you good people with the obligation of preserving the record of accomplishments in contemporary times. I cannot overly emphasize how vital a role you occupy for "without documents, there can be no history."

I am so pleased to join you in your noble pursuits for the truth. We live in an age where archivists are no longer hidden away in attics, basements or closets. The Church needs you, perhaps as never before. I applaud your work and your dedication to this vital part of evangelization.

Archivists need to have the persistence of the man in today's Gospel who came in the middle of the night clamoring for the three loaves of bread. Notice that eventually his persistence paid off and he got precisely what he wanted and needed. Keep persisting in your attempts to preserve the contents of the archives.

Remember Luke's assurance that "if you, with all your sins, know how to give your children good things, how much more will the heavenly Father give the Holy Spirit to those who seek Him."

And we exhort you to always tell the truth. Pope Leo XIII once said "the Church has no need of our lies." An honest presentation of the Church's deeds stands on its own merits.

History of the Archival Center

One of the O.C.P.'s. unfulfilled dreams was to write a history of the Archival ministry here in the Archdiocese of Los Angeles from 1962 onwards.

Happily, along came Sr. Mary Joanne Wittenburg, S.N.D., who stepped in and wrote a superb treatise, actually far better than I could have done.

Sr. Joanne Wittenburg, S.N.D.

The First Half Century

Sr. Mary Joanne Wittenburg, S.N.D.

St. Francis Historical Society

2013

The Archival Center

Archdiocese of Los Angeles

Msgr. Francis J. Weber

1999

3

Organizations

꙳ ꙳

The Zamorano Club

On May 7, 2014, the O.C.P. spoke to members of the Zamorano Club about his years with that outstanding group of bibliophiles. The text of that address is reproduced here as it appeared in the club's newsletter, *Hoja Volante.*

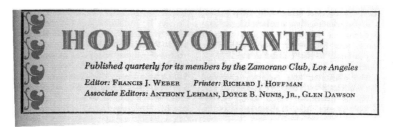

HOJA VOLANTE

Published quarterly for its members by the Zamorano Club, Los Angeles

Editor: FRANCIS J. WEBER   *Printer:* RICHARD J. HOFFMAN
Associate Editors: ANTHONY LEHMAN, DOYCE B. NUNIS, JR., GLEN DAWSON

(EDITORIAL NOTE: this issue of *Hoja Volante* honors one of the most distinguished members in the eighty-six year history of The Zamorano Club. A member since 1969, Monsignor Francis J. Weber has served the club in numerous capacities, including the presidency during the 1991–1992 season and editorship of *Hoja Volante* for a total of fifty issues. During the forty-five years of his membership, Monsignor Weber has published nearly a hundred essays in the pages of this journal. Scholar, historian, archivist, collector, writer, editor, teacher, and spiritual leader – few members have compiled a more distinguished record of achievement. Of his 170 books, the latest is *Some Memories of the Catholic Hierarchy,* published in 2013 by the St. Francis Historical Society of Mission Hills. Monsignor Weber – or the "old country priest," as he loves to be called – insists that this will be his final published volume – we'll see.)

✳ ✳ ✳ ✳ ✳

May I begin these observations by admitting that much of what I have to say is plagiarized from another presentation made early in 2005 at the behest of Dr. Gloria Ricci Lothrop, then the Editor of *Hoja Volante.*

In my eighty-year-old memory bank are many pleasant and rewarding experiences, none of which surpasses that of being a member of the Zamorano Club, a group of bibliophiles established in 1928 under the patronage of Agustin V. Zamorano who operated California's first printing press at Monterey in the mid-1830s.

I knew about the club from Lucille V. Miller, who had hosted members to a tour of the Estelle Doheny Collection at Camarillo on May 6, 1950. She gave me one of the keepsakes containing the addresses delivered on that occasion.

I was invited to a meeting of the club on October 4, 1967, at which time my friend, Doyce B. Nunis, gave a memorable lecture on "Books and Reading on the Far Frontier." Then, on November 6th of the following year, the program chairman arranged for me to address the club on "The Birth, Death, Burial and Resurrection of a California Mission Library," a talk outlining the history of the *Biblioteca Montereyenis-Angelorum Dioceseos.*

Late in 1969, I was delighted to receive a letter from Zamorano Club President, George Whitney, confirming that I had been invited to membership, sponsored by my historical colleague, Doyce Nunis.

Many years later, during my own tenure as president, I discovered that my nomination had been initially opposed by Dr. Marcus Crahan, a prominent physician and noted book collector, who contended that "having a priest at the meeting would dampen the spontaneity of conversation." In those times a negative vote by a single governor would result in blocking a nomination. Member Ray Billington told Crahan that "if you want to block this candidate because he is unqualified or lacking in clubability, I might concur, but, if you keep him out just because he is a priest, this non-Catholic will resign." Billington's intervention carried the day, Marcus voted "yes" and my name was approved. Marcus and I subsequently became close friends. Others elected to membership in that year were Alvin Brizzard, Anthony Lehman, Norman Strouse and Hugh Tolford.

Zamorano Club Members

My first meeting as a member took place on December 3rd when I joined the other Zamoranoans for sherry at the club's book-lined room in the Biltmore Hotel in downtown Los Angeles. After dinner in one of the hotel's private rooms, we returned to our club's room on the third floor to hear a lecture from Roby Wentz on "The Other Winston Churchill."

In those days when my finances were less secure, I would generally have dinner with my parents and then arrive at the Biltmore for the meeting and lecture, thus bypassing what was, for me, the costly dinner provided by the hotel. Another member who regularly joined me in that unorthodox practice was Edwin H. Carpenter, bibliographer at The Huntington Library. We engaged in many spirited conversations while waiting for the others to gather for the monthly presentation.

Even though my calendar in those years was crowded with all sorts of commitments, academic and otherwise, I considered the first Wednesday evenings of every month a "half holyday" on which Zamorano received primary priority, even though it often involved driving all the way from Anaheim or San Buenaventura.

I was able to share the privilege of being in the Zamorano Club with others over the years by helping to sponsor for membership Edward Petko, Bela Blau, Norton Stern, Anthony Kroll, Carey Stanton, Katherine Haley, Marla Daily, Regis Graden and Kenneth Karmiole.

The tenth joint meeting of the Zamorano-Roxburghe Clubs, scheduled for the weekend of September 26, 1970, took place at San Fernando Mission where I served as guide for a tour of the seventeenth of California's missions.

The day was memorable because, after leaving Mission Hills, the buses were turned back at Castaic Junction by fires raging along both sides of the highway.

The club's annual outing for 1979 was held at San Buenaventura Mission on June 28th. Zamoranoans were welcomed by the ringing of the historic mission bells. After a guided tour and a bountiful luncheon provided by the ladies of the Altar and Rosary Society, members were bused north to *Rancho Mi Solar* where Katherine Haley had arranged an exhibit of her Ed Borein collection.

Then in 1981, as part of the observance for the bicentennial of Los Angeles, members once again assembled at San Fernando Mission, this time for a tour of the newly opened Archival Center for the Archdiocese of Los Angeles. A formal dinner was served in the *gran sala* of the *convento* building featuring foods common in provincial times.

Feast of All Souls
Rancho Camulos
November 2, 2001

Each member of the Zamorano Club is expected to deliver an address occasionally and over the years I have spoken a number of times.

As part of the celebration for the American bicentennial, I read my pledge of allegiance, entitled "Happy Birthday Uncle Sam," to the club on December 1, 1976. At the end of the meeting, each member received a miniature book released earlier that year with the text of the talk.

The address to members on May 2, 1979, was entitled "California, The Golden State" which describes why the state is indisputably *"numero uno."*

In my address to members on November 4, 1981, I recalled my love for Hollywood, which dated back to childhood days when I was glued to Radio Station WLW in Indianapolis listening assiduously to "Breakfast at Sardi's." One of my ambitions in life was one day to dine in that restaurant, then located on Hollywood Boulevard.

The address given to the Zamorano Club on April 4, 1990, outlined my role as liaison for the Archbishop of Los Angeles with Christie's in the sale of the Estelle Doheny Collection.

In it I told how each of the nearly 10,000 items was identified and inventoried and then sent to New York and/or London. The ramifications of the seven auctions were described in a process that made the name of Carrie Estelle Doheny a household word in bibliophilic circles throughout the world.

Twice as many serious book people and art connoisseurs read about, saw and even caressed the book treasures as had been done in the previous half-century. Fittingly, the title of that address was "The Estelle Doheny Collection – A Personal Memoir."

"Reflections of a Newspaper Editor," the topic for a presentation to members on November 6, 1991, recalled the issues of *The Tidings*, the weekly newspaper for the Archdiocese of Los Angeles, which I edited for seventeen weeks in mid-1990.

On Ash Wednesday of 1994, I recalled some "Memoirs of the Stars," people encountered during the early years of my priestly ministry at Saint Victor's parish in West Hollywood. For that presentation, Ward Ritchie brought along his lifelong friend, actress Gloria Stuart, who was yet to star in her greatest role, in the film *Titanic*, a wonderful capstone to sixty-plus years in the motion picture industry.

"Trials and Tribulations of a Biographer," the subject for a talk on November 5, 1997, told about the book on James Francis Cardinal McIntyre. It concluded with the observation that "writing a biography can be dangerous to one's health and overall well-being." It was a consuming project that almost became an obsession. After a while, a biographer begins to identify with the person he is writing about, and therein lies the potential pitfall of losing objectivity.

In 1985 I was elected to a seven-year term as governor for the Zamorano Club. I was privileged to serve as the club's thirty-first president, 1991–1992.

Several noteworthy accomplishments were recorded during my years on the board and as president, none more important than the happy resolution of the long-debated question of inviting women to membership.

It was also during my tenure that we were able to publish a fifty-year Index for *Hoja Volante*, the club's official newsletter. Covering the years 1934 to 1984, it was compiled by Anna Marie and Everett Gordon Hager.

Of the many wonderful people in the Zamorano Club, none surpassed the gentle W. W. Robinson, longtime book reviewer for *Westways* and outstanding local historian. He was especially gracious to me personally and whenever one of my books appeared, he would mention and often elaborate on it in his monthly column for *Westways*.

The one underlying virtue of all the members was and remains their graciousness. They were all practitioners of the natural virtue of kindness. Rarely if ever did I hear a harsh word or an uncharitable remark about a fellow member.

In 1981 James Greene asked me to take over the editorship of *Hoja Volante*, the club's quarterly newsletter. Nothing further happened, however, until the end of 1983 when Hugh Tolford, by then president, formally entrusted the position to me.

The *Hoja Volante* had been published intermittently between 1934 and 1938 and quarterly since 1947. I slightly adjusted the focus to concentrate on modestly sized essays about "bookish" events and topics.

Prior to becoming editor, I had written several articles for the *Hoja Volante*, the most ambitious of which appeared in May 1972 under the title "The Editions of Palou's *Relation Historica*, 1787–1958," a chronological outline of the various editions of that monumental historical opus.

Because of the demise of Grant Dahlstrom, the previous printer, my initial issue, February 1984, was designed and printed letterpress by Richard Hoffman, who continued in that role until his own death in 1989. Richard and I were a good team and often I visited his press in Van Nuys to read, proof, tip in illustrations or otherwise participate in the overall process.

Later George Kinney and Patrick Reagh did the printing until Regis Graden, at the Nut Quad Press, in San Fernando, assumed that task. Happily I was given the freedom of introducing a number of innovations into the *Hoja Volante*. In the issue of May 1984, for example, was the first tip-in, a colorful piece of marbled paper illustrating an article by Stephen Tabor on contemporary paper marbling.

In later issues there were other tip-ins, including Tony Kroll's etching of the Zamorano logo, Carrie Estelle Doheny's leather bookplate, a print of Carl Oscar Borg's depiction of Dawson's Book Shop and a commemorative United States postage stamp featuring Robert Frost.

In addition to several dozen of my own articles on different aspects of the "book," other members of the club were encouraged to submit essays. Earl Nation, Lawrence Longo, Norton Stern, Larry Myers, Carey Bliss, Henry Clifford and Stuart Robinson became regular contributors, along with old-timers Doyce Nunis, Tony Lehman, Ward Ritchie and Glen Dawson. The greater mix of articles did much to stimulate fresh interest in *Hoja Volante*.

AUGUST 1984   NUMBER 146

HOJA VOLANTE

Published quarterly for its members by the Zamorano Club, Los Angeles

Editor: FRANCIS J. WEBER   Printer: RICHARD J. HOFFMAN
Associate Editors: ANTHONY LEHMAN, DOYCE B. NUNIS, JR., GLEN DAWSON

Zamorano World

Our distinguished maritime historian, *John Kemble*, presents a slide lecture on "The Gold Rush to California by Way of Panama" for a meeting of the Pacific Maritime Society at the Sherman Foundation in Corona del Mar. . . . Cypress College gives their American Award to *Don Meadows* for his dedicated works as a writer and historian. . . . A gala autograph party at Dawson's Book Shop heralds the appearance of *Lawrence Clark Powell's* third novel *El Morro*. Many Zamoranans are on hand for the occasion, enlivened by the sparkling, chiding, and inimitable repartee between Larry and his former school chum *Ward Ritchie*. . . . *Doyce Nunis* receives the Pontifical honor, the Benemerenti Medal, from *Timothy Cardinal Manning* at a special Papal Honors Mass. The medal was bestowed by Pope John Paul II on Dr. Nunis for his outstanding contributions to scholarship and teaching, as well as for his record of service both to the secular community and the Church, notably his long service on the Board of Trustees for the Santa Barbara Mission Archive Library. . . Msgr. *Francis J. Weber* adds two more publications to his already lengthy bibliography: *Some Fugitive Glimpses at Fray Junipero Serra* and *America's Painter—Norman Rockwell*, the latter a miniature book chosen by the Rounce & Coffin Club for inclusion in the 1984 Western Books Exhibition. . . . *Tony Lehman*, who assists Msgr. Weber with editorial duties on *Hoja Volante*, is also represented in the 1984 Western Books Exhibition by his volume *Paul Landacre: A Life and a Legacy*, a biography of a notable Southern California wood-engraver handsomely designed and

printed by *Richard Hoffman*. Tony receives further honors by being granted a Fellowship from the National Endowment for the Humanities for summer study at the University of California, Davis. . . . Non-resident member *Saul Cohen* keeps busy in Santa Fe by penning an article on "New Mexico Novels: A Preliminary Checklist" for the April 1984 issue of *Book Talk*. Saul also addresses the annual convention of New Mexico Press Women on the subject "Writers and the Law" and, only a few days later, delivers a talk on "Photographers and the Law" to the annual convention of New Mexico Industrial Photographers. . . . *Robert Vosper* and *Larry Powell* are included among fifteen librarians whose professional careers are analyzed in *Leaders in American Academic Librarianship: 1925-75*, edited by Wayne Weigand of the University of Kentucky, and distributed by the American Library Association. . . . Honorary member, *Mrs. Donald F. (Mary) Hyde* keeps busy with plans to celebrate the Centennial of the Grolier Club. . . . *Garth Huston* assumes the presidency of the American Osler Society, an office also held a few years back by *Earl Nation*. Garth additionally enlightens our Roxburghe friends in San Francisco with his lecture on "Sir Kenelm Digby's Library—Fine Binding in 17th Century England," and presents a paper at the American Association of the History of Medicine on the topic of the origin of resuscitation of drowned persons in 18th century England. . . . Finally, the State of Colorado is given a double-barrel blast of our former, esteemed UCLA librarians: *Bob Vosper* journeys to Boulder as a member of a three-man external review team for the University of Colorado Libraries

Were I asked to nominate the article that contributed the most and the one which probably would never have been published anywhere else during the decade of my editorship, it would be the two-part essay about Emilio Valton (1879–1963), the ex-priest who came to Los Angeles in 1929 and befriended Glen Dawson. Over many years, Valton had his finger in almost every level of the book trade. And he was a mystery man to the very end as the essay amply testifies.

After a hiatus of some years, I returned to act as interim editor of *Hoja Volante* for four issues in 2002. During that time, the most important article was probably Robert C. Bradbury's enumeration of the ninety-two miniature books bearing the Dawson imprint.

Over the years I edited four books for the club:

Zamorano Club Biographies and Memorial Tributes 1956 - 1997

COMPILED WITH A FOREWORD BY MSGR. FRANCIS J. WEBER

THE ZAMORANO CLUB OF LOS ANGELES, 1998

Carey Stanton's *Island Memoir* (1984), *The Zamorano Club Programs, 1928–1991* (1992), *Zamorano Choice II* (1996) and *Zamorano Club Biographies and Memorial Tributes 1956–1997* (1998).

For those who keep track of statistics, only five of our eighty confreres outrank the old country priest in club seniority. Even after forty-five years, my esteem for the Zamorano Club and my gratitude for being a member remain at fever pitch. It's been great fun and may the Lord bless those who have walked alongside these many years!

ZAMORANO CHOICE II

Selections from the Zamorano Club's
Hoja Volante 1967-1993

Compiled with a Foreword by
Francis J. Weber

Los Angeles: The Zamorano Club, 1996

The Westerners

Myths, Mythologists and the California Missions

Among the many addresses, talks, lectures and other presentations delivered by the Old Country Priest over the years, none has been more popular and repeated than the one which appeared in *The Branding Iron* of the Los Angeles Corral of Westerners in the winter issue of 1995. Because it touched so many issues discussed, we are here presenting it one last time.

If it is true that "good history drives bad history out of existence," then students of Clio must be scrupulously accurate, precise and, above all, truthful in their writings. Especially is that true of the California missions.

There might be a place for myth, legend and folklore in fiction, but not in history. The challenge about the so-called "mission myth" is that of determining what is myth and what is not! And this is always difficult because many people tend to romanticize the past by canonizing "the good old days."

In 1974, John Ogden Pohlmann wrote a superb dissertation at UCLA on *California Mission Myths,* which this author recommends highly; it is still available at University Microfilms in Ann Arbor, Michigan. Pohlmann observes, at the very outset, that "even those instances where myths and legends are revealed by modern scholarship to be totally unsubstantiated, they should never be regarded as complete falsehoods, for frequently they reflect more about the culture which circulates the myth or legend than they reveal about the previous event or era they specifically describe." Hence, the temptation to disregard totally the books of Helen Hunt Jackson, George Wharton James and Charles Fletcher Lummis must be avoided.

Perhaps the story of the California missions has been over told. It resembles an old country barn that has been painted too many times. The layers of paint become almost as thick as the walls to which they adhere. Maybe it is time for a sandblaster to remove all the paint and allow the original surface to reflect its natural luster.

My personal opinion, after thirty years of research and reflection, is that the mission system as it unfolded in California needs no apologists and certainly no mythologists. What the objective historian of the future must do is restudy (a) the missions as they operated under the *Laws of the Indies;* (b) the Mallorcan society where most of the early friars were raised and educated; (c) the demographics of the Native Americans before, during and after the so-called "conquest"; (d) missionary procedures in other areas of the world; (e) the academic credentials of purported experts; (f) the veracity of oral traditions among indigenous peoples; and, perhaps most importantly, (g) what, if any, were the alternatives to the mission system.

One is confident that when such an in-depth investigation has been made, the mission system will emerge as accomplishing what it attempted to do, namely, sharing the Christian faith with an aboriginal people. Nothing less. A good deal more. There is no place, no justification and no need for myths when telling the story of the missionary foundations along *El Camino Real.*

What is disconcerting and distressing today, however, is a whole new generation of "myths" that have arisen in the last dozen or so years, none of which is any more reliable or creditable than the yarns spun during California's "Romantic Revival" of the 1880s, and many of which are malicious, mean-spirited and untrue. Let us address the veracity or lack thereof in some of the more prominent of these myths.

(1) MYTH:
The missionaries violated the human rights of their neophytes, both before and after their conversion.
FACT:
Philip II issued directives on December 24, 1580, entrusting the viceroys, missionaries and *audiencias* with the duty of looking after the Indians so that they may be protected, favored and placated. He stated "we desire that the injuries they suffer be remedied so that they may be without molestation or vexation. The Indians are to be defended from all harm, and the laws of the *Recopilación* are to be observed exactly. Transgressors are to be punished."

The king concluded by charging missionaries "to work for this objective as true spiritual fathers of Christianity preserving for the Indians their privileges and prerogatives." These were the laws of the land, and they were observed scrupulously by the friars.

Serra personally journeyed to Mexico City in 1773 to demand and receive from the Viceroy a declaration of Indian rights, which were threatened by the military. No one then or since can equal Serra's concern and action for the rights of the California Indians.

(2) MYTH:
The accelerated death rate of Native Americans in the years after European penetration was due primarily to the diseases acquired from Hispanics or poor living conditions at the missions.

FACT:
The story of the past is forever being updated and reinterpreted. History will never stay written as long as scholars are unearthing fresh evidence and re-evaluating the old. An example at hand is the traditional explanation given for the accelerated death rate among Native Americans in the years after European occupation. Not only have statistics been misused and exaggerated, but discoveries in medical science are providing wholly new and convincing theories.

Historians have long believed that European diseases were the only cause for the heavy death toll on American Indians, but recent studies demonstrate how at least one mid-western tribe, the Omahas, was ravaged by a totally different source.

Karl Reinhard, an anthropologist at the University of Nebraska, examined the chemical contents of skeletons exhumed forty years ago from Omaha tribal graves. More than half were found to be heavily laced with lead, a substance known to have decimated ancient Romans.

Unlike such other tribes as the Sioux and Pawnee, the Omahas had more extensive contacts with Europeans from whom they obtained lead in trade for a variety of uses.

By the early nineteenth century, the Omahas had become the first gunsmiths of the Plains. They avidly exchanged items for lead with which to make musket balls. Artifacts found at gravesites also suggest that traders supplied the Indians with such items as wine bottles and food tins sealed with lead solder. Additionally, some skeletal remains showed signs of lead-based paint on their faces. Once ingested, lead was absorbed into the bones and did not readily dissipate. Depending on the quantities and the age of those exposed, lead is known to have caused retardation, developmental problems and even death.

In the case of the Omaha skeletons, twenty-two of the remains exhibited lead in dangerous to lethal quantities ranging from 80 to 400 parts per million. The skeleton of one child measured 1,000 parts per million.

The Indians in question were buried between 1789 and 1820 in northwestern Nebraska. During that time span, the population of the Omahas began to dwindle from about 1,700 until it leveled out at about 300. Previously, tribal historians had blamed the decline on epidemics spread by white traders and settlers, but according to Reinhard's studies, the chemical analysis conducted with mass spectrometers and other high-tech gear, showed surprisingly little evidence of infectious diseases on the Omaha skeletons.

Whether lead poisoning affected other tribes of the period is unknown and would not have been discovered in the case of the Omahas had it not been for an unusual resolution of a long custody fight for the skeletal remains. What happened to the Omahas could easily have happened elsewhere. In their case, history has now spoken through science. Reinhard said that "the findings have implications for the broader population as well.. Here we have a culture that almost went extinct because of the toxic elements they were coming into contact with."

Could not something like that have occurred in California? Surely such a discovery would keep a whole new generation of historians off the streets.

(3) MYTH:
Native Californians were looked down upon and treated by the friars as irrational, sub-human and animal-like beings.

FACT:
This myth revives one first posed after the fall of the Aztec capital, on August 23, 1521. Then it was asked whether the Indians of the New World were rational or even human beings, capable and worthy of becoming

and living as Christians. Obviously, this question had enormous practical implications: if the natives were not rational, then they possessed no human rights and could be treated like animals, with no property claims or governmental obligations.

Bishop Julian Garces placed this vital question before Pope Paul III, who in 1537, issued his declaration, *Sublimis Deus*, wherein he stated unequivocally that native peoples throughout the world were to be considered rational, capable and worthy of the Christian faith. The Pope had spoken, the matter was closed.

(4) MYTH:

**The missionaries should have stayed at home and their presence was
a negative factor in Alta California.**

FACT:

Those who contend that nothing in the Indian way of life should ever have been disturbed deny the inevitable progression of humankind. In a changing world, no portion of the Spanish American dominions could have been preserved in hermetical isolation. The natives were destined to change for better or worse, and the missionaries dedicated themselves to helping them change for the better.

(5) MYTH:

The presence of the Franciscans at the California missions was directly responsible for accelerating the death rate.

FACT:

Much of the criticism now directed at Fray Junípero Serra and the missions concerns the dramatic upsurge in the death rate among the Indians of Alta California after the arrival of the European missionaries. Actually, the soldiers, sailors and settlers (not the friars) spread disease wherever they went in the New World. Precisely when this started in California is a moot question, but likely the earliest expeditions left those hidden reminders behind.

It must also be remembered that none of the earliest memoirs spoke of Indian families with more than two or three children. In 1752, Father Jacob Baegert, a Jesuit pioneer in Peninsular California, noted that in Baja California "two or three children are a great burden." Reading through Baegert's letters, it is clear that he and other eighteenth-century Jesuit missionaries believed that they were dealing with a native population already on the decline. Baegert observed, for example, that few youngsters survived childhood diseases.

Baegert, who attributed the rapid decline of the Indian population in Baja California between 1700 and 1752 to "sickness and rebellion," later opined that abortion and parental neglect accounted for the low rate of live births, as well as the high infancy mortality rate. Likewise, Father Baegert stated, based on personal observation, that poor diet, inadequate attention to the ill and outright killing of infirm people contributed heavily to the decline of the adult native population.

Admittedly, during the earliest years of European presence in Alta California, the Indian population declined at an alarming rate. There were recurring epidemics of smallpox, measles and dysentery, but the greatest killer of all was syphilis, a disease passed on to children. Three out of four children succumbed the first or second year.

It is not possible to state with certainty whether the Indian population at the missions declined at a greater or a lesser rate than the unconverted Indians, for which there is no available evidence and who accounted for at least three-quarters of the Indian population during mission days. Also, it must be remembered that the friars often came across or were called to administer the Sacrament of Extreme Unction to people already at the point of dying, a factor that would inflate the normal death rate of baptized Christians in proportion to the general native population.

There were other reasons for the accelerated death rate, many of them not thoroughly understood then or now. Yet, this is not something for which the Franciscans should be singled out for blame. There is no way that the disease factor and all the other related effects of colonization could have been avoided in California. Even though statistics can be over and under estimated and possibly misevaluated, their basic thrust remains fairly consistent. Indians did indeed die, but the causes of death are still in question.

(6) MYTH:
The Indians attached to the California missions suffered dreadful deprivations and punishments during the mission period.

FACT:
The so-called Serra controversy has revealed a shocking lack of understanding not only of the mission program and its role in California, but also of the chronology of California history in general. The time sequence is vitally important: the worst violation of Indian rights in California came after, not during, the mission era. Those suffering most from the encroachments of the gold rush days were the descendants of Indians never attached to the missions.

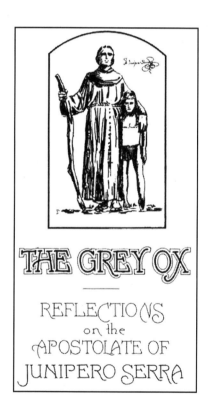

THE GREY OX

REFLECTIONS
on the
APOSTOLATE OF
JUNIPERO SERRA

(7) MYTH:
The statistics of Sherburne F. Cook are a reliable instrument of determining the death rate at the missions of Alta California.

FACT:
Few, if any, studies about the death rate during mission times have been based on the original records. Researchers have relied either on copies and summaries of the originals or on doubtful estimates, guesses and assumptions by anthropologists. The often-quoted statistics of Sherburne Cook have not withstood the scrutiny of subsequent research. Cook never utilized primary sources, but based his conclusions on transcripts made by Hubert H. Bancroft and extracts done by Thomas Workman Temple. He noted near the end of his life, in 1974, that "if time and opportunity were favorable, it would be desirable to make a definitive count of the actual entries in the register books." Indeed Cook himself, in a later study, reduced his earlier totals considerably and finally concluded that the infant mortality rate in Alta California should be "no worse than in other comparable societies in the eighteenth and nineteenth centuries." Francis Guest, archivist for the Santa Barbara Mission Archives, has suggested that a study and comparison of the death rate in Europe for the same period of time might well cast a wholly new dimension on what transpired in California.

(8) MYTH:
The catechetical program at the missions offered little challenge to the friars.

FACT:
Quite the contrary. Though Serra and other missionaries were former university professors, they found it very difficult to instruct the natives in abstract terminology. The children generally adapted easily to the rigid mission regimen, but many adult neophytes never fully embraced the Christian lifestyle. In 1830, Fray Narciso Duran wrote that even though the natives at San Jose Mission "are baptized voluntarily, they easily tire and change – because their character is fickle and childlike." As mission Indians began adjusting to the new practices, they took to living in permanent adobes, ate regular meals, learned different ways to care for their youngsters, abandoned intramural fights, raised crops, cared for livestock, learned new arts and crafts and began mixing with settlers in the *pueblos, presidios* and *ranchos.*

(9) MYTH:

The prominence of Fray Junípero Serra in California is due primarily to such propagandists as Helen Hunt Jackson, George Wharton James and Charles Fletcher Lummis.

FACT:

The fame of Serra transcends his supporters, as is evident in the Sierra Gorda region of Central Mexico where he labored before coming to Alta California and where very little had been written about him until contemporary times.

The Franciscans were active in the Sierra Gorda for roughly a quarter century, where they succeeded in fulfilling their dual goals of converting the natives to Christianity and turning them into productive citizens of the Spanish empire. That Serra and the other Franciscans were successful in the Sierra Gorda is all the more impressive in light of earlier futile attempts at bringing the peoples there into the Catholic faith.

Serra's work in Central Mexico and that of his collaborators was crucial to the later activities in Alta California because the area was a training ground for many of the friars who subsequently worked along *El Camino Real.*

Today, Serra is the most remembered of all the early missionaries working in that portion of the Lord's vineyard. He was assigned to the Santiago de Jalpan in 1750 and remained there for eight years. Happily, the activities of Serra at Jalpan were carefully recorded.

Serra's success in his earliest missionary endeavors can be attributed to the policies upon which he based his ministry: teaching his marginally agricultural people new techniques of farming and caring for livestock.

The perfecting of their agricultural pursuits allowed the neophytes to improve their standard of living, thus giving them parity with other citizens of the empire. Unlike his predecessors who relied on translators, Serra actually learned the Pame language and was able to teach and converse in that tongue.

The missionary outposts in the Sierra Gorda are very much in place today. Visitors to that remote area can still see the churches built and cared for by Serra and his companions two and half centuries ago. What is more fascinating are the verbal traditions about Serra and the good work he and others did in that region. The people there long ago "canonized" Serra and, today, he continues to walk tall in the Sierra Gorda.

Serra's missionary policies were not so easily realized in Alta California even though the lands were more fertile and easily irrigated. The natives were still at the "hunting and gathering" stage and had no traditions of farming and husbandry.

There was no common Indian language in Alta California. Within that outpost of the empire were no less than sixty-four (perhaps as many as eighty) mutually unintelligible languages, along with numerous dialects. The linguistic perplexities often forced Serra and the other friars to encourage the Indians to learn Spanish.

Despite the more challenging problems in Alta California, Fray Junípero Serra was able to establish nine missions along the coast of California, where, as earlier, he was loved and venerated by those brought into the embrace of the Catholic faith.

(10) MYTH:
The early missionaries came to California to further their careers, increase their wealth and advance their own agenda.

FACT:
Certainly the friars did not volunteer for California because they wanted to participate in the destruction of its peoples; they came to Christianize what they sensed was an inevitable trend. Like missionaries in every age, the Franciscans in 1769 were obsessed with adding a supernatural dimension to the quest for expanding the world's frontiers. Theirs was a *spiritual* conquest and their presence in California can only be explained in spiritual terminology. The mission friars provided what they believed to be the all-important and saving message of Christianity, and none of them profited personally, at least in the temporal order.

(11) MYTH:
The "lucky" Indians were those who never came into contact with Christianity, resisted its message or left the missions after conversion.

FACT:
The seemingly endless discussions about the impact of the California missions on the Indians have left some crucial questions unasked. For example, what happened to the 60 percent of the area's natives who were not assimilated into the mission system? Did their descendants prosper in later years? Did they have a lesser death and disease rate than their Christian counterparts? Did those not "contaminated" by the friars, continue to live in some aboriginal paradise? Lacking any death or other records for the non-mission Indians, only conjectural statements can be made about how they were affected by Europeans. Available evidence indicates that, if anything, the non-missionized Indians died and otherwise declined even more rapidly than the others.

(12) MYTH:
Because of the presence of the friars, the California native population was totally decimated.

FACT:
There are probably more people alive today with Indian blood in their veins than there were in the time of Fray Junípero Serra. In the years after

secularization of the California missions, few of the neophytes reverted to the wilderness and their aboriginal way of life, partly because California had changed dramatically. By that time, there were relatively few areas isolated from European contact and influence. The *ranchos* owned in 1833 by Spanish, Mexican and (soon) American landholders controlled most of the native environment, leaving less room for a hunter-gatherer culture to survive, especially along the more fertile coast.

Many of the Christianized Indians remained at the missions for the rest of their lives while others drifted away to the settlements and *ranchos*. A small percentage of the Indians engaged in farming and ranching, occupations they had learned while still attached to the once-thriving missions. Others were assimilated and became part of the *gente de razón*, inter-marrying with Spanish, Mexican and, later, American colonists. As had occurred earlier, when Indians married members of the military detachments, they acquired a social standing superior to that enjoyed by the other neophytes. Since many of the soldiers received governmental land grants upon completion of their services, their Indian spouses also shared in whatever social and economic advantages accrued to property holders.

Interestingly, many of the soldiers in California already had high percentages of Indian blood in their veins, a factor not emphasized (and sometimes vociferously denied) because of the social pressures then prevalent in Mexican society. Because a large percentage of the soldiers who married Indian wives found it politically inexpedient to identify with Native American customs and practices, most of them avoided counting or otherwise considering their offspring as "Indians." The children of those "mixed" marriages generally tended to marry non-Indians, probably because their contact and association with other natives was minimal.

However considered, America's western "melting pot" certainly included a goodly percentage of California Indians, something not true along the Eastern seaboard, where marriage with natives was not encouraged and often forbidden. Descendants of these "mixed marriages" are generously represented in today's polyglot population though, more often than not, they have lost their Native American identity. This assimilation continued well into the American period.

(13) MYTH:
The missions were "concentration camps" in which the neophytes were incarcerated.

FACT:
Believing that the neophytes were as yet unready to compete with the general population under society's complicated game rules of the 1830s, the friars felt that dispersal of the Indians from the missions would be premature. In fact, after secularization of the missions, the natives quickly lost their property and virtually became slaves in the *pueblos* and *ranchos*. Almost without exception, the Indians asked that the friars be reinstated and that the secular administrators be removed.

In Alta California, the friars used the same methods employed with great efficiency in the Sierra Gorda regions of Central Mexico. When food supplies were meager, the natives were encouraged to leave the missions, return to the wilderness and forage for themselves. As conditions improved, these absences became less frequent, although the average neophyte spent two months annually away from the mission with his or her unchristianized brethren.

(14) MYTH:
Fray Junípero Serra "beat" the Indians.

FACT:
Though the *Law of the Indies* allowed "spanking" of the natives for specified violations, the extant evidence indicates that most of the friars, Serra included, avoided that form of punishment whenever possible. The missionaries did not look upon themselves as disciplinarians and, with rare exceptions, left the "policing" of the neophytes to the military.

Every society has built-in sanctions to protect the commonwealth and the primitive communities functioning at the California missions were no exception. Whether punishments out-distanced violations has to be examined within the context of practices then in vogue in the parent society, which, in this case, was Spain. In that mother country, the penal aspect of communal life was primarily a governmental, not religious, function. While the friars in Alta California may have countenanced "spanking," most of them (a) doubted its effectiveness, (b) preferred other methods and (c) avoided whenever possible, any part in its execution.

(15) MYTH:
The "Black Legend" existed in the California missions and was epitomized by the friars.

FACT:
Contrary to the practice in the English and French settlements of colonial America, the relationship of Native Americans to Hispanic explorers and settlers along the Pacific Slope was minutely regulated by royal statutes. To the early missionaries, the *Recopilación de las leyes de los Reinos de Indias* (first published in 1552, then subsequently revised and updated) was as familiar as their breviary. Copies of this multi-volume handbook or manual were available in every mission library.

As agents for the crown as well as missionaries for the Church, the friars patterned their activity on the directives contained in the *Recopilación* where concern for the spiritual and temporal welfare of the native peoples was a recurrent theme. For example, in his edict issued in 1526, King Charles exhorted "priests and religious who might participate in discoveries and in making peace (with the native tribes) to try, with very great care and diligence to bring it about that the Indians are well treated, looked upon and favored as neighbors."

Missionaries were instructed not to allow "the Indians to be forced, robbed, injured or badly treated." The monarch went on to say that "if the contrary is done by any person, regardless of his position or condition, the justices are to proceed against him according to law; and in those cases where it is proper for us to be advised, let it be done as soon as the opportunity is available for justice to be provided and that such excesses be punished with all rigor."

(16) MYTH:
The early missionaries were intent on destroying the indigenous culture of California.

FACT:
The evidence clearly shows the exact opposite, namely that the friars came to the Pacific Slope to build on and expand the existing Indian cultures. Among the many examples of their endeavors to telescope the old with the new was their work with native languages. Where there was a single or predominant language, the friars endeavored to learn it, preach in it and preserve it. At practically all the missions, the friars compiled grammars, dictionaries and catechisms in the local language and dialects.

Examples that eventually found their way into print were Fray Felipe Arroyo de la Cuesta's grammar and phrase books at San Juan Bautista, both of which preserved the Costanoan language by allowing it to be handed down and eventually printed for new generations.

Fray Juan Cortes compiled a *Catechismo y Confesionario* for the natives at Santa Barbara and that, too, was ultimately published. Finally, Fray Jose Señan prepared a *confesionario* for the Chumash Indians which ultimately became something of a classic in the linguistic world.

In addition, there was the case of Pablo Tac, an Indian boy who was sent to Rome for ecclesial studies. As a means of preserving his own native culture, the professors at the *Colegio de Propaganda Fide* suggested that he compile a "Record of Indian Life" outlining the beliefs and history of his people. That study was eventually published and today is regarded as a primary and unique source of Indian lore.

Another cultural area that the friars built upon and expanded were the indigenous artistic talents of the Indians. Among the litany of examples would be the Stations of the Cross painted by an Indian and still very much in evidence at San Gabriel Mission. The wall embellishments at various missions, including the masterful framed vintage scene painted above the door opposite the entrance to the *convento* at San Fernando, are primary indications of how the friars encouraged and preserved local talent.

Further examples of Indian art and how the friars encouraged its portrayal at the California missions are explained in an informative booklet by Lanier Bartlett. Norman Neuerburg has codified the decoration at the California Missions and has shown how skillful the Indian artisans were.

Native American costumery was featured in many early paintings by visitors to the missions. Among those paintings, enthusiastically encouraged by the friars, was a colorful scene of an Indian dance at San Jose Mission which is presently in the collection of the Bancroft Library at the Berkeley campus of the University of California. There are others still in existence.

The musical talents of the Indians were adapted and enhanced at the missions for choral and liturgical services and this field is now being studied by Dr. Craig Russell of California State Polytechnic University, San Luis Obispo, who has produced programs of music once performed by the Indians.

One final example and one related to the preservation of native religious beliefs is Fray Geronimo Boscana's historical account of the San Juan Capistrano Indians which bears the name *Chinigchinich*. Describing the strongly moralistic religious or cult beliefs, it is the longest and most scholarly ethnological document dating from the mission period. The aboriginal religion described in Boscana's book was based on fear. Medicine men deliberately kept the Indians in ignorance about their work. The rituals were in a language unknown to ordinary people. It goes almost without saying that the missionaries were not anxious to sustain such activities.

In conclusion there was indeed a clash of cultures in Alta California between 1769 and 1840.

The missionaries knew history. Though they did not always understand how or why, they pretty much anticipated what would happen in California which probably explains why they were not overly surprised when the death rate began its sharp climb upwards. They concentrated their energies on doing what they could to alleviate or ameliorate a bad situation.

It is unfair and wrong for contemporary commentators to use the yardstick of the 1990s to measure the society of 1769 and later. The time warp throws any such comparisons into utter disarray and further confuses a true appreciation of what really occurred.

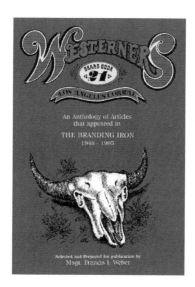

4

Cathedral of Our Lady of the Angels

Already, the standard guidebooks of prominent places in the United States are featuring the Cathedral of Our Lady of the Angels as a significant and unique architectural attraction for visitors to Los Angeles.

The Old Country Priest has written copiously on the Mother Church for Catholics in California's southland. Here is an essay on the new Chapel of Our Lady of Guadalupe and its relic of the *Tilma.*

Traditionally, portrayals of the *Relic of the Tilma* of Our Lady have been the most treasured Marian depictions in the Christian world. The celebrated Madonnas of the Renaissance, those of Raphael, Michelangelo and Murillo, are internationally famous for their beauty and artistic style. Yet there is one likeness of Mary that surpasses them all, for it was presented by the Mother of God herself to a humble Indian neophyte, on an insignificant little hill, near Mexico City, over 400 years ago.

Devotion to Our Lady of Guadalupe is the oldest Marian observance in the Californias. All the earliest missionaries from Spain visited and prayed at the revered sanctuary built near Tepeyac in Mexico City.

According to historical tradition, it was during December 1531 that Juan Diego beheld a "beautiful lady" as he crossed the hill of Tepeyac en route to Holy Mass. Identifying herself as the Virgin Mary, she told him to ask Bishop Juan de Zumarraga to build a church on the site.

Dismissed at first as a religious eccentric, Juan Diego, beatified in 1990, had two subsequent encounters with Our Lady. On his final visit to the episcopal residence, Juan brought some out-of-season roses he had found at the scene of the apparitions. As he was speaking with the bishop, Juan opened his cloak, or *tilma,* and, on the rough cloth, was an image of the Virgin as she had appeared.

Relic of the Tilma of St. Juan Diego
Cathedral of Our Lady of the Angels
Los Angeles, California

Called Our Lady of Guadalupe to avoid confusion with the medieval apparition of the Virgin at Guadalupe in Spain, the occurrences of 1531 had a greater impact upon the Western Hemisphere than any other single event during the ensuing centuries.

In 1556, a hermitage was established on Tepeyac hill to house the *Tilma*. Due to extensive flooding between 1629 and 1634, the *Tilma* was temporarily displayed in the Metropolitan Cathedral in Mexico City. Devotion to our Lady of Guadalupe was formalized in 1737, when she was named Patroness of Mexico City. A college was founded at the sanctuary and, in 1910, Pope Pius X declared her Patroness of all Latin America.

During the years 1695 to 1709, a large baroque church was erected at Tepeyac. In 1895, it was raised to the status of a minor basilica by Pope Leo XIII who also authorized the coronation of Our Lady's image.

In a 1945 radio message proclaiming Our Lady of Guadalupe Empress of the Americas, Pope Pius XII said:

> *On the tilma of poor Juan Diego was painted with brushes not of this world a most sweet Picture, which the corrosive work of centuries was most wondrously to respect. The amiable Maiden asked for a Sign from which she might show and give all her love and compassion, help and protection ... to all the inhabitants of that land and to all others who would invoke her and trust her. Since that historical moment, the total evangelization has been accomplished. Furthermore, a banner was hoisted and a fortress erected against which the fury of all the storms would break. One of the fundamental pillars of the Faith in Mexico and in all America was thus firmly established.*

In 1976, the *Tilma* was moved to a newly erected modern basilica adjacent to the eighteenth century building and it was there that Pope Saint John Paul II said Holy Mass on January 27, 1979.

As the patroness of the insurgents under Father Miguel Hidalgo, the image of Our Lady of Guadalupe appeared on the banner of the independence movement. And with the establishment of the empire and republic of 1821 and 1824, she became the official "protector" of the nation.

Today more than 20 million pilgrims annually visit the basilica, which is the largest Marian shrine in the world. An estimated 300 million faithful, representing every continent, make Our Lady of Guadalupe the single most popular devotion in the Catholic world.

The residents of the Californias, whose privilege it was to have their first church placed under the protection of Nuestra Señora de Guadalupe, in 1683, pay homage to Our Lady on her annual feast day, December 12th.

It was Fray Junípero Serra who brought devotion to Our Lady of Guadalupe to Alta California. He had arrived in the viceroyalty of the New World on December 6, 1748, when the anchor of his ship was cast in the harbor of Vera Cruz, where Mexican history began.

Serra and his companions traveled along the *El Camino Real* to Mexico City, arriving on the hill of Tepeyac on New Year's Day. In one sense it was journey's end but, in another sense, Serra's road of life was just beginning at the feet of Our Lady of Guadalupe.

In every one of the California missions, a painting of Our Lady of Guadalupe was accorded a place of special prominence. The friars were fond of reminding the neophytes that Mary's first appearance in the New World was to one of their own native Americans.

Barely a century later, on the Feast of Saint Francis of Assisi, Fray Francisco Garcia Diego y Moreno was ordained to the bishopric at the Shrine of Our Lady of Guadalupe as the proto ordinary for the Diocese of *Ambas Californias*. Once again the gentle *Tilma* of Juan Diego formed the centerpiece for the faraway vineyard of Alta California.

In mid-1941, the Apostolic Delegate to Mexico invited Archbishop John J. Cantwell to make a pilgrimage to the National Shrine of Our Lady of Guadalupe. The southland prelate was anxious to comply for many reasons, mostly because "a visit by our people to the City of Mexico would be a gracious compliment to the hierarchy and Catholics of a country that has sent so many of its children to California."

A Solemn Pontifical Mass was celebrated at the shrine on October 12th. It was a historically significant event, attended by a military delegation representing the President of Mexico. The entire diplomatic corps turned out to welcome the archbishop and his party.

Speaking over the National Broadcasting System from the *Distrito Federal*, Cantwell observed that "the missions built in California are our title deeds to show to the new-comers that we of the Old Church are in California by right of inheritance." He concluded by praying that "the traditions that made Mexico distinguished and honorable in the past may be perpetuated in a fuller measure in years to come, and that the glory of days gone by may be surpassed" by the pledge of the future.

Relic of the Tilma of San Juan Diego
Cathedral of Our Lady of the Angels
Los Angeles, California

The visit marked a thawing in the delicate relations then existing between the Church and State in Mexico. From all indications, the event was favorably received in all quarters.

Following Cantwell's return to Los Angeles, Archbishop Luis Maria Martinez of Mexico City proposed to the Canons of the National Basilica that a most appropriate way of commemorating the visit would be to present a relic of Juan Diego's *Tilma* to the Archbishop of Los Angeles. He pointed out that, even then, Los Angeles boasted a larger Mexican population than any city in the world outside the *Distrito Federal.*

The Canons agreed with the proposal and delegated a "Father Gomez" to personally bring a small rectangular piece of the famed *Tilma,* encased in a silver reliquary, to Los Angeles. Cantwell was understandably pleased with the gesture and received the relic with great devotion.

Very likely it marked the first and only time a piece of the *Tilma* had ever left Mexican soil. The archbishop entrusted the relic to Father Fidencio Esparza, a Mexican-born priest from Guadalajara who had long been active among the southland's Hispanic community.

Late in 1981, forty years after the historic trek to Mexico by Cantwell, Timothy Cardinal Manning headed another pilgrimage to the National Shrine. Upon Manning's return to Los Angeles, Esparza confided the relic to His Eminence for final disposal. It was then placed on display in the Historical Museum attached to the Archival Center for the Archdiocese of Los Angeles. The relic, the only known segment ever detached from the original *Tilma,* was draped over an artistic seventeenth-century statue of Our Lady of Guadalupe.

The snippet of the *Tilma* at Los Angeles, approximately a half inch square, was preserved in a rectangular reliquary containing four other relics of Saints Francis Borgia, Teresa of Avila, Francis Xavier and Ignatius Loyola.

Like the *Tilma* at Mexico City, the small piece of the *Tilma* is coarsely woven. It is made of vegetable fiber and consists of strips held together by weak stitching. The larger depiction of Our Lady in Mexico City can presently be seen, encased in a golden glass-covered frame, atop the main altar in Mexico City's National Basilica of Our Lady of Guadalupe.

In order to spread devotion of Our Lady of Guadalupe and to commemorate the sainthood of San Juan Diego, members of the Archconfraternity of Catholic Relics took the holy *Tilma* on several tours of the United States. Huge crowds of Catholic worshippers in twelve archdioceses and nine dioceses welcomed the relic in their Cathedrals and churches.

At the conclusion of the final tour, Roger Cardinal Mahony directed that the Holy *Tilma* be enshrined in a chapel of the Cathedral of Our Lady of the Angels in Los Angeles.

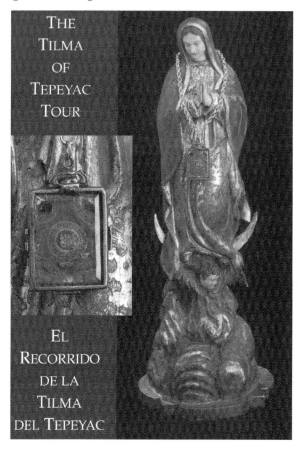

On the tenth anniversary of the Cathedral of Our Lady of the Angels, Archbishop José Gomez permanently enshrined the precious relic in the Shrine of the Tilma in the newly completed chapel of Our Lady of Guadalupe. The relic is now displayed in a golden encasement in the heart of a bronze sculpture of San Juan Diego.

The Shrine of the Holy Tilma in the Chapel of Our Lady of Guadalupe is featured in a brochure printed in 2012.

*The Cathedral of St. Vibiana, Precursor to The Cathedral
of Our Lady of the Angels*

❧ ❧

Stained-Glass Windows

(Sister Mary Joanne Wittenburg, S.N.D. has written another bro-chure. This one is on "the last of the stained-glass windows installed in the Crypt Mausoleum" which features the washing of Our Lord's feet. This window was set in place just outside the elevator to the crypt in memory of the grandparents of Msgr. Francis J. Weber, in 2014.)

The Washing of the Feet

The use of stained glass has been a tradition in the Catholic Church since medieval times. Indeed, the Minister in York, England, boasts windows containing stained glass dating from the time of William the Conqueror.

Although the windows that adorn the Crypt Mausoleum at The Cathe-dral of Our Lady of the Angels do not have as lengthy a pedigree, their history is an interesting one and offers a noteworthy link to the earlier Cathedral of Saint Vibiana.

The last of the stained glass windows installed in the Crypt Mausoleum of the Cathedral of Our Lady of the Angels in 2013 features the washing of the Lord's Feet

CATHEDRAL
OF OUR LADY OF THE ANGELS

The story of the Crypt Mausoleum windows began in 1922, when the Archdiocese of Los Angeles was still the Diocese of Monterey-Los Angeles. Wanting to "erect a respectable Catholic Church for the City of Los Angeles, Bishop John J. Cantwell embarked on an ambitious two-year renovation project designed to expand and modernize Saint Vibiana's. Among his planned alterations was the installation of new stained-glass windows.

Since the bishop's brother, Father William Cantwell, was traveling in Europe at the time, the bishop suggested that he visit several stained-glass firms in Germany and Ireland in order to identify someone for the commission. Father ultimately suggested the Franz Mayer Company in Munich; "an old firm," he noted in a letter to his brother, "70 years standing, [with] a reputation that they are living up to and not living on."

An interesting sidelight is that the only stained-glass window in Rome's Saint Peter's Basilica, portraying the descent of the Holy Spirit, was designed, fabricated and installed by the Franz Mayer Company.

Accordingly, in June 1922, Bishop Cantwell ordered fourteen large windows depicting scenes from the life of Christ for the cathedral for a total of $6,560 – a price which included packing and shipping to Los Angeles.

The windows that the bishop chose were to be done in a revival style, that is, in a manner resembling a baroque illustration. Most likely, more than twenty-five artists and numerous apprentices in Mayer's studio worked on the windows during the eight months it took to complete the commission.

The pieces of glass were first fired. Next a master or another craftsman – perhaps an apprentice who was nearly a master – would trace on the details in fine black lines; then the pieces of glass would be fired again for ten minutes at 1200 degrees. The drapery was given a three-dimensional effect by firing enamel paint into the glass.

The piece was then painted a soft half-tone and finally the artisan rubbed in the highlights. The appearance of silk damask in the figures' robes was created by placing a stencil over the painted glass and then rubbing off the paint through the holes in the stencil. Finally a master would add the half tones while others would do the background or the trees or a sunset. Each color, each object incorporated into a window had a symbolic meaning according to the rules of iconography. Lastly, the apprentices worked on the borders – firing silver nitrate into the glass to turn it gold, adding the details, and on occasion purposely leaving a fingerprint in order to mark their work.

At the dedication of the windows in the refurbished cathedral, the brilliantly lighted edifice was "radiant in the beauty of its enlarged and newly adorned sanctuary, its handsome stained-glass windows [and] its redecorated walls and arches." A reporter concluded by relating how "the bright sunlight of a cloudless California morning, falling softly throughout multi-colored windows, touched with its softened splendor the marbles of the sanctuary and the pilasters of nave and aisle."

For the next seventy-five years Mayer's windows graced the walls of the Cathedral of St. Vibiana – admired but perhaps not fully appreciated. All that changed in 1994 when the Northridge earthquake precipitated the closure of St. Vibiana's. Shortly afterward, Walter Judson, head of the Judson Studios in Los Angeles, received a phone call from Roger Cardinal Mahony asking him to get down to the cathedral as soon as possible. "We want to see if we can save the windows!"

The first challenge which the craftsmen encountered was removing the windows themselves. According to Walter Judson, the windows had originally been installed with an old-fashioned putty that had become as hard as concrete. As a result, the men had to dig the putty out from between the steel sash and the lead of the windows and then ease the windows out.

This task was complicated by the fact that a number of the windows were actually oversized. As a result, when the workmen first fitted them into the sash, they crumpled back some of the lead in order to shove them into place. The result was a very, very tight fit.

Once the windows had been safely removed, the Judson craftsmen cleaned, flattened and repaired them. In instances where the windows were cracked, the artists used a reversible adhesive to glue the pieces of glass together again. So skillfully was this done that, as Walter Judson noted, "If you can even find any of those cracks, they look just like a hairline – they're very small."

Finally, new lead was placed around the outside of all the sections and, in a few cases, within a window itself. Lastly the restored windows were crated and stored until such time as they could be backlighted and incorporated into the new cathedral's crypt mausoleum.

MAUSOLEUM

of the Cathedral of Our Lady of the Angels

The installation of the stained-glass windows provides visitors with an opportunity to appreciate Mayer's artistry and the Judson Studio's craftsmanship in a way that was not possible in Saint Vibiana's. As Walter Judson pointed out: "At the old cathedral the windows weren't really clerestory windows and they weren't really aisle windows. They were sort of halfway in between and they were inset into the wall so when you walked into the church you really didn't notice them."

Stained-glass windows of Cathedral Mausoleum

In the Mausoleum, this is not the case. Now it is possible to see each window up close as well as to step back and study them from a distance and thus appreciate what has been described as examples of "the most beautiful glass of the nineteenth century in Germany."

Time capsule located in the Cathedral Mausoleum

CATHOLIC COMMUNITY FOUNDATION
Los Angeles

Update on the Brother Hilarion O'Connor, OSF, Fund for the Arts

Above, from left: Msgr. Kevin Kostelnik, Msgr. Francis Weber, Kathy and Howard Anderson, and Brother Hilarion O'Connor with several of Howard's 21 Missions of Old California, on display at the Cathedral of Our Lady of Angels now through December 31, 2015

Thanks to all who supported the October 4th event honoring Brother Hilarion O'Connor and the creation of a new endowed fund at Catholic Community Foundation of Los Angeles in his name for the arts at the Cathedral of Our Lady of the Angels. Those attending enjoyed a private reception to view works of art in the new chapel honoring the canonization of Junipero Serra and 21 original oil paintings by artist Howard Anderson on loan to the Cathedral for this exhibit.

Cathedral pastor Msgr. Kevin Kostelnik greeted over 200 guests and introduced the program, which included remarks from Anderson on his Mission collection and from Msgr. Francis Weber, the archivist for the Archdiocese and foremost authority on Padre Junipero Serra. The keynote address was made by Brother Hilarion, who said "I've been involved in the construction of the Cathedral from the very beginning and it was always our intention to bring great art to the Cathedral. This new fund provides us with an opportunity to work with artists and benefactors to make that happen."

5

Santa Cruz Island Memoir

Island Memoir (1984)

(A homily delivered on the island each year on the Feast of the Holy Cross.)

Some of you have seen and even read *An Island Memoir*, which is Carey Stanton's book about Santa Cruz Island. If you don't have a copy, I would recommend that you get one. Not only is it an accurate portrayal of this islandic paradise, but it is fast becoming a rare volume – as, indeed, are all books about the islands of California.

I would like to recall, ever-so-briefly, how that book came to fruition. And while I freely admit that this memoir doesn't really fit into the context of a normal homily, let me also point out that Carey always made the rules for the chapel on this island and I know he would approve of this digression. He was always able to poke fun at himself. He once had me look up the history of *padrons* in Canon Law. Then, he unilaterally declared himself *padron* of Santa Cruz Island, even though he wasn't even a Catholic. Those fine points never bothered him.

It is not uncommon that talented people speak more eloquently than they write. Carey Stanton was one such person, as this short reflection amply illustrates.

Over many years, Carey spoke frequently about Santa Cruz Island. I recall hearing him address the Kiwanis Club at San Buenaventura, where he received enthusiastic and sustained applause even after a thirty-minute panegyric.

Shortly after becoming a member, Carey was invited to speak before the Zamorano Club of Los Angeles. The announcements for the March 2, 1983, meeting noted that his presentation would be "a Discussion of Historical Accounts of Santa Cruz Island in Literature from Cabrillo's Log to the Present."

The Chapel at Santa Cruz Island

As usual, Carey's presentation was a stellar performance. Because of illness, I wasn't able to be present, but Marla Daily graciously sent me a typed transcription of the talk. A while later, I suggested that Carey give some consideration to having his talk printed, possibly in book form. Rashly, I offered to "edit" the manuscript.

Carey enthusiastically welcomed my offer, little realizing what that would entail. Even when I casually mentioned that the treatise would need some "drastic surgery," he didn't appear perplexed. Marla sweetened the overall proposal by agreeing to compile a bibliography for the volume.

In a letter to me on November 6th, Carey was a bit defensive, noting that "if I am supposed to have written this, I guess it should be in my style." By the end of his letter, however, he backed off, observing that "this is really going to be fun," a statement that he probably later regretted.

We didn't disagree about the factual content because, in that area, Carey was pretty much on target. There was a minor squabble about whether Richard Henry Dana mentioned Santa Cruz in his classic book. He didn't, but it took the intervention of Maurice Neville, a friend of Carey's from Santa Barbara, to convince him.

Of the four drafts, the first was the hardest. On November 27th, he wrote "I disagree with you strongly about style. I do not feel it is the editor's job to be changing words around. If that were true Scott Fitzgerald would not be known, among other things, for his style. That credit would go to Maxwell Perkins, Fitzgerald's editor at Scribners and his lifelong friend. I feel that an editor lets the author's style be his own."

*The Old Country Priest waiting to begin Mass. Chapel of the Holy
Cross – Santa Cruz Island*

I gently pointed out that Carey wasn't F. Scott Fitzgerald, nor was I
Maxwell Perkins. It just wasn't a valid analogy.

Back and forth by mail, on the telephone and in person, Carey continued to fuss about this or that stylistic suggestion. After a while, a pattern
emerged and, happily, he would conclude with something like "Okay,
if you insist, but this one time only."

Near the end of the editing process, Carey made an end run and demanded that all kinds of changes be made – most of them reversions to

the original manuscript. When I offered to step aside and to allow him to resurrect the earlier version, he backed off completely.

On February 23, 1984, Carey reluctantly approved the final draft, noting that "there is little similarity between the final version and what I wrote." Actually, there wasn't much difference. The facts held, only the manner of expression was altered.

By the time we arrived at the final draft, the text looked pretty good, so much so that I recommended that the Zamorano Club publish the book as their keepsake for the joint meeting with the Roxburghe Club of San Francisco.

Initially, as we entered the galley stage, Carey tried to do some re-writing, but that was nipped in the bud when I explained that it cost $8 a line to change a single letter. Carey wasn't cheap, but he was thrifty.

In my humble opinion, *An Island Memoir*, printed by Richard Hoffman at Van Nuys, was a superb book. It won Ronce and Coffin recognition in 1985 and even today is considered both a well-written and a typographically attractive book. The whole enterprise revealed a lot about its author. He was stubborn, insistent and cagey, but he always knew when to quit pushing.

I found him both a challenging and an affirmative person and I will always cherish the friendship we shared.

CAREY Q. STANTON

February 2, 1923 • December 8, 1987

Interment

La Capilla de la Santa Cruz del Rosario

Santa Cruz Island

Memorial Service

All Saints bythe Sea

Montecito

December 17, 1987

The Rock Star and the Old Country Priest (2015)
(By Marla Daily)

Rock star, Joe Walsh and Roman Catholic priest, Monsignor Francis J. Weber, were born almost 15 years and 620 miles apart: Walsh on November 20, 1947, in Wichita, Kansas, and Weber on January 22, 1933, in Indianapolis, Indiana. The unlikely duo met west of the west, on Santa Cruz Island, California, as mutual friends of island owner Carey Stanton (1923–1987). For more than a quarter of a century their friendship has flourished. And here is how it came to be:

Justinian Caire (1827–1897) first acquired sole title to Santa Cruz Island in 1880. Subsequently he asked Bishop Francisco Mora, who served Monterey-Los Angeles from 1878 to 1896, for permission to erect an island chapel for use of his family and friends. The bishop agreed. Father Gaspar Genna inaugurated the chapel when it was completed in 1891. Through subsequent years various priests ventured out to Santa Cruz Island. One such visitor was the celebrated Father Thomas Sherman, son of the famous Civil War general, who celebrated Mass on the island Christmas Day, 1929.

On April 10, 1937, Santa Cruz Island changed hands when Edwin Stanton (1893–1963) bought the western 9/10ths of Santa Cruz Island (five parcels) from Justinian Caire's descendants. (The eastern end of the island, divided into two parcels, was retained by Caire family descendants.) With this transition came disuse of the chapel, until 1968 when Edwin Stanton's son and heir, Carey Stanton, physician and historian, desired Mass to be offered annually in the chapel on May 3rd, the Feast of the Holy Cross.

Msgr. Francis J. Weber had written a "cold" letter, offering his services, which Stanton heartily accepted, and thus began an annual 50-year tradition for Msgr. Weber that spanned from 1968 to 2017.

As the 35-year-old priest was initiating annual Mass on Santa Cruz Island in 1968, a talented 21-year-old musician from Kansas, Joe Walsh, began playing lead guitar for the three-member band The James Gang. In short order he became the band's star attraction. In 1974 Walsh released his first official solo album, *So What*. An invitation to join the Eagles band followed in late 1975, and his addition turned out to be a grand success.

Joe Walsh paid his first visit to Santa Cruz Island in 1976 in a visit arranged by Marla Daily, friend of Walsh and personal assistant to Carey Stanton. Over their first long island weekend together, Stanton and Walsh became fast friends. Walsh delighted in touring the miles of island country with bourbon-drinking ranch manager Henry Duffield.

The Old Country Priest and Joe Walsh in the San Fernando Mission Chapel
during the shooting of the documentary West of the West.

In October 1976, Walsh reciprocated with an invitation for Stanton to join him as his guest at the opening night of the Eagles' *Hotel California* concert held at the Forum in Los Angeles. As 17,000 attendees stomped their feet and raised their Bic lighters to welcome the band onstage, Stanton twisted pieces of paper napkin and placed them in his ears. For years, Stanton delighted at the retelling of his extraordinary experiences that evening – accompanying Joe in his dressing room backstage, and later departing the Forum with him in his limousine, as female fans flung their bare-breasted bodies along the windshield!

Carey Stanton died on his beloved island on December 8, 1987. Mass on May 3, 1988, was a seminal event, with Carey Stanton now in his final resting place outside the chapel door. Msgr. Weber graciously insisted on keeping Carey Stanton's chapel tradition alive, and Joe Walsh suggested he provide the musical accompaniment.

And so it was meant to be that the Old Country Priest met the Rock Star on Santa Cruz Island, in a tiny chapel west of the west. Over these many years, from 1988–2017, the two, without fail, celebrated the Feast of the Holy Cross in this very special House of God. To this day, every May 3rd the notes *of Amazing Grace* can be heard filtering through the century-old Eucalyptus trees as the breezes blow the notes over the Main Ranch.

ço ço

Memories of an Old Country Priest

Three Volumes—1465 pages

6
Funeral Eulogies

✟

Sir Daniel Donohue (1919–2014)

Homily Preached in the Cathedral of Our Lady of the Angels

For those among us who find it hard to imagine that Daniel Donohue's life has ended, I have good news: "It's not true!" And that's not just a wishful sentiment of a longtime friend. In the Preface for today's Liturgy, we are reminded that "for God's faithful people, life is changed, not ended. When the body of our earthly dwelling place lies in death, we gain an everlasting dwelling place in heaven."

There is abundant confirmation of this notion from all kinds of human sources. In *Newsweek* magazine, for example, not a journal known for its theological expertise, deaths are listed under the heading of "transitions" and transitions they surely are because Christians look upon death as the beginning of a whole new plain of existence with God. Daniel Donohue has died to this world, only to be born into a new existence where the frailties of this life are wiped away.

In earlier days, certain Jesuits and a few other religious took a fourth vow of allegiance to the Holy Father. I have always suspected that Daniel Donohue took such a vow – surely he practiced it to a remarkable degree.

Daniel was a man of great and charming humility. I was always fascinated, for example, how someone who could talk so knowingly for endless hours about the Church, its past and present leadership, its often torturous history, its shortcomings and successes, rarely spoke about his personal background and how he came to be such a pivotal person in the life of the universal Church.

DONOHUE

So let me here fill in the public record by recalling some of the details in the life of this truly remarkable gentleman. He was born at Newark in 1919, the son of Daniel and Julia (Walter) Donohue.

Along with the other two Donohue children, Eugene and Rosemary, Daniel studied at Saint Aloysius Grammar School, which was staffed by the Sisters of Charity of Emmitsburgh. Entering the city's Jesuit-operated Saint Peter's Preparatory School in 1937, he completed his secondary education at Graymoor and then joined the Franciscan Friars of the Atonement as a postulant.

He was sent to the community's monastery in Washington, D.C. There he studied philosophy at The Catholic University of America, along with the other disciplines associated with the ministry inaugurated by the famed ecumenist, Father Paul Watson.

Daniel's father, a pediatrician and specialist in internal medicine, was a benefactor of Brother Mathias Barrett, a highly respected and pioneer member of the Order of Saint John of God.

With the expiration of his temporary vows as a Franciscan, Daniel affiliated himself with the Hospitaller Brothers of Saint John of God at their foundation in Los Angeles. He journeyed to the west coast in 1940 and it was there that he spent the remainder of his life.

In 1947, Daniel took solemn vows as a Brother of Saint John of God. He was attached to the community's motherhouse, located on West Adams Boulevard. With the exception of his years of graduate study at Mount Saint Mary's College, Brother Daniel spent most of his years at the motherhouse and at Rancho San Antonio.

Because his father had known and studied at Fordham University alongside Francis J. Spellman, later the Archbishop of New York, Daniel was early on personally acquainted with many members of the American hierarchy, including Coadjutor Archbishop J. Francis A. McIntyre who came to Los Angeles in 1948. When Daniel expressed a desire to study for the priesthood, Archbishop McIntyre suggested that he become a clerical candidate for the Diocese of San Diego.

While waiting for his dispensation, Daniel worked briefly for United States Steel Corporation in their newly formed psychological screening program, an experience that served him well in later life.

In 1951, Daniel was accepted at Immaculate Heart of Mary Seminary in San Diego. By a strange, but surely providential twist of circumstances, Daniel was assigned temporarily as a special assistant to Charles Francis Buddy, the dynamic and colorful Bishop of San Diego.

As time progressed, there was less and less time for study and more and more allotted to coordinating the multitudinous activities of Bishop Buddy. Daniel took up residence at the Episcopal residence and became, in fact if not in title, *aide-de-camp* to the bishop.

The almost three years in that capacity proved to be among the most interesting of Daniel's life. He traveled with the bishop, looked after his house, arranged his appointments and acted as intermediary with clergy and laity.

While accompanying Buddy on an *ad limina* visit to Rome, Cardinal Spellman suggested to Daniel that his position in San Diego was ambivalent and needed redirection. After a ten-day retreat and considerable thought, prayer and consultation, Daniel concurred that his vocation in life would find its maximum fulfillment outside the clerical ministry.

Daniel had known Bernardine Murphy since 1940, when she came regularly to visit the Brothers at their residence in Los Angeles. On several occasions, he had advised her about benefactions to charitable organizations. Their relationship grew closer in the months after he left San Diego and, on January 16, 1954, they were married at a ceremony witnessed by Cardinal McIntyre in the archbishop's chapel in Fremont Place.

A few years later, Daniel and Bernardine purchased the Villa San Giuseppe on Waverly Drive, a Hollywood mansion erected by car magnate Earle C. Anthony, owner of KFI radio station.

In 1957, the Donohues established the Dan Murphy Foundation, a charitable trust funded by the Murphy fortune which had been accumulated from various sources, including California Portland Cement. With first Bernardine and later Daniel Donohue as chairman of the Board, the Dan Murphy Foundation became active in supporting charities, mostly those associated with the universal apostolate of the Roman Catholic Church.

After Bernardine's sudden and unexpected death on March 5, 1968, Daniel continued the traditions of charity inaugurated by his wife. Personally and through his position as chair of the Dan Murphy Foundation, he became one of the most generous benefactors of the Holy See and the local Church for over forty years.

I doubt that this little man with a big heart would want me to recite or otherwise dwell upon even a short list of his knighthoods, awards or citations. That he was named a Gentleman-in-Waiting to the Holy Father, by Pope Paul VI, at the request of Timothy Cardinal Manning, says it all. Nor do I think he would want you subjected to an enumeration of his benefactions and those of the Foundation which he chaired for so many years. Might I just borrow the words chiseled on the tomb of Sir Christopher Wren in Saint Paul's Cathedral in London: "If you are looking for his monument, just look around you."

I would only say this, as an ecclesial historian, that Daniel has very likely channeled more funds to the Catholic Church and its charitable works than any other single person in our nation's history.

In a recently published book, Daniel Donohue is aptly described as the "linchpin" of this new Cathedral of Our Lady of the Angels. And, in an oral interview in February of 2003, Daniel said that being involved with the planning, designing, executing and dedicating of this great house of worship was the culmination of his life service to the Church.

Daniel once told me that for many years he had daily recited that part of Psalm 102 that says: "Do not take me away before my days are complete." He confided that since the cathedral's dedication, he no longer needed to say that prayer!

The story of Daniel's sixty-year association with the cathedrals in Los Angeles, old and new, is told elsewhere. I would just say that despite his love and affection for this building, Daniel rejected out-of-hand the initial suggestion that he be interred here, especially in a place of honor.

It was just another manifestation of his personal humility which only Cardinal Mahony's coaxing eventually overcame.

I was in Rome in October 2003. Upon coming out of Gamarelli's tailor shop, I noticed a humungous black limousine pulling up. A regal-looking man from Rhode Island emerged from the back seat and charged towards me, announcing that he was a Gentleman-in-Waiting to the Holy Father. Trying to think of something appropriate to say, I asked him if he knew Daniel Donohue. "Oh yes," he said, "but he has been inactive for years." I couldn't resist responding. "Well, not really, he has just finished spearheading the erection of the third largest church in the North American hemisphere."

Some years ago, at one of the many occasions when Daniel was honored, a speaker began by saying that "there were three great virtues – faith, hope and Daniel J. Donohue." Actually that's not too far off base. While most people spend their lifetime taking, Daniel spent his giving away. He always felt that he was only a steward of God's bounty.

There was much about Daniel Donohue that was "priestly." A journalist for the Los Angeles *Times* wrote an essay about him on October 18, 1982, in which he referred to Daniel as a "priest." I recall asking Daniel what he thought about the article with all its inaccuracies. His reply said a lot about him: "Well, I felt quite honored to be mistaken for a priest."

Remembering Daniel as a priest might really be a good thing. One of the great contemporary lay theologians contends that "the Church is far too important to be left entirely to the care of the clergy." Once Cardinal Conslavi was summoned into the presence of Napoleon who was irritated about the antics of certain churchmen. The emperor thundered at the cardinal: "Eminence, you must know that I could destroy the Church if I so wanted." The cardinal smiled and said: "Your Majesty, priests have been trying unsuccessfully to do that for centuries."

Daniel never equivocated on what he felt were really pivotal issues. I remembered being awfully proud of him on one occasion during the many months of meetings when this cathedral was in the planning stages. He spoke out rarely, but when he did, people listened.

One day the question came up about whether the central cross in the sanctuary would have a *corpus* attached. Someone argued against the *corpus* in deference to the interests of ecumenism. Each member of the committee had something to say. When it was Daniel's turn he spoke out, softly but authoritatively: "This issue is not negotiable. There will be a *corpus* or I will walk." Matter closed.

Interestingly, the crucifix, which you see in the center of the sanctuary, has become one of the most popular devotional features of the Cathedral, venerated by hundreds each day.

While always a perfect gentleman, Daniel never hesitated to speak out when confronted by viewpoints and practices he felt were unworthy of or unbecoming to members of the hierarchy or lowerarchy. After beginning by saying, "may it please Your Grace," he would then unapologetically express himself to nuns, priests, bishops, archbishops and even cardinals. One of those exalted lordships told me afterwards: "I wish I had the courage to speak out the way he does."

While I am not here to launch Daniel's cause for beatification, I can testify that chief among the virtues that he practiced heroically was **gratitude.** He was ever mindful and expressive of God's blessings in his life. Monthly he had at least one Mass offered in gratitude. When once I asked him why, he gently reminded me that no less a theologian than Thomas Aquinas characterized "ingratitude" as the black sin. In fact, Thomas went so far to say that "it was blasphemous to withhold the proper signs of appreciation."

> The same filial spirit which animates all prayer gives rise also to thanksgiving. The first canticles which the Gospel presents to us are cries of gratitude: the *Benedictus*, the *Magnificat* and the *Nunc Dimittis*. The great prayer of Christians is Eucharist. We bless God for all His benefits, for His creation, His providence, above all, for the mission of His divine Son, for His incarnation, birth, life, death, resurrection and ascension, for the gift of the Spirit which fructifies the Church and remits sins.

The Gospel chosen for this Mass was a favorite of Daniel's because it emphasizes the importance of gratitude. Ten men were cured of leprosy and only one bothered to return and thank the Lord.

Daniel balanced petition with gratitude. And he never complained when this or that petition went seemingly unanswered. "God hears all petitions," he would say, "but He answers them in His good time, not ours."

One of Daniel's most charming and enduring talents was that of storytelling. I once asked him why he so frequently flavored his conversation with stories. He reminded me that "the Lord almost always spoke in parables." And parables are basically message-laden stories.

Daniel further noted that many of the Lord's listeners quickly forgot his theological and scriptural messages, but they rarely forgot his parables.

And that's still true today. The best teachers and preachers are the ones who have mastered storytelling. Probably the only thing you good people today will remember from this homily is the story or parable than I am about to repeat, one that features the "orange." I have one here which I picked before leaving Mission Hills.

Daniel often recalled the accomplishments of his father-in-law, Dan Murphy, who was one of the west coast's most gifted pioneers and financers. One of his classic stories was occasioned by my question about Murphy and his extensive influence on California's history. Here was part of his response in story form.

When Dan Murphy was young, he recalled how on Christmas morning all the kids would rush to see what treasures were in their stockings hung by the fireplace. The greatest treasure for those living in the east would be an "orange," something easterners had rarely seen. Oh, they drank orange juice, but there was no way to get an orange itself to the east before it spoiled.

Dan Murphy determined to solve that problem. He spent many years looking for a way to transport oranges thousands of miles to the east coast intact. The result was the refrigerated railroad car, which Dan Murphy helped to design and finance.

Then, as Sir Daniel concluded his story, "that's why kids, then and now, identify a fresh orange with the birthday of Jesus."

In all the times I ever visited Daniel, he rarely failed to tell a story or a parable – usually with a religious overtone. He was truly a "giant of the storytellers."

In the course of human life, one runs across many kinds of people. There are some who resemble wheelbarrows, effective only when pushed. A few are like canoes that have to be paddled and others are similar to kites, needing to be restrained. A handful behave after the fashion of kittens, content only when petted; and then there are those who react like a basketball, bouncing in all directions; others recall the image of balloons, full of hot air. A few are content to be trailers, towed along by others.

Daniel J. Donohue was like none of these. He was something like a faithful old railroad watch, full of good works – his message clearly visible for all to observe, his personality etched in the purest of gold and his tireless talents ticking away on behalf of others.

And finally, may I inject a personal observation. I remember thirty-five years ago, while convalescing at my father's home from spinal surgery, I was praying the breviary when my Father came to tell me that Msgr. Hawkes was on the phone. "What did you do now?" he said.

Anyway Msgr. Hawkes said the cardinal wanted me to know that the Dan Murphy Foundation had approved our request for erection of a new archival facility in Mission Hills. Msgr. Hawkes concluded that wonderful news by saying: "I hope you add Daniel to your prayer list."

The eventual building served as the archdiocesan participation in the bicentennial celebration for the City of Los Angeles. It became the first independent archival facility erected under diocesan auspices in the United States. And, fittingly, it was located within the shadow of a California mission.

In his address at the dedication, on September 13, 1981, Daniel mentioned his late wife Bernardine Murphy, who, he said, "was always interested and knowledgeable about history from the standpoint of art and science."

Let me conclude this observation by saying that I have indeed kept Daniel on my daily prayer wheel all these years. Soon, I hope to meet up with him in eternal life where he can once again regale me with his wonderful treasure trove of stories.

Today, the universal Church, the noble State of California, the grateful City of Los Angeles, the bereaved community of the local Church and a host of friends, admirers and collaborators formally enshrine Daniel J. Donohue among that select group of individuals who became legends while yet alive. It was indeed a privilege to know and love him.

In Loving Memory

Daniel J. Donohue

K.M., K.G.C.H.S., K.C.S.G.

July 30, 1919 - December 3, 2014

Memorare

Remember, O most gracious Virgin Mary,
that never was it known that anyone who fled
to thy protection, implored thy help,
or sought thine intercession was left unaided.

Inspired by this confidence, I fly unto thee,
O Virgin of virgins, my mother;
to thee do I come, before thee I stand,
sinful and sorrowful.
O Mother of the Word Incarnate,
despise not my petitions,
but in thy mercy hear and answer me.

Amen

Allow me to conclude this eulogy with the same words I did sixteen years ago for Daniel's brother Eugene: *Show me a man of integrity, a man with an open heart, a man of many friends and a man unafraid of death and I will show you another Solomon or maybe even another Moses.*

Dr. Gloria Ricci Lothrop (1934–2015)

(Reprinted from *Hoja Volante*, #268 – February 2015)

Mankind, with all its sophisticated complexities, is still and always will be subjected to a time sequence ordained by Divine Providence. The God who creates the soul and sustains its existence also summons that soul to Himself in His time, not ours.

Recognizing that divine economy and grateful for a participation in it, we come today in thanksgiving for His having shared one of those precious souls with us.

A life well spent speaks its own eulogy. The words uttered by others can only be faint echoes of what a person really accomplished for God and neighbor in a lifetime.

This much we do know – that for over eighty years Gloria Ricci Lothrop moved among her family and friends as a gracious, courageous and forceful lady. In her wake, countless people came to know what it means to be cheerful in time of adversity, optimistic in moments of sorrow and determined in periods of pain.

By profession a historian, by research a talented writer and by dedication an exemplary practitioner of her Catholic faith, Gloria Ricci Lothrop met the challenges of daily life with forthright courage and dedicated virtue.

Her books, articles, book reviews and lectures at the University of California at Northridge and in halls of other research centers form a gigantic chapter in Western American history.

Gloria can only adequately be remembered when placed in her unique niche in the historical annals of Southern California. She was a formidable woman, as those of us who knew her can readily testify.

She belonged to the Doyce Nunis tradition of local historians. As most of you know, Doyce was a pathfinder among his peers and Gloria was among the most loyal of his followers.

GLORIA RICCI LOTHROP

Doyce subscribed to Ray Ballington's notion that all history is local. In his almost half century as editor of the *Southern California Quarterly*, Doyce wrote about, published and championed local history, almost to the exclusion of everything else.

To Doyce, history moved upwards beginning with the family, the neighborhood, the township, the city, the state and the nation. To him, Gloria, myself and others, all history is local.

Whether it be political, religious, institutional or whatever, all historical efforts begin in the home, the Church, business and neighborhood, and only when those components are fitted into the puzzle of life can one hope to understand the happenings of the world, the nation and the community.

The key to Gloria's contributions, and they were many and pivotal, is local. Her writings, lectures and personal interests, whether they involved women, Italians or others, never wandered far off course.

And one other thing, Gloria was a superb teacher. She knew well how to manage the components that make for clarity in teaching.

I once asked a Scripture scholar why the Lord almost always spoke in parables. He reminded me that parables are nothing more or less than stories. Jesus was a storyteller *par excellence*.

Gloria's success as a teacher was her ability to embellish and weave important events into stories. She knew, as do so few others, that students and listeners often forget the subject matter of a lecture or a sermon, but they seldom forget a well-structured and interesting story. Always a positive, direct and outspoken person, Gloria would appreciate but surely not encourage our making of this moment into an occasion of sorrow.

Rather she would endorse and repeat the words of Saint Augustine that "it is not our judgment, but our nature which shuns death."

She would remind us, ever so gently, that death is a vital and necessary part of living. [Saint Augustine phrased that concept well when he said that] "we grieve over the necessity of losing our friends in death, but always with the knowledge that we shall meet them again."

John Henry Newman put it another way when he observed that "we mourn the blossoms of May because they wither, but we know that May will eventually have its revenge upon November, by the revolution of that solemn circle which never stops – which teaches us in our height of hope ever to be sober and in our depth of desolation never to despair."

Death closes one door, only to open another. She whom we have known in life, we know now in God. It's a different kind of relationship, but no less real.

Dying is the beginning of a glorious adventure. Surely, if a milligram of musk gives out perfume for seven thousand years, and a milligram of radium emits energy for seventy thousand years, then the human soul, which is far more precious in God's sight than musk or radium, will live for seven times seventy thousand years, or for eternity.

For His own reasons and in His own way, God leaves the imprint of his presence wherever He goes and in whatever He does.

Surely that presence was visible in the life of her whose earthly remains lie before us today. Gloria was always and everywhere a determined, forthright and scrupulously honest person whose companionship, friendliness and loyalty pervaded the atmosphere of her presence.

IN LOVING MEMORY OF

Dr. Gloria Ricci Lothrop

Dec 30, 1934 - Feb 2, 2015

God looked around His garden and found an empty space. Then He looked down upon the earth and saw your tired face. He put his arms around you and lifted you to rest. Gods garden must be beautiful, for He only takes the best. He saw the roads were getting rough, and the hills were hard to climb, so He closed your weary eyes and whispered, "Peace be Thine." It broke our hearts to lose you, but you did not go alone, for a part of us went with you, the day God took you home.

Saint Paul had the likes of Gloria in mind when he told the Hebrews how looking at the lives of those who faithfully follow Christ inspired him with new reason for seeking the city which is to come.

Though plagued by a long succession of illnesses in recent years, Gloria never allowed the thought of defeat to cross her mind.

She accepted her fate and met its challenges with a faith and determination that inspires those of us who remain behind.

That's why today we honor not a human body broken by pain and suffering, but a supernatural soul proven by faith and hope. This good person taught us how to live by showing us how to die.

Were she to offer a last bit of advice, one is inclined to think that she might put it this way.

> JUST THINK
>
> Of stepping on the shore and finding it
>
> HEAVEN;
>
> Of taking hold of a hand and finding it
>
> GOD'S HAND;
>
> Of breathing a new air and finding it
>
> CELESTIAL;
>
> Of feeling invigorated and finding it
>
> IMMORTALITY;
>
> Of passing from storm and tempest to an
>
> UNKNOWN CALM;
>
> Of waking and finding you're Home!

Finally, may I thank those who helped to make this memorial today a reality. Among others would be Cecilia Rasmussen, longtime columnist for the *Los Angeles Times,* the members of the Zamorano Club who long ago recognized Gloria as an outstanding and esteemed "woman of letters" and finally the music makers for this Mass. [May I tell you a secret – the music for this ceremony will be repeated *verbatim* for my own departure – the only condition being that Charlene outlives me and she is already in her nineties!]

Goodbye Gloria. See you soon at the throne of God.

Msgr. George Parnassus (1927–2013)

"George of West Hollywood"

When Msgr. Murphy asked me to say a few "pious words" at tonight's rosary, I asked him if "I had to tell the truth." He said, "of course." That restriction will be hard to follow, but I will do the best I can.

The clerical pedigree of "George of West Hollywood," as he was known to his fellow priests, is indeed impressive. He lived long enough to be among the less than one percent of the local clergy to have observed sixty years of priesthood.

In the very year that John J. Devlin came as pastor to Saint Victor Parish, in the then Village of Sherman, his future successor was born to George and Rosalie Parnassus in Pasadena. The Parnassus name was legendary in the boxing world. The elder George, a manager, matchmaker and promoter, known to his contemporaries as the "Golden Greek," was responsible for staging more than a hundred championship matches in the Olympic Auditorium. George married Rosalie in 1924 and from that bond came two sons, William, a prominent local physician, and George, destined to become an ecclesial fixture in West Hollywood.

After attending Loyola High School, George the younger enrolled at Los Angeles College, the minor or preparatory seminary for the Archdiocese of Los Angeles. Upon completing six years of collegiate and graduate study at Saint John's Seminary in Camarillo, George was ordained priest in Saint Vibiana's Cathedral by James Francis Cardinal McIntyre on May 30, 1953. During the early years of his ministry, Father George served as curate at Santa Isabel (Los Angeles), Our Lady of Mount Carmel (Newport) and Saint John Chrysostom (Inglewood.)

After completing his master's degree, Father Parnassus taught at Pius X and Saint Monica secondary schools. He became Vice Principal at Fermin Lasuen High School in 1960 and, two years later, returned to

Downey as Vice Principal of Pius X, a position he occupied until 1963. He was then advanced to the Principalship for a three-year term. Somehow, during those years, the busy priest found time to teach religion and marriage courses at Immaculate Heart College in Hollywood.

A candidate for the doctorate in history at the University of Southern California, Father Parnassus was named to the Domestic Prelacy by Pope Paul VI in December 1968. Later, he was sent to the archdiocesan seminary college at Camarillo as spiritual director. Meanwhile, he served as Chair of the western regional division of the National Conference of Seminary Spiritual Directors, an organization comprising sixty (arch)dioceses and thirty religious communities.

After completing a brief period as administrator at Saint Barnabas parish in Long Beach, Msgr. George Parnassus was posted to West Hollywood in 1977 as administrator and later pastor, where he served until his retirement.

When the new Church of Saint Victor was erected in 1961, financial limitations had dictated that only the shell of the church was completed. It remained for Msgr. Parnassus to furnish this parochial jewel box with artistic stained-glass windows, handsome chandeliers, mosaic stations of the cross and other accoutrements that qualify the church for inclusion among that select roster of Southern California's "most prayerful and attractive houses of worship."

Now, I am not here to canonize or even beatify George of West Hollywood. Great people need no eulogies. May we only say that spiritually, intellectually and in every other way, the earthly sojourn of George Parnassus measures up most perfectly to Robert Louis Stevenson's definition of one who has achieved the maturity of manhood:

> That man is a success:
> Who has lived well, laughed often and loved much;
> Who has gained the respect of intelligent men and the love of children;
> Who has filled his niche and accomplished his task;
> Who leaves the world better than he found it;
> Whether by an improved poppy, a perfect poem or a rescued soul;
> Who never lacked appreciation of earth's beauty or failed to express it;
> Who looked for the best in others, and gave the best he had.

On a holy card given out at the time he became a priest, in 1953, was a quotation from Saint John Chrysostom, which said that "according to the mind of Christ, a good shepherd may be compared to many martyrs. A martyr dies but once for Christ; the shepherd dies a thousand times for his flock."

Throughout the years of ministerial life, George was "a people's priest" whose demeanor was appreciated and recognized by laity and clergy alike. He genuinely liked people – all kinds of them – the rich and the poor, the learned and the ignorant, the simple and the mighty, the orphan and the needy, the homeless and the forgotten. He was most at home in what we used to call the "box" where people flocked to tell him their sins, listen to his advice and receive absolution.

Sertillanges once observed that "One has no faith in the jewel merchant who sells pearls and never wears them." George Parnassus lived what he preached and people instinctively knew that. He wore the pearls of priestly service where everyone could see them. He was the ideal role model for the American priest. He worked hard, laughed often, recreated sparsely, listened much, counseled wisely and prayed a lot. He had some difficult assignments, but he never complained. He was the good and faithful servant spoken about in Holy Scripture. He was a company man – and his company was the Lord.

Through it all, George of West Hollywood was always happy. His joy didn't rest on a better definition of the priesthood or even on the experience of its effectiveness. Rather it rested on the total trust which he placed in the Lord who called him out of weakness to participate in His ministry.

And so, eulogizing George of West Hollywood would be redundant. Everyone has his or her memories of George as they knew him. He was one who performed well all the priestly tasks; he recited his breviary, he read Holy Scripture, he made his meditation, he said the rosary, he did his spiritual reading and he practiced the virtues. Truly he did all things well. And he did them in an unobtrusive, almost hidden way. In a busy world, he found time for the Lord, for his parishioners, his friends and even strangers.

What you saw was what he was – a good priest, a faithful ambassador of Christ, a reflection of the Good Shepherd.

Msgr. John A. Mihan (1932–2015)

May I begin these remarks by saying that I will refer to Monsignor John A. Mihan in the only terminology I have used for well over a half century, "Jack." That's the way I knew him and that's how I will remember him for whatever is left in my own earthly sojourn.

Someone once remarked that truly prominent people are those who choose their parents carefully. On that note, Jack scored extremely well. Arnold and Virginia Mihan were God-fearing, church-attending, devout people who lavished a lot of love and attention on their three children, Nancy, Richard and Jack.

Arnold was controller for the City of Los Angeles – Virginia was the spiritual anchor of her family and the one who attended daily Mass and watched out for the family's spiritual treasures.

The genesis of Jack's call to ministry goes back sixty-nine years, long before the Archdiocese of Los Angeles had a vocation director with an office at the chancery or any structured recruitment program. In those days, a goodly percentage of vocations to the priesthood and the religious life were actively encouraged, carefully discerned and lovingly nurtured by that resourceful army of consecrated women who staffed the Catholic schools here in Southern California and throughout the nation.

Let me sketch the scenario for you – one that could no longer happen – but one that worked amazingly well. The year was 1946 – the school was Saint Brendan – the nun-principal and 8th grade teacher was Sister Mary Rosario Paul, a wonderful religious who never wrote her name without proudly annexing the initials BVM.

It was March and the exams for entrance to the local Catholic high schools were approaching. For the boys, the options were Loyola and Cathedral High. Sister Mary Rosario Paul insisted that they gather forty minutes early each morning for a special crash course on how to pass the entrance exams.

One morning, she announced that two of the 8th grade boys would be taking the exam for the minor seminary and then, out of the blue and without any prior consultation, she announced to all the world that "Jack Mihan and Frank Weber would be going to the seminary!" No one was more surprised than the two of us. After class I asked Jack: "What's a seminary?" to which he replied: "I have an uncle who's buried there!"

That's how two 8th graders, by God's grace, first learned about their priestly vocation. It was a little unorthodox, perhaps, and there were many hurdles ahead, but that was the beginning of our twelve-year-long trek to ministry.

That scenario couldn't happen in today's Church when there are few if any Sister Mary Rosario Pauls left. Today it takes a whole staff of recruiters and elaborate programs to do what one nun did in those earlier times and for many years before and after.

Over subsequent years Jack and I lived in the same parish, traveled to the seminary in the same car and offered our first Solemn Masses on the same day in the same church.

On the day of our first assignment, we were the only two members of our class who didn't receive appointments. Later we discovered that we were both destined for graduate work at the Catholic University of America, something that was temporarily delayed because of two unexpected deaths among the clergy.

Finally, Jack and I had the good fortune of sharing one of the truly great pastors in the archdiocese, Father Thomas F. Fogarty, who probably directed more young men to the priesthood than any other of his contemporaries. He served as archpriest at our first solemn Masses on the same day here at Saint Brendan's Church in Hancock Park.

The Year 2015 has been an interesting and eventful time for the people of God in Los Angeles. For myself, I lived to see one of my heroes named a saint and now another called home to God.

When I told my sister on the telephone about Jack's death, she said, "Oh, this has been a bad year for you." "Not at all," I responded. "The Lord has given California a new saint in the person of Fray Junípero Serra, the archdiocese has been blessed with three new bishops and this Old Country Priest has acquired a new dog." I reminded her that Job put it all in prospective when he said, "The Lord gives, The Lord takes away. Blessed be the name of the Lord!"

There were three major challenges to Jack's life in the fifty-six long years of his priestly ministry, all of which he met and mastered with admirable grace. He was an *educator, a pastor, and a patient,* and in each of those roles he left behind an example for others to emulate.

Some future chronicler will surely devote considerable time assessing the many contributions that Msgr. Mihan made to Catholic education here in the archdiocese.

Upon returning with his doctorate from The Catholic University of America, he gradually introduced a long litany of new and modern techniques which transformed an already large and efficient system into an educational showcase. He remained at that pivotal position for an eventful seventeen years and later helped to inaugurate what evolved into the Archdiocesan Education Foundation.

In 1987 Jack was named pastor at Corpus Christi parish. He wasn't a stranger to the area for in the 1950s we had a classmate who lived on nearby Swarthmore Street and many of our weekends were spent in the Palisades.

Jack remained at the parochial helm for several years. Not being part of the "touchy, feely generation," he probably never told his parishioners how much he loved them but that was the reason he wanted to stay there for the duration of his ministry. The Lord denied him that request.

Several months ago, Jack needed an outing. We brought him out to San Fernando Mission for lunch. I recall asking him what must have seemed a strange question. "Do you miss education?"

"Well I'm still in education," he replied. He continued by explaining that he had just finished reading a life of Saint Therese of Lisieux. Therese suffered from tuberculosis and often had to spend considerable time in bed.

One day her superior charged into her room and said "Get to work, you have things to do in the kitchen. You didn't enter religious life to spend the day in bed."

Therese gently but forcibly replied "Reverend Mother, God called me to religious life to do His will and today His will is that I stay in bed."

Finally, like Therese of Lisieux, Jack served the final years of his education ministry in bed, not at a desk.

In his eighty-three years on Planet Earth, Jack could and occasionally did step out of character. An example was his use of a motorcycle. Actually it was a motorbike, which his mother often referred to as a "murdercycle." She was more right than wrong. Jack once totaled it and almost himself in an accident that caused him to lose a whole year of schooling.

In biblical times, the Cedars of Lebanon in the Holy Land were the oldest, most durable and handsome of all the trees known to humankind. When the occasional one fell, the whole countryside went into mourning and later into jubilation for its long and faithful service as God's instrument among His people. Today, we bid adieu to one of California's Cedars of Lebanon. Sorrowful for his loss, we are jubilant for his towering presence among us these many years.

Any member of our class would readily agree that Jack was the most intelligent and gifted of us all. He would have excelled in any profession or he could have lived off his family inheritance. Instead, he freely chose to respond to the vocation of serving others in the priesthood. That says about all anyone could say about this fallen Cedar of Lebanon. For myself I am proud and grateful to have known Jack and for having been his friend.

There were many facets to Jack's personality. Though he never actually taught in a classroom, he was a natural-born educator, pedantic to the point of exhaustion.

And as many of you know, he was not a man of a few words. He would explain, repeat and elaborate an issue over and over again. But that was Jack the educator who personified the old dictum that "repetition is the mother of learning."

Today we live in a convoluted society where the priest who gets in trouble receives all the publicity. Bishop Sheen once remarked that "If the priest weren't important to the people, no one would care when the rare one falls by the wayside."

So what more can we say about Jack and the rest of that priestly army who say their prayers, serve their people, work long hours, keep their promises, recite the divine office, live out the Beatitudes, obey their bishops and teach the little ones.

With head high and shoulders erect, Jack walked along California's *El Camino Real* for almost seven decades. It was a long trek, with valleys, hills and even a few mountain tops. He didn't slacken his pace in severe storms or long droughts. He knew what priesthood was all about long before the learned fathers of Vatican Council II codified it all.

At their ordination, priests make special promises of poverty, chastity and obedience. Jack Mihan excelled in that trinity of pledges. His face would enhance any vocational poster.

Now I am not here today to propose Jack Mihan for canonization. But, secretly I suspect his would be a fairly easy process.

Last evening I pulled out some holy cards issued for various members of our ordination class in 1959. Jack's had the following description of priesthood from the great Pere Lacordaire.

To live in the midst of the world without desiring its pleasures:

To be a member of each family yet belonging to none:

To share all sufferings; to penetrate all secrets; to heal all wounds;

To go from men to God and offer Him their prayers;

To return from God to men to bring pardon, peace and hope;

To have a heart of fire for charity and a heart of bronze for chastity;

To teach and to pardon to console and to bless always

My God what a life!

And it is yours, O Priest of Jesus Christ!

Goodbye Jack. One last favor I would ask of you. Give our love to the Big Man when you see Him.

Msgr. Laurence O'Leary (1927–2012)

(Never delivered. Bishop Joseph Sartoris preached)

The person we honor by our presence today was many things to many people – a priest, a pastor an administrator. And he excelled in all of those roles.

But it is my contention that Laurence O'Leary will be most remembered as a **missionary** whose spiritual outreach touched peoples on every continent of old Planet Earth for fifty-nine priestly years.

Perhaps most of you knew this fine man as a gentle and effective priest who came to this parish thirty-three years ago in his role as pastor.

Here he baptized the converts, catechized the youngsters, provided Catholic education, married young people and buried the dead. He was always there for you and he would appreciate your being here today for him.

I came to know Msgr. O'Leary in his earlier years as head of the Propagation of the Faith office and Director of the Lay Mission Helpers and Mission Doctors, a post he occupied for many eventful years.

The good monsignor was in on the very beginning of the Lay Mission Helpers when that unique organization was founded as an extension of the Papal Volunteers and a reflection of the American Peace Corps.

The story of the Lay Mission Helpers has been eloquently related by Bob Dellinger and those of you who may want to read about Msgr. O'Leary, the **missionary**, would surely profit from reading that superbly written book.

Suffice to say here that for several decades Larry personally visited every single one of the Lay Mission Helpers in places whose very names I can't even pronounce.

And though I could easily provide some pretty good arguments for his beatification, I am not here today as the postulator for his cause.

During his time as pastor here in Brentwood, Msgr. O'Leary functioned well and admirably in a host of positions, and in all of them he left behind a distinctive roadmap of success and accomplishment. He built a hall, refurbished the church, rounded out the property and expanded the school.

When I last visited him, he gently but rather threateningly warned me not to extol his memory, "Tell the truth. That would be more effective than any of your stories." And believe me, that was an accurate appraisal.

Actually it is easy to comply with Monsignor's advice. After all, **a well-lived life is its own legacy**. Our lately departed friend could be characterized in a trinity of words – priesthood, priesthood and priesthood.

Though he may have lacked physical stature, he surely was able to walk tall among the leaders of the Church. Nothing beyond that really matters.

Archivists are full of secrets. Let me share one about Msgr. O'Leary with you. Many years ago, when Fulton J. Sheen was appointed Bishop of Rochester, Larry was proposed to succeed him as National Director for the Propagation of the Faith in New York. The **only dissenter** was O'Leary himself.

He begged Cardinal Manning to allow him to stay in Los Angeles. In his defense he quoted the words of Fray Junípero Serra: "In California is my life, and there, God willing, I hope to die."

Happily for all of us, the cardinal blocked the nomination. And plans were eventually set in motion for 0'Leary to come here to Brentwood. You all know the rest of the story.

Catholic folklore is often as interesting as Catholic theology and, sometimes, equally accurate. In any event, Cardinal Manning liked to invoke Irish folklore to the effect that on the day of a priest's death, a percentage of all the graces derived from the sacraments he dispensed, all the good works he inspired and all the fine examples he gave redounds to his own spiritual benefit.

And, if that be true, and I suspect it is, there was indeed a noble reward waiting for Msgr. Lawrence O'Leary when he returned his soul to the Lord.

Great men need no eulogies. We would only say that spiritually, intellectually and in every other way, the earthly sojourn of Laurence O'Leary measures up most perfectly to Robert Louis Stevenson's definition of one who has fulfilled his spiritual objective:

> That man is a success, who has lived well, laughed often and loved much;
> Who has gained the respect of intelligent men and the love of children;
> Who has filled his niche and accomplished his task;
> Who leaves the world better than he found it

Whether by an improved poppy, a perfect poem or a rescued soul;
Who never lacked appreciation of earth's beauty or failed to express it;
Who looked for the best in others and gave the best he had.

On the memorial card for his mother, Larry recalled a meditation, which seems to have special meaning today:

> On the wings of death and sorrow
> God sends us new hope for tomorrow
> And in His mercy and His grace
> He gives us strength to bravely face
> The lonely days that stretch ahead
> And know our loved one is not dead
> But only sleeping and out of our sight
> And we'll meet in that land
> Where there is no night.

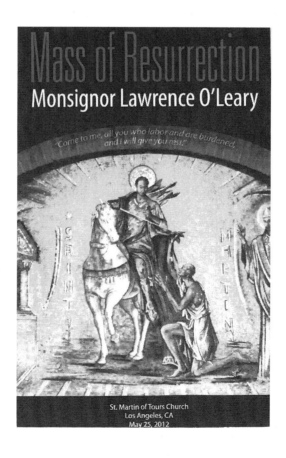

Thom Davis (1950–2015)

Thank you for joining us today in paying a final tribute to our long-time friend whom we fondly recall simply as "T. Davis."

One of this era's great biographers once noted that we can rather accurately describe a person by looking at his role models or heroes.

By his own testimony, T. Davis had only one hero, Fray Junípero Serra. He once told me that his earliest association with Serra was in a comic book that he traded with a friend as a youngster. And how fitting it was that he returned his soul to the Lord during the octave of Blessed Junípero Serra's feast day.

We can only fully understand T. Davis and his contribution to our local scene by examining how Serra challenged, inspired, motivated and influenced this good man in his daily life.

Years ago, when the California Catholic Conference wanted to honor Serra on the 200th anniversary of his death, Bishop Thaddeus Shubsda of Monterey was asked to establish the Serra Bicentennial Commission. I was to chair the board and to select a handful of members to serve on that commission.

T. Davis was among those answering the call for members and he became our most active supporter. Our objective was threefold: to have a US postage stamp issued for Serra, to prepare a series of columns for the Catholic newspapers of California and to arrange for a trek to Mallorca, Serra's birthplace in Spain.

Happily everything went as scheduled and most of the members subsequently also traveled to Rome for the beatification of Serra. But it didn't stop there for T. Davis.

He was in his element as a follower and proponent of Serra for canonization. And this was the activity that shaped the rest of his life. Oh, he had his family priorities, but Serra always occupied center stage.

In most recent times T. Davis was consumed with writing a biography of Father Zephryn Engelhardt, the Franciscan friar who laid the historical framework of all future activity about Serra. Thom's work was never finished, but I hope to work with Becky to complete it as a final tribute to this good man.

But, for the moment, let's get back to heroes. Let me go a step further because I find it hard to separate T. Davis from his hero.

And that's perhaps a good thing because that hero will soon be officially recognized by Church and State as a founder and hero for all of us here in California. I suspect that in God's mercy, Thom will soon join Serra, his hero in heaven.

This was the context in which I knew T. Davis the best. Oh, he did other things. He touched many people by his ministry, he influenced and prayed for Becky, Graham, his extended family and on and on.

Those were all good things and things to remember. But I suggest that we all remember T. Davis and his hero together as a team for good here on old Planet Earth.

And I am quite confident that Thom opened a lot of doors, as did his longtime hero Fray Junípero Serra.

Personally, I doubt if Serra really cares about his own canonization. After all, heaven is a state of perfect happiness and what more could canonization add to that? What can a formal recognition of his stature as a saint add to Fray Junípero Serra's reputation or enjoyment?

Then, why have Thom and so many people worked so hard and prayed so long for the event that will occur at the National Shrine in Washington D.C. on September 23rd?

It's because **we** need to have Serra canonized. In that status he will become a beacon for those of us still working out our salvation here on old Planet Earth.

Saint John Paul II suggested that we honor those "dry martyrs" who were willing to accept isolation, humiliation, rejection and social opprobrium for their beliefs.

Such great people as these are not surprised at encountering hostility in the world. On many occasions Jesus clearly warned His followers that they would face persecution. He even extorted them to "rejoice and be glad" when they were so treated.

The Holy Father's call for heroes has long been echoed in the literary world. Samuel Johnson, for example, said that "almost everyone will be found to have some hero or other, living or dead whose character he endeavors to assume, and whose performances he labors to equal. When the original is well-chosen and judiciously copied, the imitator achieves excellence."

Thomas Carlyle maintained that hero-worship is a natural human tendency. "All people look for heroes because of inadequacies in their human nature. That people often tend to complete themselves vicariously is really not unreasonable. People look to those whose lives and examples provide clues about life's questions. When such persons are identified, they become authentic heroes."

Hero worship is so ingrained in the human psyche that failure to find one can result in the discovery of pseudo-heroes and that can and often does lead to disastrous consequences.

Saint John Paul II further reminds us that "the Catholic Church has a treasury of admirable people where everyone can browse for heroes. In the Church heroes are called saints, most of whom have never been formally canonized. By imitating the heroes of holiness, people can achieve ultimate completeness."

Thomas Carlyle, who was there at the beginning of the modern age, viewed heroes as a solution to modern society's evils. Authentic heroes

helped society in the nineteenth century and they can help people today. A society that rejects its heroes is spiritually doomed.

In Loving Memory of

THOMAS LESLIE DAVIS, JR.

April 15, 1950 - July 4, 2015

But the Lord stood with me

and gave me strength.

2 Timothy 4:17

"ALWAYS GO FORWARD, NEVER TURN BACK"
JUNIPERO SERRA, O.F.M.

San Fernando Mission Rey Church

Mission Hills, CA

In response to the Holy Father's pleas for identifying and praising
heroes, from all walks of life, we bystanders stand on their shoulders
and walk in their footsteps.

So I would propose today, as we honor and recall Thom Davis, that
we portray him as a role model for ourselves.

Role models leave large footprints as they move along the pathways
to salvation. In Thom's case, I would single out three ways he showed
us how to live more useful and beneficial lives.

1. He not only *loved* his family and others, he *liked* them;
2. He accepted and profited by his own shortcomings and physical
   challenges;
3. And finally, like Fray Junípero Serra, he always looked ahead – never
   backward.

Unlike Serra, his hero, T. Davis will probably never be canonized. But
I would suggest that he will be long remembered as one who bravely

and successfully faced the world. He conquered, profited and learned by its challenges.

I can only speak for myself, but, for me, it was a unique pleasure to know Thom, to admire his determination and to walk in his footsteps.

Rosemary Donohue (1918–2015)

Before beginning, may I thank Msgr. Kevin Kostelnik, the rector of this magnificent Cathedral, for setting the scriptural and theological stage for my remarks.

Kevin, Msgr. Jeremiah Murphy, pastor of Saint Victor's Parish in West Hollywood, and I have prayed as a team for all the funerals of this "trinity of Donohue siblings," Eugene, Daniel and now Rosemary.

And, what a singular privilege we have had in representing the local Church in paying tribute to these unique religious personages in California's southland.

Seldom in the history of the United States has a single family been as generous to the Catholic Church as that of the New York physician, Daniel Donohue, and his wife, Julia, whose children are all remembered as outstanding heroes and role models for the local church.

Today we bid adieu to Rosemary Donohue who graced Planet Earth with her presence for almost a hundred years.

To have known that great lady and to have been known by her was a great blessing that we will all cherish until the day we join her in eternal life.

The pedigree of Rosemary's accomplishments for the community, the Church in California and the nation as a whole is long and impressive, something of a roadmap in and around this Golden State.

In her early days Rosemary had a long and remarkable career as a fashion giant with such firms as Lord and Taylor where she was acknowledged nationally as a visionary in modern fashion designs.

Some of you may remember Bullocks Wilshire, a department store of elegance where woman went to adorn themselves with elegant dresses and other vestures of the fashion world. My own mother worked there and once I asked her if she had ever met Rosemary Donohue.

"Oh yes," she replied, "she used to come every year or so to update the sales force on contemporary fashion designs."

When I asked her to describe Rosemary, she said something I have never forgotten: "If the world had more Rosemary Donohues, it would be a far better place."

Later Rosemary worked alongside Daniel, her brother, and his wife, Bernardine, in organizing and directing the Dan Murphy Foundation.

It was in that capacity that she had a large part in the design and building of this Cathedral which is already known worldwide as one of the nation's unique ecclesial accomplishments. Here, most appropriately, she will soon be interred to await the final call of our Blessed Lord.

Rosemary was indeed forceful, courageous and outspoken – characteristics associated with the Church's great pioneers and founders.

She informed me once that I would be asked "to preach her homily at the proper time." I was likely chosen because she had outlived the long litany of priests more qualified than I for this task.

"Well," I responded, "what do you want me to say?" Without the slightest hesitation, she said "Talk about the role of women in the Church. Tell the *oldsters* to be proud that they are women, remind the *middle aged* to rejoice in their calling and, finally, tell the *young ones* how happy and fulfilling is their membership in the contemporary Catholic Church." Oh yes, she said, and "keep it short."

So in deference to her forcefully expressed wishes, allow me to fulfill that mandate by reflecting ever-so-briefly on the role that women have and are playing in our Catholic community.

A feature story in a recent issue of *Time* magazine referred to Los Angeles as the "Orient of the Western World" and, in that regard, I thought you might like to hear a Chinese version of the creation story:

"Lord, I need a companion," said the first man on earth. So God took the beauty of a flower, and the song of a bird, the color of the rainbow, the laughter of the wave, the gentleness of the lamb, the cunning of the fox, the fickleness of the showers and the waywardness of the clouds and wove them into a female which He gave to man."

There has always been a rich treasure of womanhood in both the Jewish and Christian traditions. Before Sarah was *loyal*, before Rebekah was *wise*, before Rachel was *beloved* of her husband, they were, first of all, women.

In the gospels, Elizabeth prophesied, the women of Samaria and Canaan professed their faith, the woman in the Temple gave all she had, the widow at Nairn mourned for her only son, Martha and Simon's mother-in-law prepared the meals and the Magdalen wept for her sins. Each was a woman – some wives, some single women, some widows and one divorced.

In the apostolic generation, Priscilla and her husband offered St. Paul the hospitality of their home; the charitable Dorcas made dresses and cloaks for those in need; and Phoebe was a deaconess "who gave great help to the apostles." Wives, widows and single they were, but their names are now immortalized in the book of life. . . .

The Russian scholar, Nicholas Berdyaev, said that we are entering the "feminine age of history," an era he equated to be an "age of mercy."

Maybe so, but I strongly suspect we entered the feminine age about the year that Rosemary Donohue reached adulthood.

Those who belittle or underestimate the Catholic attitude toward women really know very little about the Church or her history.

In most of the last century, for example, there have been more Catholic female college presidents, hospital administrators, school principals and more women signing checks than is true even today in America's corporate world.

And for the chauvinist who dared to criticize God for creating man before woman, may I remind him that one always makes a rough draft before the final masterpiece.

Were the Lord to add an appendix to the New Testament, Rosemary Donohue would likely be included. She epitomizes the best in Catholic womanhood. She could be best characterized and remembered by words earlier part of the Talmud which says:

> God did not create woman from man's head that he should command her, nor from his feet, that she should be his slave. But rather from his side, that she should be near his heart.

The Donohue chapter in the religious annals of California and the nation is now closed. And what a glorious chapter it has been. She and her brothers, Eugene and Daniel, belong to the canon of history. May they continue, from their place in Heaven, to bless and pray for us.

May I conclude my memories of this wonderful lady by recalling what I said at the funerals of her brothers.

> Show me a person of integrity, a person with an open heart, a person of many friends and one unafraid of death and I will show you another Solomon or maybe even another Moses.

Goodbye Rosemary – please leave a light on for me and others who will soon follow in your footsteps.

🕸osemary 🕸leanor 🕸onohue

🕸ntered 🕸ternal 🕸ife
🕸obember 13, 2015

🕸eb. 🕸lsgr. 🕸ebin 🕸ostelnik
🕸rincipal 🕸elebrant

🕸obember 23, 2015
🕸athedral of 🕸ur 🕸aby of the 🕸ngels

Msgr. Jeremiah Murphy (1937–2017)

As I return to this beautiful church to memorialize the life of Msgr. Jeremiah Murphy, I can't help recalling that I preached the first sermon ever delivered from this pulpit – over half a century ago.

I remember that Louella Parsons, the gossip columnist for William Randolph Hearst's newspaper chain, was in the congregation. After Mass I made the mistake of asking her if she liked my homily. She smiled and said: "It'll do until something better comes along."

A lot has happened along Holloway Drive since then. The legendary John J. Devlin was pastor in 1960. He was truly a great priest, educator and churchman and, happily, his example here in West Hollywood is reflected in his successor thrice removed.

For a long time, Jeremiah Murphy has been God's anointed agent on the local scene. When people needed an exemplar, advisor or just a shoulder to cry or lean on, he was a vivid portrayal of Jesus walking alongside His followers on the roadway to Emmaus. What you saw was what he was.

As a priest, Jeremiah Murphy touched all the bases. He offered Holy Mass daily (sometimes multiple times), he recited the Divine Office (in season and out), he made the sacraments available whenever called upon, he prayed the rosary every day and he dutifully performed all the other duties of the modern high priesthood.

As educator he taught in the seminary and in two Catholic high schools, completed the requirements and was awarded two doctorates and administered the secondary school system for this, the largest archdiocese in the United States.

As churchman, Msgr. Murphy became the face of God's people in Hancock Park and then here in West Hollywood, and this he did for several years beyond his physical ability to even walk.

As a priest in this epicenter of the world's motion picture industry, he leaves an indelible imprint of spiritual authenticity. The old has been honored, the new updated and the modern refurbished.

The next pastor of West Hollywood will inherit a congregation ready for whatever theological and religious surprises the future may bring. And his parochial breastplate will bear the unmistakable image of a physically incapacitated but very active shepherd.

While he served his people as an invalid in these later years, Murphy was anything but a passive pastor. A lady reporter from the local newspaper once told me that whenever she needed to know what was happening in West Hollywood she would phone St. Victor's Church and push button #1, Murphy's private number. She said that wherever she went she could see the shadow of his car in the foreground.

I know of one time when a phone call came to the rectory in the darkest hour of the night. A crying voice desperately pleaded for a priest at Cedars-Sinai hospital and none was available. Somehow, defying all the laws of gravity and good sense, Jeremiah and his caregiver got up, dressed and drove to Cedar's where he anointed the dying person. The next day, the caller came by to thank "the priest" and only then did she realize that he was totally paralyzed.

And here, I would like to interrupt myself for a brief moment to thank Monsignor Murphy's three care-givers who were with him 24/7 for the last years.

In the Epistles for the Weekdays of Lent, Saint Paul enumerates and comments on the virtues as they have evolved in the New Covenant.

The caregivers for Msgr. Murphy personify those virtues and I would ask you to join me in tribute to these practitioners of those virtues.

I might also mention that Jeremiah had prophetic moments. For example, he sensed that the end of his earthly sojourn was near. Just a few days ago, when I last talked with him on the phone, he ended the conversation in these words: "Frank, I want to thank you for being such a longtime friend." Before I could respond, he terminated our phone call.

Entered Into Life
August 19, 1937

Entered Into Eternal Life
March 1, 2017

An Irish Blessing

May the road rise to meet you,
May the wind be always at your back,
May the sun shine warm upon your face,
The rains fall soft upon your field
and, until we meet again,
May God hold you in the palm of
His hand.

Father Murphy was a breath of fresh air at Queen of Angels seminary where he arrived as spiritual director in 1970s. His was a hard act to follow in the classroom and his weekly sermons in the Chapel brought a whole new spiritual dimension to the teenage seminarians of the 1970s. Those of us brought up in the Church of an earlier era were made to feel a little bit out of touch by comparison.

In the world of minor seminaries, the era of the 1970s was reinventing itself. Though the students probably didn't realize it, those years were more challenging to the teachers than the students.

One of his innovations at Queen of Angels was his insistence on visiting the homes of the students. Recalling Archbishop Cantwell's observation "show me the stone from which a young man is hewn, and I will tell you whether he is fodder for the priesthood," Jerry personally visited every single family whose son aspired to be a priest.

Murphy had the rare and remarkable ability to speak the language of teenagers. At Queen of Angels, we all took turns in the confessional. Murphy made it easy for the rest of the faculty by being the "Confessor of Choice" for the great majority of the seminarians.

Of all the priests who taught at Queen of Angels seminary, I am the only one still residing there. Even after all these years at least once a month someone will ring my doorbell and, invariably, he asks for Father Murphy. The rest of us are only memories, but Murphy is the one whose presence in their lives made a real and lasting difference.

In later years he lived at Saint Basil's Church in the Wilshire District. Murphy's appearances in the pulpit were eagerly anticipated by the parishioners of those days. Msgr. Hawkes told me that, once, when Bishop Fulton J. Sheen was scheduled to preach the *Tre Ore* on Good Friday, he was unable to come. He called to "see if that young priest from Queen of Angels could take my place." Few priests there were who could step in for "Uncle Fultie." Murphy had every ingredient for preaching except Sheen's pectoral cross.

Nor did the monsignor allow his crippled body to interfere with the obligations of his extra-parochial commitments. He maintained his seat at the Dan Murphy Foundation and on the board of Don Bosco Technical Institute, which meant all-day activity at quarterly meetings throughout the archdiocese.

And like his namesake from the Old Testament, Jeremiah was devoted to his siblings, Kathleen and Patrick and their extended families. His kinship bespoke a deep and close relationship which he valued highly.

One of Jerry's heroes was James R. Wooden, longtime basketball coach at UCLA. In 1999, Wooden wrote his memoirs wherein he spelled out his ten reflections for greatness. We discussed those many times and I would like to mention them here because they so accurately reflect the one who's earthly remains lie before us today.

1. Failure to prepare is preparing to fail.

2. Make each day your masterpiece.

3. Do not be disagreeable when you disagree.

4. What is right is more important than who is right.
5. Discipline yourself, so others won't need to.
6. Treat all people with dignity and respect.
7. True happiness begins where selfishness ends.
8. Be more interested in finding the best way rather than having your own way.
9. Goals attained with little effort are seldom meaningful or lasting.
10. Ability may get you to the top, but it takes character to keep you there.

And so there you have a glimpse of Jerry, the pastor of souls. He loved the people of West Hollywood and he would want me to say that today.

Catholic folklore is often as interesting and meaningful as Catholic theology. The late Cardinal Manning liked to invoke Irish folklore to the effect that on the day of a priest's death, a percentage of all the graces derived from the sacraments he dispensed, all the good works he inspired and all the fine examples he gave redound to his own spiritual benefit. And, if that be true, and I suspect it is, there was indeed a noble reward waiting for Msgr. Jeremiah Murphy when he returned his soul to the Lord on Ash Wednesday.

Over the past decade I made it a practice to call him at least once a week. Each time I asked him, "how are you feeling?" He was one of those rare persons who responded "fine" even when everyone knew that wasn't the case. I must mention that he was exceedingly pleased when Archbishop Gomez extended his term of service because, as he said, "I am still able to get around."

Great people need no eulogies. We would only say that spiritually, intellectually and in every other way, the earthly sojourn of Jeremiah Murphy measures up most perfectly to Robert Louis Stevenson's definition of one who has fulfilled his spiritual objectives. He once wrote that a person is a success

Who has lived well, laughed often and loved much;

Who has gained the respect of intelligent men and the love of children;

Who has filled his niche and accomplished his task;

Who leaves the world better than he found it;

Who never lacked appreciation of earth's beauty or failed to express it;

Who looked for the best in others and gave the best he had.

On the memorial card for his father, Jerry invoked a meditation which has a special meaning today:

> On the wings of death and sorrow God sends us new hope for tomorrow;
> And in His mercy and His grace, He gives us strength to bravely face;
> The lonely days that stretch ahead and know our loved one is not dead;
> But only sleeping and out of our sight and we'll meet in that land
> where there is no night.

In one of his masterful exhortations, Pope Saint John Paul II invited Catholics to celebrate the recent jubilee year by honoring their heroes.

I think it was Thomas Carlyle who suggested that "hero worship" is a natural human tendency. "People look for heroes because of inadequacies in their human nature. Individuals often tend to complete themselves vicariously and that is really reasonable."

Once again Pope John Paul II reminds us that the Catholic Church has a treasury of admirable adherents where everyone can browse for heroes.

Authentic heroes have helped society in earlier times and they can help society today. A society that rejects its heroes is spiritually compromised.

I once wrote a book on the *Catholic Heroes in Southern California*. Because the heroes cited in that book were deceased. I am here today to enroll Jeremiah Murphy in that list of personal heroes.

Why? Because everyone needs heroes – even priests. A hero is one we look up to for a host of reasons, especially his practice of virtue.

Each of God's special friends is asked to bear a distinctive cross and what made that cross more burdensome for Murphy was the necessity of having to depend on others for moving about his parish and wherever else his vocation required him to sanctify.

Once again, Jeremiah measured up to the challenge. The Cure of Ars, who set the standard for parish priests, once said that "God leans heaviest on those whom he loves the most." By that yardstick, the Monsignor gets an A+.

When Monsignor Murphy's earthly world became burdensome by the lack of bodily movement, he was virtuous enough to accept that challenge as an opportunity for further growth in the spiritual realm. And here too, "the Murphy man" won another gold medal. He regretted only that his ability to help others was diminished.

It's a pleasure for me to express my esteem for Monsignor Murphy by proclaiming him among my cherished heroes.

Hopefully and prayerfully I anticipate seeing him again in the eternal life we all anticipate with hope and gratitude.

Finally, Thank you Lord for allowing us to know and love Msgr. Jeremiah Murphy in this life and, hopefully to be with him in eternal life.

Monsignor
Jeremiah Timothy Murphy

Ordination Date
May 1, 1963

7

Selected Memorials

Over the past century plus, the Old Country Priest has preached at numerous memorials and funerals – a goodly percentage of which were not Catholic. Here are a select few of those for whom he had the last word:

Earl C. Adams (1893–1986)

How appropriate it is to honor the memory of Earl C. Adams in these historic surroundings. This church symbolizes the world that Earl loved and the one in which he was the most at home.

He was, like this church, a refugee from another century. And further, like this humble house of worship, he contributed mightily to keeping alive the values that have made this area of the Lord's Vineyard the leading metropolis in the Western world.

The passing of Earl Adams gives pause for reflecting not so much on what he did for ninety-three years but on what he stood for. Earl was among the few high priests of the legal profession and, like all great jurists, his ideals will long outlast his human accomplishments.

A valid portrayal of Earl Adams must begin and end with the profession in which he excelled for almost seventy years. He was always and everywhere a purveyor of the law, one whose entire value system was anchored to the notion of justice.

And justice is the virtue practiced by those who live and die by the natural law. That law, etched onto the souls of every human being, is nothing more than the Judeo-Christian term for The Decalogue, the Ten Commandments.

Earl had the unusual ability of being able to couch the application of his chosen profession in terms of the people for whom laws are made. And though he shunned the reins of leadership for himself, he was constantly on the lookout for those who shared his view that law must be accommodated into the framework of human needs and aspirations.

Imagine, just for a moment, how one man thus influenced this and future generations by his friendship and support of candidates for public office!

Is it any wonder that he became the trusted confident of presidents, congressmen and governors? And they listened to him not because he wielded power, but because he personified what good government is all about.

Beyond justice, that virtue which most characterized Earl Adams was kindness. Oh, he could be and often was firm, stubborn and even adamant on an issue, but he was ever kind and gentle. I once heard someone suggest that the term "gentleman" was coined to describe Earl Adams.

Whether as a husband for sixty-four years, or a father or grandfather, whether as a confrere in the legal profession or a fellow collector of art or maybe just a friend, Earl Adams always had time for a smile, a compliment, an encouraging word. He was an upbeat man in a downbeat world.

We all came to know Earl for different reasons. In my own case, I knew him as a Westerner and member of Zamorano. But it didn't take long to figure out that Earl was a cut above being a devoted lover of the west, a fervent collector of books or an avid connoisseur of English silver.

He was an outstanding Christian gentleman whose presence tolerated no preferment or reservations. He had the remarkable ability of conferring his total interest and concern on those with whom he spoke and worked. No matter how exalted or lowly, a person was king of the mound in Earl's presence.

I once asked Earl if it bothered him that the Lord leaned rather heavily on him in his final years. His unhesitating response was typical of the man: "Certainly not. He carried me for eighty years and I can well afford to carry him for the rest of the journey." Then he added this footnote: "You know, the man who hasn't suffered really hasn't lived. I think the way a person suffers says a lot about his priorities." To that we can all say, "Amen."

From this day forward, Earl Clinton Adams becomes a part of the past which he loved so intensely. He moves from being a collector of books to being a subject for books.

I strongly suspect that historians will come to recognize this kind and gentle man as one of the great patriarchs of California's legal profession, one whose contributions will far outreach the fallible confines of the humanity in which they were unfolded.

Ethel Bossert (1904–1992)

The Feast of Our Lady of the Angels in the year of our Lord, 1986, richly deserves to be remembered by the Catholics of Southern California. For on that day, Ethel Bossert closed out a sixty-year career of uninterrupted service to the Church of Los Angeles, a record unparalleled in the Golden State's religious annals.

A private person to the very last of her days in the Chancery Office, Ethel confided very little for the public record. This much we know – that she was born in Los Angeles, at the old Clara Barton Hospital. She and her brother attended elementary school in Ocean Park.

Her first contact with the Catholic Church came during her teen years as a student at Saint Mary's Commercial School in Boyle Heights. Shortly after her conversion, Ethel became a member of the first class at Conaty (Catholic Girls) High School. In 1926, after completing her education at Venice High, Ethel took a "temporary" position with Steve Sullivan, who was spearheading the drive to raise funds for Los Angeles College, the preparatory seminary for the Diocese of Los Angeles-San Diego.

She was assigned a desk in the chancery, which was then located in the Higgins Building, at 108 West Second Street, across from Saint Vibiana's Cathedral. When the drive was finished, Bishop John J. Cantwell invited Ethel to join Mary Sinclair and Pat Powers on the permanent curial staff. Though she worked at numerous tasks in the next six decades, Ethel was associated mostly with the chancellors of the diocese, including such outstanding churchmen as Bernard J. Dolan, Joseph T. McGucken, Alden J. Bell and Benjamin G. Hawkes.

In the spring of 1932, when the diocesan offices were relocated, Ethel took up her work on the seventh floor of the then new Petroleum Securities Building, on West Olympic Boulevard at Figueroa. She recalled the ever-gracious Carrie Estelle Doheny insisting that she and Mary Sinclair take their meals with the staff of the Doheny Oil Company on another floor of the building.

The chancery was relocated in August 1951, this time to 1531 West Ninth Street and there Ethel rounded out her service to the Archdiocese of Los Angeles. She alone has the distinction of having worked for all four of the southland's archbishops!

While researching an article for the golden jubilee of the archdiocese, we noticed that the earliest letters relating to that epochal event bear the initial "b," an indication that they were typed by Ethel Bossert who, in 1936, had already logged ten years of service to God's people!

In Loving Memory of
Ethel V. Bossert

BORN
Los Angeles, California

PASSED AWAY
March 26, 1992, Los Angeles, Calif.

FUNERAL MASS
Tuesday, March 31, 1992, 11:00 a.m.
Holy Cross Mausoleum Chapel

INTERMENT
Holy Cross Cemetery

Almighty God, through the death of your Son on the cross, You have overcome death to us. Through his burial and resurrection from the dead You have made the grave a holy place and restored us to eternal life. We pray for those who have died with Him in the hope of rising again. God of the living and the dead. may those who faithfully believed in You on earth praise You forever in the joy of Heaven.   Amen.

Pierce Brothers Cunningham & O'Connor

Los Angeles Mortuary

Though her mark remains on tens of thousands of letters, reports, memoranda and journals, Ethel always preferred to work behind the scenes. Only once did she emerge from the shadows, and that time by obedience. It was January 1929, and she appeared with Bishop Cantwell in a photograph published in the Los Angeles *Times*. The late Monsignor John J. Devlin, for whom Ethel worked in her earliest days at the chancery, once remarked that she was "the most professional, qualified and loyal person" he had known in all his long and distinguished ministry.

That testimony, made a quarter century earlier, was echoed by Timothy Cardinal Manning, who said that "for half a century and a decade more, Ethel Bossert served the Church in Los Angeles in a manner unique among its handmaidens. She was intimate to all the doings that were transacted at the headquarters of the Church. In that capacity she preserved a confidentiality that made her a treasured person. No one's light will ever shine brighter."

Richard Hoffman (1912–1989)

With a sense of quiet reverence, we open our lips to speak about one whom we loved and venerated in life. Like a broken alabaster box, the good odor of Richard Hoffman's life penetrates our minds and fills our hearts with the most pleasant of human memories.

And while we join with Ruth and the Hoffman family in their profound sense of loss at Richard's passing, we don't fault the summons of the Lord. Richard was a strong-willed man who would have and did rebel at prolonging his life in a world where he could no longer be an active participant.

A lifelong and committed Baptist, Richard expressed his faith more in type than in words. I suspect that his notion of the resurrection, for example, was closer to that of Benjamin Franklin than Thomas Aquinas.

The nation's premier printer put it this way: "Here lies the body of Benjamin Franklin, printer. Like the covering of an old book, its contents torn out and stripped of its lettering and. gilding, food for the worms. But the work will not be lost. It will appear once more, in a new and more beautiful edition, corrected and amended by its Author."

During his long and productive years, Richard cherished life because it afforded him the opportunity of doing what he did best – printing. Yet Richard wasn't afraid of death, because he knew how to live. Long ago he recognized that the Lord and He alone gives meaning to life and validity to death.

The story is told that when David Thoreau was dying, someone tact-fully inquired whether he had made his peace with God. He answered, "why should I do that now; I never quarreled with Him."

Thoreau and Richard were realists. A realist doesn't know anything more about the future than the non-believer, but he's convinced that God will most assuredly provide for those who faithfully profess His name and abide by His commandments.

Richard's could have been the words of the poet, who said:

When death shall beckon with outstretched hand

And whisper softly of an unknown land;

I shall not be afraid to go,

Though it's over a path I do not know.

I take death's hand without a fear

For He who safely brought me here;

Will also take me safely back.

Despite the many things I lack

He will not let me go alone

Into the valley that's so unknown.

So I reach out for God's kindly hand,

And my journey to the Promised Land.

Now others will pay tribute to Richard the family man, Richard the printer, Richard the teacher and maybe even Richard the lionhearted – all roles in which he excelled.

But there was another Richard I got to know and love during those many Wednesday drives to Zamorano – Richard the man who loved his wife and bragged about his children, the man who dwelt on the virtues of others while overlooking their failings, the man who recog-nized his own shortcomings and endeavored to rise above them. That was Richard the Teddy Bear, a man who liked people, enjoyed simple conversation and related to human foibles.

Oh, Richard was a renowned printer, an acclaimed raconteur and a discerning collector. But I suspect God loved Richard most for his simplicity – a virtue one comes across rarely enough in modern times.

We celebrate Richards's life today in the words Origen used in his commentary for the Book of Job. Let us rejoice at the time of earthly demise "because those who seem to die, do not really die." They are more alive than ever.

"Lord, for your faithful who die, life does not end, but life is changed; with the destruction of our earthly bodies, an eternal dwelling place is made ready and waiting."

Dr. Norman Neuerburg (1926–1997)

Though he was not a card-carrying or dues-paying Catholic, Norman Neuerburg probably knew more about the Church's theology, patrology and history than 95 percent of its certified adherents.

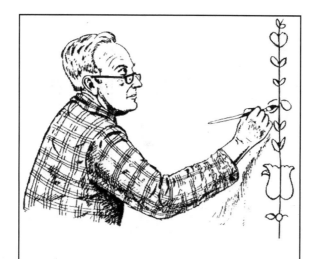

Memorial service for
Dr. Norman Neuerburg
(1926-1997)

San Fernando, Rey de España Mission
Mission Hills, California
December 28, 1997

I asked him last year when he was going to sign up and his response was "I am getting readier and readier." Certainly he was in total accord with Catholic doctrine and practice.

We have a lot of funerals here at San Fernando Mission and one day, not so long ago, I noticed that Norman was sitting in the back of the church during the whole of a funeral service. He told me afterwards how much he enjoyed and was comforted by the scriptural readings read on that occasion – the very ones used today.

The moving and very human account of Our Lord arriving at Bethany just after the death of his personal friend, Lazarus, provided an occasion to remind Martha and Mary and all of us about the resurrection on the last day.

Christ remarked to Martha: "Your brother will rise again," to which she replied, "Oh, I know that he will rise again in the resurrection on the last day." Then Jesus gently interrupted her and said: "I am the resurrection and the life; whoever believes in Me, though he should die, will come to life."

Those are powerful words from the Big Man Himself. And, isn't it comforting to know that there is yet another and a better life to come – one that will never end. That's why Christians are or should be happy and joyous people even when the shadows of death fall upon their loved ones.

The preface for the Resurrection liturgy shouts out for all the world to hear: "The sadness of death gives way to the bright promise of immortality. Lord, for Your faithful people, life is changed not ended. When the body of our earthly dwelling lies in death, we gain an everlasting dwelling place in heaven."

Now, the notion of the resurrection of our bodies is not something peculiar to Catholics. All Christians embrace that concept. Let me give you just one example.

Winston Churchill planned his own funeral, which took place in Saint Paul's Cathedral in London. He included many of the great hymns of the eloquent Anglican liturgy. At Churchill's direction, a bugler positioned high in the dome of St. Paul's intoned after the benediction the sound of "Taps," the universal signal that proclaims that the day is over. But then came a most dramatic turn, as Churchill had instructed. As soon as "Taps" had been played, another bugler, perched on the opposite side of the dome, played the notes of "Reveille": "It's time to get up! It's time to get up! It's time to get up in the morning!"

That was Churchill's testimony that at the end of history, the last note will not be "Taps" it will be "Reveille." These bones will rise again!

Norman's approach to life was upbeat and positive because he believed in the resurrection of the dead. Oh, he had his sorrows and disappointments, but he would remind us that Christ had first to die before he could rise from the tomb.

For the person who uses life well, as did Norman, death seems spontaneous, without the least pretense, not the destruction, but the fulfillment of life.

So, let us not be like those who always seem to be pallbearers of the past. Let us utilize, by living, the qualities of the dead. Truth is ever new. Like the grass of morning, moist with glistening dew, all the old virtues are waiting to spring up afresh.

The only thing that now separates us from Norman is that wholly human creation called time. Until the hourglass runs out for each one of us, I find it easy to picture Norm speaking with J. Paul Getty, Edith Buckland Webb and Maynard J. Geiger. And what wonderful conversations they must be having.

In Memory of

Dr. Norman Neuerburg

Born

February 3, 1926

Los Angeles, California

Passed Away

December 12, 1997

Los Angeles, California

Interment

York Creek Cemetery

New Braunfels, Texas

Sister Madeline Rose, C.S.C. (1905–1980)

Mount Saint Mary's College

The names of far less than one percent of the world's population will be remembered in the annals of history. Fifty years after a person's death, hardly a trace of his or her human existence can be found or substantiated.

Yet every person who has, is or will walk the face of Planet Earth is vitally important to God. And everyone is given a task to perform, a vocation to fill and a soul to save.

Today we celebrate the birth to eternal life of Sister Madeline Rose – a person who fought the good fight, who kept the faith and who now reaps the reward promised by God to those who love and serve Him.

Sister Madeline Rose was one of the Lord's very ordinary people, yet she leaves an indelible mark on her community which we can all admire and emulate.

No one could come here, meet her and not be impressed by her joyful, enthusiastic and contagious personality. Her glasses were tinted with love – everything she saw was good, delightful, funny, glorious and pleasant.

And what a pleasure it was to know someone with those characteristics in this age of somberness.

The sermons were always inspiring, the food always delicious, the weather always lovely and on and on. Maybe she was a little unrealistic in her appraisal of things, but then again so was Christ.

Those who came in contact with Sister Madeline Rose came away a little happier and a lot more joyful. She was one of those rare people it was always fun to speak and joke with.

She was a musician after the fashion of Oscar Hammerstein who once wrote that "love wasn't put in your heart to stay, love isn't love until you give it away."

One of the Sisters told me yesterday that once at a party, Sister Madeline Rose pinned a sign on the back of her habit which read: "Kiss me even if you don't know me."

How typical that was! She obviously decided, early on is life, to subscribe to the old Lincoln adage that says "most folks are about as happy as they make up their minds to be."

The secret of Sister Madeline Rose's lifestyle was a supernatural love – motivated and inspired by Christ. To her, the neighbor was nothing more or less than a reflection of the Savior. And who would frown at the Lord?

She didn't learn the lesson of love from dusty old theology books. Her spiritual orientation was acquired on her knees.

Scientists tell us that people are greatly influenced by their individual body chemistry. And surely that is true to some extent.

But there's one chemical that cannot be measured out in a laboratory and that chemical is love. Fill up any body with love and it will overflow into the lives of others.

By reason of her vows, Sister Madeline Rose leaves us today no material legacy. But what she does bequeath is vastly more pleasing and infinitely more acceptable – a heritage of good works and happy memories.

From her place in heaven, one can almost see her rushing down the hallways, laughing and singing her way through eternity. That's the kind of legacy Holy Cross can long be proud of.

Mark Thomas (1963–1979)

Those of us gathered in this historic church today have come together for a host of reasons: some to pray for a son, a brother or a friend, others to honor the memory of a classmate and still others to mourn for a young man who figured one way or another into our own lifestyle.

Whatever our motive for being here, we who are Christians want it clearly proclaimed and understood that we harbor no resentment towards God for His unexplained and premature intervention in Mark's life.

You see, it is part of our Christian faith that life is freely given and freely taken by God. There is nothing arbitrary about God. There is a time to be born and a time to die – and He alone determines the circumstances, time and manner.

God is our heavenly Father. We believe that His decisions are always in our best interest – even in times such as this when human sensitivities find it difficult to accept His time sequence.

What a boring place heaven would be without teenagers – and Mark will forever be a teenager as now he begins to share eternity with the Lord and Master he has loved and served these past sixteen years.

In an address to a group of young people at the Vatican, Pope Paul VI once observed that the whole aim of Christian life is "service to the truth which Christ has bequeathed to the world." He concluded by saying: "What a noble mission it is to bear witness to Christ."

The Mark we've known and esteemed was one of those witnesses. Oh he wasn't perfect at it, but then again few are. What's really important is that he tried and that's all the Lord wants from any of his followers. He doesn't need our success – only our determination to try.

As are many young people these days, Mark was a little confused and perhaps even scornful of the manner in which the older generation has messed up the world. He rebelled at those who said one thing and did another.

And Mark didn't like structure – probably because intuitively he sensed that sincerity needs no artificial barriers.

But through it all Mark never lost confidence in his own determination to make the world a better place by his presence. And that's the "stuffing" of real greatness.

Though he didn't live long enough to study philosophy, Mark exemplified the wisdom of Socrates who long ago advised: "Ask not that you live long, but that you live well."

Those of us who knew Mark, in his good times and in his bad ones, feel no hesitation in saying that he may not have lived long, but he did live well!

Mark was a Christian and for a Christian the light that flickers out at midnight symbolizes not the end of an old day but the promise of a new dawn.

And so today, we joyfully repeat and affirm those meaningful words of Psalm 116: "Precious in the eyes of the Lord is the death of His faithful one."

For Mark, life is not ended today but changed. With the destruction of his earthly body, God has prepared for Mark an eternal dwelling place in the perfection and company of the saints.

Isabel Piczek (1927–2016)

Before reflecting on Isabel's singular contributions to our lives here in Southern California, may I speak about the combined Piczek imprint on old Planet Earth. I say that because she and her sister are almost inseparable both in time and talent.

As I look back on my priestly ministrations along California's *El Camino Real*, nothing stands out more prominently than my acquaintance with Isabel Piczek and her late sister, Edith.

These good people, surely among the most outstanding ecclesial artists of contemporary times, were motivated by the realization that art speaks a message for all humankind.

From their modest and unobtrusive studios, in the Echo Park district of Los Angeles, these Hungarian-born artists produced some of the finest murals, mosaics and stained glass in America and Europe.

The Piczeks inherited their talent from their father, an art professor of considerable renown in one of Hungary's leading universities.

They completed their training in the School of Fine Arts in Budapest. Shortly after the Communists took over their homeland, the sisters escaped to Vienna.

Later, they literally painted their way across war-torn Europe, finally arriving in Rome at the outset of the 1950 Holy Year. In the Eternal City, Isabel and Edith won the celebrated *Galleri di Roma* prize and were commissioned to create a 377 square foot fresco mural at the Pontifical Biblical Institute, an unheard of distinction for women.

At the invitation of the Canadian hierarchy, the sisters set up studios in Hamilton and Toronto. Then in 1955 they came to the United States, where their first commission was a 2,880 foot mural for the cathedral at Reno.

Since 1958, the Piczeks have lived and worked in Los Angeles at their Construction Art Center with artistic masterpieces adorning numerous churches, convents and public buildings on three continents and in seven countries.

Probably the most celebrated of their many works are the stained-glass windows, murals and mosaics at Guardian Angel Cathedral in Las Vegas. Within walking distance from the Strip, on Desert Inn Road, is the masterful ten-year project "Toward the Total Christ."

Locally, the Piczek art can be seen at Saint Phillip Church (Pasadena), Saint Mary Magdalen (Camarillo), Saint Victor (West Hollywood), Saint Bridget of Sweden (Van Nuys), Saint Catherine Laboure (Torrance) and Our Lady of the Assumption (San Buenaventura).

Their talents have a decided ecumenical attraction too. The Air Force Chapel at Nellis Air Base, Messiah Baptist Church and B'nai David Synagogue in Los Angeles are perhaps the three finest examples of their outreach, award-winning art.

Here at San Fernando, Rey de España Mission, we are surrounded by the artistic beauty of the Piczeks. From the giant portrayal of Pope John Paul II's arrival in 1987 (over the entrance to the Church), to the mural of Our Lady of the Archives (on the northern wall of the Archival Center) to the six panels outlining the history of the Archdiocese of Los Angeles, to a stained-glass window over the choir loft of the Church, to the dozens of cartoons and assorted expressions of beauty adorning the walls of our other buildings, visitors are daily reminded of the Piczek genius for expressing their devotion to Almighty God.

Over the years, Isabel and Edith described their "aesthetic partnership" in terms of a "mystical realism" which they looked upon as part of the modern visual and spiritual revolution in ecclesial art. The unassuming sisters saw their vocation as a "cultural and religious mission."

Feeling compelled to be "always moving forward," they were ever concerned that the old ways will disappear or trap those who insist on a piety not in keeping with the times.

Proposed sketch of Our Lady of the Archives

Believing that much of modern art has a dehumanizing effect, the Piczek sisters portrayed the destiny of humankind in forms of glass, paint and tile, while acknowledging that authentic artwork is implanted on the soul of the observer. And that's a philosophy almost as beautiful and attractive as their works of art.

Edith went home to the Lord four years ago and early on the morning of September 28, 2016, the Feast of the Archangels, Isabel joined her half-sister before the throne of Almighty God.

How appropriate it was that her going forth from old Planet Earth occurred on that angelic feast day. Always the angels were a part of her artistic expression.

Someone observed that had there been a fourth archangel, it would have borne the name Isabel.

It was my pleasure and privilege to have known these two remarkable ladies for well over a half century. What an honor it has been to witness their unique contribution to the artistic history of the Roman Catholic Church around the world!

Isabel literally prayed her way through her long and productive life in the sense that everything she did was an expression of her profound faith and devotion.

Whether it was her murals, her stained glass or her ceramic tile, Isabel imprinted her unique style on the figures that came from a lifetime of devotion and dedication to the spiritual life.

Happily I can disclose that a book is now being prepared outlining the artwork of these fine ladies. Surely it will be a finer tribute than I could give on such an occasion as this.

Today we come to pray and thank Almighty God for these two artistic comets who have brightened the life of a world left far better by their presence.

I called Cardinal Mahony as soon as I heard about Isabel's demise. He was departing for the Holy Land and he promised that today he would pray for her at the Shrine of Our Lord where it all began for the Catholic world.

Isabel and her late sister were pioneers not only in the world of artistic creations, but in their very way of life.

Once when I chided Isabel about her scholarly defense of womanhood, she pulled out an old copy of *Time* magazine, which repeated the classic version of the creation story.

> Lord, I need a companion,
> said the first man on earth.
> So God took the beauty of
> a flower, and the song of a
> bird, the color of the rainbow,

the laughter of the wave, the
gentleness of the lamb, the
cunning of the fox, the
fickleness of the showers
and waywardness of the
clouds and wove them
into a female which He
gave to man.
And the woman's name was "Eve."
Or was it "Isabel".

Just yesterday we installed a Shulmerich G5 Series digital carillon here in the Mother Church for San Fernando Valley.

Today it will ring for the first time as a tribute and a farewell to Isabel Piczek, who will long live on in her art and service to the God of all Creation!

Suppose now we all pause to pray for Isabel and Edith as they go ahead of us to the throne of God.

Thomas Gardiner (d. 2016)

Those familiar with California history know that the redwood trees of Mariposa County are long-lived. When one dies, it is a noteworthy event that usually gets wide attention in the local newspapers and national airways.

In the Holy Land are relatives of the redwoods, known as the Cedars of Lebanon. They live for over a century and one hears often about the longevity of those familiar trees in the pages of Holy Scripture.

And when our own Thomas Gardiner died, his passing was likewise notable in many respects – it was analogous to the death of a Cedar of Lebanon.

The parallel goes even further. When a redwood or cedar tree is ready to die, it does so graciously and with profound dignity.

Because he knew how to live, Thomas Gardiner knew how to die. When the signs began to appear, he embraced them with the same enthusiasm that he had exhibited throughout his long and eventful life.

As a Catholic, Tom knew that we are all visitors on planet Earth, not permanent residents. Fittingly, he spent his last days getting ready.

We are all here for a reason and that reason is to serve, praise and love the Lord both in the way we live and in the manner we die.

Those of us who live as Christians see death for what it really is – the joyful returning of the faithful soul to the Lord who created it. We see those sentiments spoken in the Preface for the Mass of the Resurrection:

For those who, like Tom, bear the indelible imprint of Baptism, "the light that flickers out at midnight symbolizes not the end of an old day, but the promise of a new dawn."

Because it's often hard to say goodbye, perhaps we could better say "until we meet again!"

For all of us, the mystery of death is probably best explained in one of the ancient Prefaces for the Requiem Mass; "Lord, for Your faithful who die, life does not end, but it is changed; with the destruction of our earthly bodies, an eternal dwelling place is made ready and waiting."

To have known Tom Gardiner, to have been edified by his unashamed love for wife and family, to comprehend his devotion to the Church, is to understand what Socrates had in mind when he said: "ask not that you live long, but that you live well."

This Tom most assuredly did. Oh, in the past months, Tom may have been a little hard to live with at times – but so were the saints. But when a person travels in that exalted company, he soon discovers how to fit all the jagged pieces of the human puzzle into their meaningful place.

The reason why Tom doesn't need a eulogy is that his life was an open book – a book which any reviewer would immediately consign to the best sellers list.

May we only say that spiritually, intellectually and in every other way, the earthly sojourn of Tom Gardiner measures up most perfectly to Robert Louis Stevenson's definition of one who has achieved the maturity of manhood.

Tom Gardiner's sojourn here on planet Earth lasted for eighty-two years. And, with God's grace, he learned to sidestep bitterness and most of the other vices associated with human life.

Holy Scripture speaks of people living into their eighties as being "strong." But those so-called "strong years" aren't necessarily happy ones. By that time most everything hurts and the simplest chores are burdensome.

Though he remained a loving husband, an attentive father, a loyal parishioner and a valued friend, Tom was called upon to endure much of his purgatory here on earth.

But, he did it well and I suspect that his entry into the Beatific Vision is near at hand.

That being the case, let us all rejoice because that's where we all want to be.

And, when we achieve that goal. I suspect Tom Gardiner will have everything in place for one gigantic welcome. Another Gardiner in the Garden of Eden!

Teresa Feeney (1929–2016)

I was watching television last Monday evening. Just as the camera panned over the United Nation's headquarters in New York City, I noticed that the flags of the United States, and its close neighbor, Ireland, were both at half-mast.

My fascination with this rare phenomenon was satisfied a few moments later when Kevin Feeney called me to say that his mother had just died. How perfect a gesture that was to mark the demise of a wonderful lady who held dual citizenship in these two countries.

Born in County Longford Ireland and seeing no future there, she became a globetrotter in 1950. She eventually settled in New York where she married a fellow Irishman, Tom. A few years later they joined the westward movement to California where they settled in beautiful downtown Burbank.

It was there that Teresa began her career with Penney's Department Store, a relationship that lasted for over a quarter century during which her two sons were born and raised.

Happily for San Fernando Mission, Teresa then volunteered her services at the Old Mission where her second-born had joined the staff in 1983. Her older offspring became a priest and is now the *officialis* for the Diocese of Corpus Christi in Texas.

Teresa was an "upbeat" person who always elevated the tone of the conversation. I recall once overhearing her response to a woman who told her on the phone about plans to visit all the California missions. She wanted to know how many missions there were, where they were located and which were the most popular. Without hesitation, Teresa casually responded; "There are twenty-one missions but you needn't travel to each one. Just come here to San Fernando, the most beautiful, the most authentic, the most accurately restored of them all."

She concluded the conversation by telling the caller that the Gift Shop at San Fernando Mission was known internationally for the quality of its wares and the courtesy of its employees!

Always a positive, direct and outspoken person, Teresa would appreciate but surely not encourage our making of this moment into an occasion of sorrow.

Rather she would endorse and repeat the words of Saint Augustine that "it is not our judgment, but our nature which shuns death."

A life well spent speaks its own eulogy. The words uttered by others can only be faint echoes of what a person really accomplishes for God and neighbor in a lifetime.

This much we do know – that for almost ninety years Teresa Feeney moved among her family and friends as a gracious, courageous and forceful lady. In her wake, countless people came to know what it means to be cheerful in time of adversity, optimistic in moments of sorrow and determined in periods of pain.

For His own reasons and in His own way, God leaves the imprint of his presence wherever He goes and on whatever He does.

 Surely that presence was visible in the life of her whose earthly remains lie before us today. Teresa was always and everywhere a determined, forthright and scrupulously honest person whose companionship, friendliness and loyalty pervaded the atmosphere of her presence.

Saint Paul had the likes of Teresa in mind when he told the Hebrews how looking at the lives of those who faithfully follow Christ inspired him with new reason for seeking the city which is to come.

Death closes one door, only to open another. She whom we have known in life, we know now in God. It's a different kind of relationship, but no less real.

Dying is the beginning of a glorious adventure. Surely, if a milligram of musk gives out perfume for seven thousand years, and a milligram of radium emits energy for seventy thousand years, then the human soul, which is far more precious in God's sight than musk or radium, will live for seven times seventy thousand years, or for eternity.

Teresa would remind us, ever so gently, that death is a vital and necessary part of living. Saint Augustine phrased that concept well when he said that "we grieve over the necessity of losing our friends in death, but always with the knowledge that we shall meet them again."

John Henry Newman put it still another way when he observed that "we mourn the blossoms of May because they wither, but we know that May will eventually have its revenge upon November, by the revolution of that solemn circle which never stops – which teaches us in our height of hope ever to be sober and in our depth of desolation never to despair."

When I recalled that Mother Teresa of Calcutta would be canonized this year, I thought how appropriate it was and that there will now be a second Teresa, this one of San Fernando, added to the long list of heavenly inhabitants.

Teresa was surely not rich by earthly standards yet she left something for everyone in this church today, namely the example of a well-spent life. No greater treasure could be requested of anyone. She was no theologian, but she knew how to practice the virtues and she did it well. We leave here today richer for knowing her.

Were Teresa to offer a last bit of advice to those of us who are left behind, one is inclined to think that she might put it this way:

JUST THINK
Of stepping on the shore and finding it
HEAVEN;
Of taking hold of a hand and finding it
GOD'S HAND;
Of feeling invigorated and finding it
IMMORTALITY;
Of passing from storm and tempest to an
UNKNOWN CALM;
Of waking and finding you're Home!

An Irish Blessing

May the road rise up to meet you,
May the wind be always at your back,
May the sun shine warm upon your face,
The rain fall soft upon your fields,
And until we meet again,
May God hold you in the palm of his hand.

8

Cardinal Manning Memoir

(This address, entitled "Timothy Cardinal Manning – Some Personal Remembrances," was given at Saint John the Baptist de La Salle Hall in Granada Hills on March 5, 2014.)

No ecclesial figure in the Golden state's history served so long and so prominently at the helm or near the helm of Peter's bark than he who became Archbishop of Los Angeles in 1970. Trained in the noble tradition of the Cantwell years, seasoned in the expansionary complexities of the McIntyre archiepiscopate and steeped in the spirit of Vatican Council II, Timothy Cardinal Manning left an impressive imprint on the pilgrim Church of Our Lady of the Angels.

Old Country Priest

a.k.a. Msgr. Francis J. Weber

will be commemorating the
Silver Anniversary
of the
Demise
of
Timothy Cardinal Manning

on June 23, 2014
at a gathering in the Parochial Hall
of Saint John Baptist de la Salle
10738 Havenhurst Avenue
Granada Hills
at 7:15 in the evening

You are cordially invited
Admission is free,
but for our planning we would appreciate it if you would
make reservations by contacting our office at (885) 389-2035

My remarks this evening are more personal than biographic. My book about the cardinal's accomplishments is already part of the record and needs no further explanation.

Here I would like to reflect on my personal association with His Eminence whom I consider to have been a truly outstanding pioneer along California's *El Camino Real.* Let me just begin with a quick overview of his life and then launch into some of the reasons why I could and can call him a true friend.

First of all, let me sketch briefly an overview of Timothy Manning and his place in the historical annals. One of the four children of Cornelius and Margaret (Cronin) Manning, Timothy was born November 14, 1909, at Ballingeary, County Cork, Ireland. In 1915, he enrolled at the local National School and seven years later advanced to the educational facilities operated at nearby Cork City by the Christian Brothers. His preparation for the priesthood began in 1923, at Mungret College, a secondary school staffed by the Society of Jesus for the foreign missions.

The Manning home, Ballingeary, Co. Cork, Ireland

The youthful clerical aspirant was attracted to California by an appeal on behalf of the Diocese of Los Angeles-San Diego. Leaving Ireland in October 1928, he traveled to Menlo Park where he joined the student body of Saint Patrick's Seminary.

He was ordained to the priesthood by Bishop John J. Cantwell on June 16, 1934, in Saint Vibiana's Cathedral. His initial assignment was that of curate at Immaculate Conception Church in Los Angeles. The following year, Father Manning was sent to Rome for post-graduate studies at the Pontifical Gregorian University, where he received a doctorate in Canon Law in 1938. Upon his return to Southern California, Father Manning was named secretary to Archbishop Cantwell, a post he occupied for eight years. In 1943, he was made a papal chamberlain and, two years afterwards, was promoted by Pope Pius XII to the domestic prelacy.

On August 17, 1946, Msgr. Manning was appointed Titular Bishop of Lesvi and Auxiliary of Los Angeles. Episcopal orders were bestowed on October 15 by Bishop Joseph T. McGucken, then Apostolic Administrator for the Diocese of Monterey-Fresno. At the time and for a goodly while thereafter, Bishop Manning was the "Benjamin of the American Hierarchy."

With the appointment to Los Angeles in 1948 of Archbishop J. Francis A. McIntyre, Manning was named Chancellor. From 1953 to 1967 he also occupied the pastorate of Saint Gregory's, a parish on the western rim of downtown Los Angeles. On November 29, 1955, he became Vicar General of the archdiocese.

Upon the realignment of ecclesial boundaries in Central California, Bishop Manning was named to the newly erected Diocese of Fresno on October 24, 1967. His work in the eight counties of the San Joaquin Valley was described as "a servanthood of justice and reconciliation." In eighteen brief but intensely fruitful months, he created a diocesan housing commission, established four new parishes and five missions, approved formation of a priests' senate, authorized a task force to marshal resources for inner city and minority groups, shared the bitter anguish of the Delano labor dispute and visited each of the eighty parishes scattered through the 35,239 square mile jurisdiction.

The prelate was recalled to the scene of his earlier priestly labors on May 6, 1969, as Coadjutor to James Francis Cardinal McIntyre. Assigned to the titular See of Capri, Archbishop Manning was re-named Vicar General and given the pastorate of Saint Brendan's Church. Upon the retirement of Cardinal McIntyre on January 21, 1970, Archbishop Manning became Chief Shepherd of the Church of Los Angeles. He received *the pallium,* symbolic of the metropolitan office, on June 17, 1970.

In addition to pursuing administrative and expansionary policies, Archbishop

Manning established a priests' senate, an inter-parochial council and a clerical personnel board. He energetically supported a host of ecumenical involvements and warmly endorsed and participated in the Cursillo movement. He personally chaired the Commission for Liturgy, established a spirituality house and erected an Archival Center, to mention but a few of his many activities

In his concern for and identification with the archdiocesan founded and sponsored Lay Mission Helpers, Manning visited missionaries in South Africa, Rhodesia, Ghana, Kenya, Malawi and Uganda. It was while en route to another segment of that far-flung apostolate early in 1973 that he received word that Pope Paul VI once again had honored the People of God at Los Angeles, by naming him to the College of Cardinals.

Though the Catholics of Orange county were given their own diocese in 1974, Los Angeles continued to expand and, by 1984, was acknowledged as the largest ecclesial jurisdiction in the United States. In 1985, with the acceptance of his retirement by Pope Paul VI, Cardinal Manning turned the reins of leadership over to his successor. He died in Los Angeles on June 23, 1989.

My earliest association with Manning came shortly after I entered Los Angeles College, the old preparatory seminary for the Archdiocese of Los Angeles in 1946. I was one of the favored few chosen to represent the seminary community at his episcopal ordination at Saint Vibiana's Cathedral on October 15th.

My first personal encounter with the new Auxiliary Bishop of Los Angeles came a few weeks later when Father Robert T. Brown, the rector of the seminary, asked me to pick up a *Pontificale* at the archiepiscopal residence in Fremont Place. I nervously rang the bell and Manning answered the door himself. He invited me to wait in the parlor while he fetched the book. When he returned, he brought with him a brownie, hot from Mary Boyle's oven. When I left, he said, "Thank you Frank. I'll see you again soon." I recall being very impressed that he would remember the name of a fourteen-year-old seminarian. When I mentioned the incident to him years later, he responded: "Oh yes, that was the day you came for the *Pontificale*." As Chancellor, Manning made it a point to know all the seminarians by name.

Throughout his years in the southland, Archbishop John J. Cantwell visited the Little Sisters of the Poor on December 27th for the celebration of his feast day. That tradition was continued after Cantwell's death by his auxiliary, Bishop Timothy Manning.

In 1958, several of us seminarians accompanied the bishop to the big, red brick building on East Second Street for the event, after which the Sisters provided everyone with a sumptuous meal.

As had long been customary, the bishop administered Confirmation to any of the patients who had not received that sacrament. Two of us, ordained deacons only a few weeks earlier, acted as chaplains for the ceremony. After arriving back in the sacristy, the bishop casually asked me which of three oils he had used for the anointing. After checking, I discovered that I had given him the wrong oil, probably because it was the only vial in the wooden container that was uncorked.

He was annoyed, to say the least, and asked me to bring the recipient into the sacristy where he performed what was then known as a "sanation," this time using the correct oil.

It wasn't a particularly pleasant way to begin my life in major orders, and the bishop never forgot that unhappy incident. He frequently recalled, usually in the presence of others, that "Father Weber's first association with Confirmation resulted in the nullification of the sacrament."

From the very outset, the then Auxiliary Bishop Timothy Manning was supportive of my historical work. I discovered, long after the fact, that he had encouraged my being sent for graduate studies under Msgr. John Tracy Ellis at The Catholic University of America.

Thereafter, he was always ready and eager to assist in whatever projects came along. The first of my major "challenges" occurred in 1961. In those times we needed permission to write for secular journals and the customary procedure was to pass articles by the local ecclesiastical censor for approval. I had sent an essay on the *"Real Patronato de Indias"* to Dr. Gustav Arlt for consideration in a future issue of the *Historical Society of Southern California Quarterly*. Had he approved it, I planned to process it through the normal channels. Arlt never responded but, some months later, much to my embarrassment, the essay appeared in the issue for June 1961.

I hastily wrote to Manning explaining the situation and offering to send him a copy as soon as one arrived in Washington. He answered immediately, saying that he had already read the article and that I need "have no further worries about the matter." He later gave me a blanket permission to write whenever occasions would arise and never did he question me about anything that later appeared in print under my name.

Among my most cherished memories is that of being in the *Piazza di San Pietro* for the opening session of Vatican Council II in October of 1962. Having just finished my graduate studies at The Catholic University of America, I was in Rome working on my dissertation about Bishop Thaddeus Amat. While there, the then Auxiliary Bishop Manning invited me to his suite in the Michelangelo Hotel where he confided to me that I would be teaching history at Queen of Angels Seminary upon my return to Los Angeles.

Manning had lived in Rome for several years as a student priest and he knew all or most of the back alleys of the Eternal City. He and Archbishop Joseph T. McGucken devoted a whole day to taking me in and out of museums, churches and other historic places, most of which are not even mentioned in the local guide books. Manning accompanied me to the archives at Propaganda Fide where he met the director and further enhanced my credentials there. I was especially moved when, upon leaving Rome, Manning gave me a rosary which he had received two days earlier from Pope John XXIII. Later, I gave it to my mother and she used it daily for the rest of her life and was buried with it.

It was Bishop Manning who early in 1963 encouraged me to launch "California's Catholic Heritage," a column that ran weekly in *The Tidings* and sporadically in other Catholic newspapers for over thirty-two years for a total of 1,124,400 words. Manning read every column and often made useful and constructive comments about the topics covered. In the first of the eleven volumes of collected essays, issued in 1967, he wrote the Preface in which he noted that:

> *From the rich but hidden records of our past [Weber] has gleaned episodes and drawn profiles. We are provided with an inspiration for the present day, a connecting link with the past and raw material for a definitive history at a later time.*
>
> *It is to be hoped that students in our seminaries and schools will be stimulated through these essays to an introduction to historical research, which will stand them in good stead in later responsible years. It is devoutly wished that through the inspiration of these pages pastors of parishes will sense the value of passing events as seen through the perspective of history since they move forward through "the inaudible and noiseless feet of time." From this collection also we underscore the importance of all records and sacredness of archives. Finally, the skill has to be acquired to clothe these skeletons in the sympathetic words of popular language so that they will be readable and praiseworthy.*

My relationship with Manning was probably unique, in that he was always open and frank. I recall one time, after reading remarks I made in *The Tidings* occasioned by the twenty-fifth anniversary of my column, he proclaimed, in an unguarded burst of candor, that humility was not one of my "more outstanding virtues." I didn't take offense, because he was more right than wrong. An amusing incident in which I played a minor role occurred in 1967, when Manning was named Bishop of Fresno. When I asked if he was taking Clare Berger, his long-time secretary, he replied: "Well, I'd like to, but I could hardly ask her to uproot herself and move north." Later, I addressed a similar question to Clare and she said "Yes, but I suspect that he has someone else in mind." I then told Manning that Clare wanted to go. He was delighted and off they went only to return eighteen months later.

I suspect that Manning's kindness and encouragement for the archives was the result of a guilt trip that went back to the years when he was chancellor. In those times, the chancellor was nominally in charge of archives and Manning openly confessed that he didn't know where or how to properly care for the documents, papers and other materials that comprised the archives.

Cardinal Mindszenty visits the Chancery Archives

While admitting ignorance about the mechanics of archival management, Manning understood the value of recording history. In 1961, when he wrote the article on the Archdiocese of Los Angeles for the new *Catholic Encyclopedia*, he laboriously rewrote and revised until his completed essay was a model for other entries.

It was a happy day for Manning when he came to Mission Hills, in 1981, to bless the new Archival Center for the Archdiocese of Los Angeles. Ours was the first building of its kind ever erected in the United States and that was a distinction he enjoyed. It was Cardinal Manning himself who commissioned Isabel and Edith Piczek to design and fabricate the mosaic tableaus adorning the eastern wall of the building. The panels portray the geographical history of the Church in Los Angeles, since its inception in 1840 as the Diocese of *Ambas Californias*.

After he retired, Cardinal Manning drove out to the Archival Center every Friday to work on various historical projects. We proudly put his name on our masthead and boasted to being "the only Catholic archives in the world with a cardinal on staff." He unraveled our sacerdotal files by writing in and correcting details that only he could recall after over a half century in California's southland. There was always something for him to do and we were sorry when he left for the day.

The Archival Center in Mission Hills

One of the cardinal's projects, and one about which he was uniquely qualified, was that of recording how the parishes of the archdiocese got their saintly names. Though this was originally intended as an in-house project, we felt that others might be interested, so we published a series on the subject in *The Tidings*.

The Cardinal was most generous to the Historical Museum attached to the Archival Center. We have a case crammed with items associated with his years as priest, bishop, coadjutor, archbishop and cardinal. He publicly accused me once of wanting to have him "stuffed" when he died, so we could continue to have a cardinal on staff.

Manning dreaded confrontations and, whenever possible, he avoided them. In October 1970, we had a major crisis over the style and lack of leadership at Queen of Angels Seminary. The eight archdiocesan priests on the faculty signed a petition asking for Manning's intervention. Though he admitted privately to agreeing with the petitioners, the archbishop refused to take a public stand, much to the annoyance of both sides. Instead, he appointed a review board which held numerous interviews but brought about no effective improvement. When all the hearings were completed, Manning invited himself to dinner one evening and talked his way out of what could have been a unpleasant situation. It was a vintage Manning performance, solving nothing but motivating us to look further for a compromise.

For a host of reasons irrelevant to this context, Manning and his advisors decided in the mid-1970s to remove the relics of Saint Vibiana from her place of prominence in the cathedral bearing her name. She was to be re-interred in the basement vault that had earlier housed the remains of Bishop Thaddeus Amat. I was instructed to remove the relics and waxen form, take them to a local mortuary, have a new casket made and then return them for interment. The sanctuary was being reconfigured at the time and was full of scaffolding. As the mortician and I were exiting the sacristy door, he bearing the relics and I carrying the waxen figure of Vibiana, part of the scaffolding, without any warning, broke loose and came crashing down to the floor, missing the two of us by inches.

When the incident was related to Manning, he instantly decided that Saint Vibiana would be placed in a marble sarcophagus at the south side of the sanctuary, replacing one of the side altars. Thereafter, he liked to recall what Richard Cardinal Cushing said about Saint Philomena: "There may be some confusion about her place in heaven, but somebody up there is answering her prayers."

Manning was always extremely kind to me personally. I was the first one he named to the archdiocesan Board of Consultors. And, I remember vividly the day when Father Clem Connolly called me in Anaheim and said the Cardinal wanted to talk to me. I waited and, when he came on the line, he began by saying: "Good morning, Monsignor." I answered, "No, Your Eminence, this is Father Weber," to which he replied, "I was right the first time. It's now Monsignor Weber." It was one of the few times in my life that I was speechless.

One day late in 1975, as I walked by his office, Cardinal Manning came out and told me that he was thinking about a personnel change at San Buenaventura Mission. He thought it "would be appropriate" if I were to go there to replace retiring Father Aubrey O'Reilly, the pastor. His proposal caught me totally off-guard and so I asked for a while to think about it. He said "okay but write me in the morning asking for the position."

I was initially reluctant to even consider the offer. No one else wanted me to take the position, not even the Vicar General. But, eventually, I decided that I would go, even though it meant two weekly seventy-five mile trips back to Los Angeles to care for the archives. But I was young then and nothing was insurmountable. What I embraced with little or no enthusiasm became the happiest five and a half years of my life. And, during those times, Manning always remained supportive, even to the extent of coming a year later to consecrate the historic mission church.

It was while at San Buenaventura, on April 2, 1976, that I was stabbed inside the Old Mission church by a deranged young man who was either coming down or going up on an LSD flashback. Happily, the wounds were superficial and that evening I was able to attend a confirmation ceremony in Santa Paula.

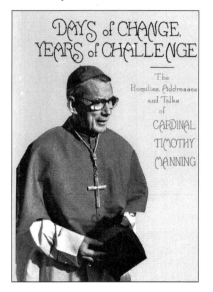

Cardinal Manning proclaimed that I had become "a confessor to the faith" inasmuch as the incident had occurred inside church while I was officially carrying out parochial duties. He told me that I could have the term "confessor" chiseled onto my tombstone. My hint about a raise in salary, however, fell on deaf ears!

The publication of his homilies, addresses and talks was not a project the Cardinal initiated. Originally he adamantly refused to discuss the possibility of such a book and even after listening to the reasons why such a volume was desirable, he registered unmistakable reservations. Following his retirement, our relationship became a bit more informal and I no longer felt restrained by his earlier veto.

Ever so gradually, he began taking an interest in the project, becoming almost enthusiastic as the months unfolded. He would drive out to the Archival Center and together we read through his voluminous writings, selecting a cross section that merited a more lasting format. Early on, we dismissed the notion of an in-depth biographical study as premature. Such works demand the perspective of time and it would be several decades before historians could begin sifting through Manning's papers, objectively appraising his contribution to the Church in Southern California and in the world at large.

Anyway, it is my personal conviction that Cardinal Manning will be longer remembered for what he said than for what he did. His God-given charisma shone brightest in the pulpit, on the podium and from the printed page. Except for identifying the occasion of each entry and indicating its source, it was thought best to avoid editing and otherwise commenting on the selections in this trilogy of books. Each entry easily stood on its own merit.

The Cardinal disdained administrative responsibilities and, whenever possible, he would delegate them to others. He always wanted to answer in the affirmative. Whenever queries came his way, he either agreed immediately, refused to answer at all or passed them on to his Vicar General who never had the slightest reluctance in saying "no." Those pastors unwise enough to try an end run around the Vicar General would occasionally approach Manning directly with requests to erect or demolish this or that building, to begin or close down one or another activity or approve or endorse some other questionable project. The Cardinal would listen attentively, praise the motivation behind the request and then suggest that the visitor "stop and check with Monsignor Hawkes on the way out about financing."

The door to Manning's office was always ajar and, if there was no one with him, he delighted in having visitors. He never passed the archives without coming in. High among the regrets of my lifetime was not keeping a log of our conversations on those occasions. He always had a morsel of "news" or "gossip" and he apparently felt that the archivist, like his confessor, never spoke out of turn. And, for the most part, that was a correct assumption.

While he rarely spoke uncharitably, it wasn't hard to read his views about persons or events. He always exhibited profound respect for the

Holy Father, Pope Paul VI, for example, but he admitted to not always understanding the cross currents of Vatican diplomacy.

Manning's care for and concern for the sick and aged was evident in many ways. Whenever possible, he devoted Saturdays to visiting priests and others in the hospitals and rest homes of the archdiocese. When my father was in the Elizabeth Manor on Alvarado Street, the Cardinal would stop almost every week. When he died, Manning was unable to attend the actual funeral, but he came to San Fernando Mission the previous day to offer Holy Mass for our local community. He surely preached more funeral homilies than any other American prelate and, when impeded, he would send a personally written note of condolence.

The Cardinal is greeted by Pope John Paul I

I was one of four priests invited to accompany the Archbishop to Rome in 1973 for his investiture in the College of Cardinals, an honor I will long cherish. My role was that of gathering information for a memorial book that was issued to commemorate that historic event. During the trip to the Eternal City, aboard one of TWA's 747s, I had the opportunity of sitting for a while with the Cardinal-elect and, knowing that he would soon be looking for an editor for *The Tidings*, I confided a desire for that position. He gave every indication that my candidacy would receive careful consideration at the appropriate time.

Later that year, I was summoned into the Cardinal's office for an interview. From the very outset, however, I could sense that he was ill at ease. It was an encounter that I suspect he would have liked to avoid. In any event, he told me that Msgr. Patrick Roche would soon be retiring from *The Tidings* and that he had decided to entrust the editorship to Roche's longtime associate, Al Antczak. He didn't see any reason for further discussion.

But I did. In one of my more brazen moments, I asked him why he was giving the position to a layman, something that hadn't been done for forty-eight years. Was not the Catholic press an arm of the clerical ministry – and so on and on. He gave me the usual response about the shortage of priests, the era of the laity, the recommendation of Msgr. Roche, seniority, none of which reasons he meant and none of which I believed. So I pressed him further until, in a rare burst of impatience, he said: "Do you really want to know the reason?" I said, "Yes." "He'll make a better editor than you would." As much as it injured my psyche, I liked that answer because I knew it was the real one. On the way home, I tried to sort it all out in my mind. And then, all of a sudden, the thought came to me – "You know, he's right." And with that, all the hurt and rebellion went away, never to return. It didn't matter so much losing out to someone better qualified for that or any other position. Al measured up to Manning's expectations and his tenure as editor was indeed impressive in every way. I had my chance later, if only for a short while.

Manning was always a private person who personally disliked the limelight. Contrary to the recommendations of his closest collaborators, he adamantly refused to sanction any official city-wide observance upon his return as cardinal to Los Angeles, beyond the rather simple liturgical services that took place at Saint Vibiana's Cathedral.

Archbishop Timothy Manning and James Francis Cardinal McIntyre

It might have been that same shyness that kept Manning from playing a larger role in the American Church. Though he could have exercised a strong influence among his episcopal confreres, Manning rarely did so. He addressed that assembly only a handful of times in his forty-three years as a member. I once heard him express dismay that a bishop from Northern California spoke out on an issue at his very first meeting!

When the name of his successor at Fresno was announced, Manning expressed surprise and admitted that he had not been consulted. When asked whether he would have any input in determining his replacement at Los Angeles, Manning told me "they will probably give me a veto, but I won't exercise it." He did feel that his replacement would need to be more dynamic and communicable with the press and public officials. He later expressed satisfaction that his successor more than measured up to those aspirations.

Shortly after he became Archbishop, Manning selected his own burial plot among the sacerdotal pioneers buried at Calvary Cemetery. Choosing not to be interred alongside his predecessors in the Mausoleum's Episcopal Vault, he opted for a grave outside All Souls Chapel and there he had a simple marker erected with only his coat of arms and room for a death date.

I suspect he would not be overly pleased with the humongous granite slab subsequently placed over his grave. Knowing my penchant for moving around deceased bishops (Alemany, Amat, Mora, O'Connell), he more than once threatened to send a bolt of lightning from heaven if ever I attempted to disturb his remains.

Though I assiduously recorded the accomplishments of Timothy Manning in the archives, I never expected or aspired to be the cardinal's biographer. When the life of Cardinal McIntyre appeared at the bookstalls, I suggested to Cardinal Mahony that it might be wise to visit Manning's birthplace, interview his sister, relatives and close friends and otherwise prepare the way for an eventual biography. Mahony graciously and enthusiastically concurred and even obtained a grant from the Dan Murphy Foundation for the project.

When I wrote Manning's niece, Breda Lucy at Gougane Barra, and told her of my imminent journey, she wrote back to say that "the cardinal told us that one day you would make a visit." I interpreted that as Manning's endorsement for personally taking on the burden of writing his life, surely an ambitious undertaking for an old priest of mediocre health.

Unlike many of his contemporary clerics in high places, Manning's path to the archbishopric had nothing whatsoever to do with his own aspirations. Prior to 1967, his name wasn't even considered for that position. But, in God's providence, he outlived whatever restrictions were attached to his episcopal appointment and he ultimately outperformed most others who might have had a greater claim to the position.

The book on his life outlined the very substantial contributions made by Timothy Manning to those whose lives he touched during the fifty-five years of his sacerdotal ministry. What it says about the "person" of Timothy Manning is not quite so obvious. He was a very private, almost shy man who effectively hid himself behind his public role as priest, bishop, archbishop and cardinal.

It does nothing to diminish Manning's stature to agree with the general perception that he "was not a dynamic leader." In Manning's case, he compensated for that deficiency by allowing others to act in his stead. He began his role as archbishop by openly defying conventional wisdom and opting to leave in place the organizational structure and staffing of his predecessor who had a genius for reducing, if not almost eliminating the bureaucracy typical in the post Vatican Council II era.

Manning's concept of leadership was akin to that played by the conductor of a symphony. "He need not be himself skilled in a particular instrument, but he can be the unifying force for bringing out harmony." He felt that "team action rises above one's personal likes and dislikes."

The key to understanding Manning's leadership abilities is to make a clear distinction between leading and administering; he excelled in the first and delegated the latter. In an open message written at the time of the cardinal's death, a chum from seminary days at Menlo Park agreed that Manning "was not a great administrator. He left the responsibilities of managing the varied affairs of a sprawling archdiocese to the associates, clerical and lay he trusted, supported and appreciated. But the desk was not where he could do his best for God and God's people."

Rather, "the hallmark of the cardinal's priesthood was his love and commitment to his people. He was forever in their midst, blessing, honoring, remembering, dedicating, encouraging." That theme was echoed by others. A writer for a local newspaper, after extolling the Cardinal for his accomplishments, admitted that "he disliked administration, according to those who knew him, and willingly delegated most of the day-to-day operation of the archdiocese to chancery aides."

Yet, Manning was clearly God's man for the time, a wholly different kind of leader from his predecessor. He was "a theologian, a man familiar with the dynamics of history, a man of sensitivity chastened by but not hardened by suffering."

The pitfalls associated with that elusive *charism* known as "leadership" were well expressed by a befuddled college professor who admitted he was never quite sure whether his students were following him or chasing him. The paramount quality associated with leadership and its obvious master key is intelligence, the ability to reason and intuition.

Beyond a competence based on training and the gradual accumulation of experience and skill, the leader's mind needs enough resiliency to weigh, logically and objectively, all the alternatives before arriving at ultimate conclusions. To emotional balance, tested self-discipline and a strong sense of personal morality must be added a fair, honest, frank, kindly, straightforward and firm integrity. Keeping in mind the distinction between leading and administering. Timothy Manning emerges with high marks.

Though he was occasionally given to periods of melancholic depression, Manning endeavored to be an optimist. In an interview with the cardinal conducted at Rome during preparations for the Holy Year, Wally Burke said that Manning, "a veteran observer of the ebb and flow of faith and morals, has become neither cynical nor pessimistic. Instead he is sensitive, gentle, outgoing and has an optimism laced with Irish good humor and wit. He is optimistic about the role of religion, despite the changing times. He quoted the cardinal as saying:

> I feel that this is one of the greatest moments in the history of the whole Church. I say that because while the Church is making the great transition into the technological age, naturally she is suffering the effects of change which all institutions suffer.

He rarely lost his temper. When something went wrong with a relationship or an unpleasant encounter, Manning would apologize. He classified his own temperament as "passive and phlegmatic" which, he admitted, was "a common trait among the Irish." While denying that his temperament influenced his actions "in any dominant way," he agreed that it did have a bearing on his writings. When queried as to whether he avoided confrontations, Manning responded "whenever I can," observing that "nothing is gained by confrontations." One of the more astute priests of the archdiocese once observed that he had "never seen the cardinal give the impression of being restless. The burdens of his office rest lightly on him." He saw that as "a grace, for a man of sensitivity cannot be cold or casual about decisions that have a deep and lasting effect on other people."

Manning instinctively saw the good in people and only later that which was tainted by the frailty of human nature. Especially was that true with his fellow priests. When the antics of some errant cleric were related to him, he found it difficult to comprehend. On one occasion, after listening to an especially unpleasant incident, he replied: "That's hard to believe. I knew his mother and she was such a lovely lady."

Those who knew him before and after Vatican Council II uniformly testified that he absorbed much of the spirit of the council. The post-conciliar Manning was considerably more flexible in his demeanor with others. Apart from his role as archbishop, Manning's more attractive human traits jumped out at people, even reporters. One writer for a prominent local newspaper recognized the cardinal as "a purposely non-controversial prelate who sees his role best characterized as 'servanthood' for Catholics."

A personally spiritual man, Manning did all the things traditionally associated with priesthood and he did them well. He recited his breviary, read Holy Scripture, made his meditation, said the rosary, did spiritual reading, practiced the virtues and made a daily holy hour. In a busy world, he found ample time for the Lord.

Though not innovative by nature, Manning seized upon suggestions of others and often encouraged proposals, ideas and plans presented by subordinates. His permissive nature served him well because it allowed him to divert attention from himself. Having no identity crisis, he was not threatened by the accomplishments of others, but was perfectly content when the credit for this or that project went to others. Manning often remarked that "there is always plenty of credit to spread around." He was fond of a quote from Alexander Pope that reflected his own philosophy: "Be not the first by whom the new is tried; nor yet the last to set the old aside."

By choice, Manning lived simply. A news account told how the cardinal lived "in a three-room apartment at the priests' house on Second and Main in the skid row area. His lifestyle, like his living quarters, was a model of Christian simplicity and a witnessing to Gospel values which his clergy and people admire and appreciate."

However one cuts the cake, Timothy Manning emerges as a truly remarkable figure on the national and local ecclesial scene of the American Catholic Church.

Finale

I would like to conclude these remarks by remembering a little lady known only as Marguerite, who unknowingly, provided an interesting insight in the "hospitality" practiced by the late Timothy Cardinal Manning. It all started in the 1960s when Marguerite appeared out of nowhere with a phone call to the archives, which were then housed in the Chancery Office at 1531 West Ninth Street in downtown Los Angeles.

She wanted to know if the archives would be interested in having some photographs of early churches in the area. I readily agreed and scheduled an appointment to see her. The photographs proved to be of little or no value. They were predominantly magazine reproductions of Protestant churches, most of them unidentified. And, to make matters worse, her visit took a half hour out of an otherwise busy day.

A month later, she called again about some other object she thought was valuable. The second visit was more frustrating than the first, and this time it was almost an hour before she departed. This scenario went on monthly for several years. I grew to dread her visits and the utter waste of time they entailed. I used every imaginable excuse to stall or postpone those totally unproductive encounters. But she never backed off and, the following month, she would call again.

It all seemed so wasteful. After all, I was busy teaching at the seminary, working two days a week in the Archives and doing weekend parochial work in West Hollywood. My lack of enthusiasm must have been patently obvious.

Then, one day, as I was hurrying down the hallway at the Chancery, I saw this little lady come out of the then Bishop Manning's office. I wondered if she had come to report me for not giving her a more hospitable reception. I went down to Clare Berger's office and there found, to my utter astonishment, that Marguerite came regularly to see the bishop and he gave her not a half hour but a whole hour. And he left instructions with Clare that he was always "available" to Marguerite.

At the next opportunity, I asked the bishop about our mutual visitor – why did he bother seeing her? How did he manage to fit her into his busy schedule? And why was he so courteous and patient with her? He told me that she had been coming for years, noting that she had become a needed contact with reality in a mostly office-oriented ministry.

Giving time and attention to Marguerite, he observed, was probably the most rewarding part of his day. He concluded by observing that "Christ probably would have preferred her company to that of some important personage absorbed by the ceremonial tasks that fill a busy calendar."

I left his office a humbler person that day and, thereafter for almost a dozen years, I welcomed and even grew to anticipate the little lady's visit each month. When Marguerite died early in 1983 she left instructions that I was to go through her simple effects and take whatever was useful for the archives. Her possessions were meager but what I treasured most, then and now, was the opportunity that Marguerite provided for discovering and then practicing the virtue of hospitality.

Now there were other encounters and memories about Cardinal Manning that stand out in this old country priest's mind. But these are surely enough to assure a place for this truly significant man-of-the-cloth in California's Catholic Hall of Fame.

9

Miniature Books

*C*hronological listing of miniature books written, edited, compiled and/or published by Francis J. Weber.

1. What Happened to Junípero Serra?
2. Up 65 Years to Larchmont
3. An Earthquake Memoir
4. Christmas in Pastoral California
5. Hollywood's "*Padre* of the Films"
6. Jake Zeitlin and the Big Red Barn
7. Following Bernhardt Wall
8. Mayor of Indianapolis
9. California on United States Postage Stamps
10. *Catholica* on American Stamps
11. Interfaith in Action
12. California. A Bibliography of Its Miniatures
13. Happy Birthday Uncle Sam
14. The Meanest Mother in the Whole World
15. Christmas Cards
16. Ramon Mestres: *Padre* of the Restoration
17. Five Magic Words
18. Sir Harry of Carmel
19. *El Pueblo de San Jose de Guadalupe*
20. Solemn Consecration at San Buenaventura
21. Mickey's Golden Jubilee

22. Eulogy for a Cardinal
23. California the Golden State
24. A Visit to Santa Catalina
25. *Minibibliophilia*
26. Hollywood
27. The Missionary Rationale
28. Chapel of the Holy Cross
29. Los Angeles: A Bicentennial Salute
30. Maynard Geiger, Archivist-Historian
31. Father Was a Dictator
32. The Spruce Goose
33. America's Painter – Norman Rockwell
34. The Holy Year of 1983–1984
35. The Goodyear Blimp *Columbia II*
36. The XXIII Olympiad
37. A Birthday Memoir
38. Silver Jubilee Memoir (1959–1984)
39. The Grand Conclave
40. A Letter of Junípero Serra
41. The Cable Cars
42. Fray Junípero Serra
43. John Henry Cardinal Newman (1801–1890)
44. Haley's 1986 Visit to Planet Earth
45. Value Versus Worth
46. The National Archives (1934–1984)
47. San Xavier del Bac
48. The Serra Landing Monument
49. The Magic Kingdom
50. The World's Most Widely-Read Book
51. Grand Conclave 3
52. Msgr. Benjamin G. Hawkes
53. The Unfinished Psalter
54. The Great Pardon of Portiuncula
55. *Los Regalitos de Fray Junípero*
56. Peter Arrives in the Promised Land
57. Father Flanagan of Boys Town

58. Angel's Flight
59. Knute Rockne
60. The Rose
61. C.E.D.: "The Lady"
62. Pope John Paul II at San Fernando Mission
63. Baltimore's Cathedral
64. Jan Styka's Crucifixion
65. Los Angeles International Airport
66. Our Lady of Montserrat
67. Nation's Christmas Tree
68. small PAXweber
69. Yosemite
70. Californian at *Santiago Compostela*
71. Immortal Little Willie
72. *Gaspar de Portola*
73. The Holy Grail
74. A Short Story
75. Majesty
76. Buffalo Bill
77. San Simeon
78. Farmers' Market
79. John Carroll and the Vernacular Liturgy
80. Ellis Island
81. FDR's Little Books
82. Editing *The Tidings*
83. Christopher Columbus
84. Cambridge American Cemetery
85. *Magnificat*
86. Pledge of Allegiance
87. *Las Golondrinas*
88. San Diego, The City and the Saint
89. Mission Goes to Sea
90. Explorer of California
91. Dean of Microbibliophiles
92. Saint Brendans
93. Wendell Willkie

94. The Passing of the Backhouse
95. Remember Pearl Harbor
96. Queen Mary's Miniature Library
97. Ecclesial History
98. A Bibliography of California's Miniature Mission Books
99. The "Replanting" of Frederick
100. On Reaching a Hundred

The following descriptions are taken from
Darleen Cordova's booklet, *Weber's 101 and Counting.*

101

Alexander S. Taylor, California's First Bibliographer

Weber, Francis J. New Britain, CT: REM Miniatures, 1994. 2 9/16 × 2 1/8. 18 pp. White leatherette. Matching slipcase with black pull ribbon. Printed applied paper label on book cover and slipcase. Frontispiece. 33 numbered copies in special subscription edition.

102

William Randolph Hearst

Weber. Francis J. San Fernando, CA: Junipero Serra Press, 1995. 2 3/8 × 1 5/8. 27 pp. letterpress by John Lathourakis at Tabula Rasa Press. Gilt brown cloth. Rust and gold marbled endpapers. No postage stamp, per Weber. 150 copies.

103

The Rose Parade

Weber, Francis J. Miniature Book Society, 1995. 2 15/16 × 2 1/4. 12 pp. letterpress by Regis Graden at Nut Quad Press. Gilt red cloth boards with green spine by Mariana Blau. Decorative endpapers. 150 copies.

104

Franciscan Missions of
Fr. Zephyrin Engelhardt, O.F.M. and Edward Borein

Weber, Francis J. New Britain. CT: REM Miniatures, 1994. 3 × 2 1/4. (26) pp. Wine cloth boards, pictorial label. Matching slipcase with yellow pull ribbon. Engraved illustrations by Anthony Kroll. Two tipped-in photographs of Engelhardt and Borein. 50 copies.

Msgr. Weber and Darleen Cordova at San Fernando Mission, June 28, 2013.

105

Mont-Saint-Michel

Weber. Francis J. Los Angeles, CA: Mar Michel, 1996. 2 1/4 × 3. 11 pp. letterpress by Regis Graden at Nut Quad Press. Gilt "taupe" cloth boards by Earle Gray Bookbinding Co. French postage stamp of Mont-Saint-Michel opposite colophon. 500 copies.

106

Dogs at the California Missions

Weber. Francis J. New Britain, CT: REM Miniatures, 1997. 2 13/16 × 3 1/16. 12 pp. Black cloth boards. Matching slipcase with green pull ribbon. Pictorial label by C. Ernest Massmann. Frontispiece color photo of Pixie J. Weber, Sheltie-in-residence at Mission San Fernando by Robert E. Massman. Typography, design, layout and binding by Robert E. Massman. Possibly contains 4 USA postage stamps of dogs. At the end of the book is an original tipped-in 1976 etching from "Dogs: Ten Etchings" by Michael O'Mara. 40 numbered copies in regular edition (plus 10 lettered copies in a more deluxe issue).

(Thank you, Caroline Brandt for assisting with this description, and to Msgr. Weber for clarifying there was not a second edition, but 10 "more deluxe" copies, possibly dark green cloth boards with matching slipcase, also with a tipped-in full color photograph of Pixie as frontispiece and a limited, signed etching of another dog at the end (which is different from the dog shown in the regular edition.)

107

Via Crucis

Weber, Francis J. Los Angeles, CA: Mar Michel, 1997. 2 7/8 × 2 1/8. 12.pp. letterpress by Regis Graden at Nut Quad Press. Gilt brown cloth spine, tan paper boards by Mariana Blau. "*Via Crucis*" stamped on spine. (1966) Hashemite Kingdom of Jordan Via Dolorosa postage stamp used as frontispiece. 504 copies.

108

Franciscan Crown Rosary and the City of Los Angeles

Weber, Francis J. Los Angeles, CA.; Mar Michel.1998. 2 7/8 × 2 1/8. 15 pp. letterpress by Regis Graden at Nut Quad Press. Red leather spine and gray cloth boards by Mariana Blau. No title on cover or spine. Tipped-in seal of the City of Los Angeles used as frontispiece. 500 copies.

109

The Last Supper

Weber, Francis J. San Fernando, CA: Junipero Serra Press, 1998. 2 3/8 × 2 7/8. 10 pp. by Castle Press of Pasadena. Gilt wine cloth boards by Roswell Bookbinders of Phoenix. Italian postage stamp of Last Supper used as frontispiece. Decorative endpapers. 400 copies.

110

Earl Warren, Chief Justice of the United States,
A Personal Memoir

Weber, Francis J. San Fernando, CA: Junipero Serra Press, n.d. (1999). 2 1/4 × 1 1/8.10 pp. by Nut Quad Press. Navy blue leather spine. White paper boards with all-over blue by Mariana Blau. USA. 29¢ postage stamp of Earl Warren used as frontispiece No limitation given. (200 copies).

111

The Shroud of Turin

Weber, Francis J. Los Angeles, CA: Mar Michel, 1999. 2 5/8 × 2 1/8. 15 pp. letterpress by Regjs Graden at Nut Quad Press. Gilt green cloth cover with beige cloth spine by Mariana Blau. Italian postage stamp frontispiece depicting Shroud of Turin. 500 copies.

112

Our Lady of the Angels

Weber, Francis J. Los Angeles, CA: Mar Michel, 2000. 2 1/4 × 2 1/16. 12 pp. letterpress by Regis Graden at Nut Quad Press. White silk moiré spine, gilt white paper over boards by Mariana Blau. Frontispiece. No limitation given.

113

The First Mass In California

Weber, Francis J. Monterey, CA: Old Monterey Book Company, 2000. 2 7/16 × 2 1/8. 18 pp. letterpress by Roger Hilleary and David Salinas. Printed mustard yellow cloth spine, blue and gold paper over boards. USA 29¢ postage stamp of Juan Rodriguez Cabrillo used as frontispiece. 80 copies.

114

The Bayeux Tapestry

Weber, Francis J. Mission Hills, CA: Junipero Serra Press, 2003. 3 1/4 × 2 5/16. 17 pp. letterpress by Regis Graden at Nut Quad Press. Printed light yellow wrappers. Color frontispiece. 275 copies.

115

The Veil of Veronica, A Personal Memoir

Weber, Francis J. Mission Hills, CA: El Camino Real Press, 2004. 3 1/8 × 2 1/8. 27 pp. letterpress by Regis Graden at Nut Quad Press. Dark brown cloth with title stamped in reddish orange. (Weber says "orange" but others call it "red".) Color frontispiece. Illustrated. 150 copies.

116

Blessed Teresa of Calcutta

Weber, Francis J. Mission Hills, CA: El Camino Real Press, 2004. 3 × 2 3/16. 18 pp. letterpress by Regis Graden at Nut Quad Press, Sky blue cloth with title stamped in silver. 2003 Vatican City postage stamp of Mother Teresa used as frontispiece. No information on bindery. (Note per Weber: This book was chosen by the judges for the Western Book Exhibition). 190 copies.

117

The Ronald Reagan Presidential Library

Weber, Francis J. Mission Hills, CA: El Camino Real Press, 2005. 2 7/8 × 2 1/8. 13 pp. letterpress by Patrick Reagh. Silver-stamped green cloth by Mariana Blau. USA 37¢ postage stamp of Reagan used as frontispiece. Color photograph of five presidents mounted on page 12. Decorative endpapers. 150 copies.

118

John Paul The Great, A Eulogy

Weber, Francis J. Mission Hills, CA: El Camino Real Press, 2005. 2 13/16 × 2 3/16. 12 pp. letterpress by Patrick Reagh. Gilt red leatherette by Mariana Blau. 2003 Vatican City postage stamp of Pope John Paul used as frontispiece. Seal of papal coat of arms on page 4. Decorative endpapers. 150 copies.

119

Bob Hope Memorial Garden.

Weber, Francis J. Mission Hills, CA: El Camino Real Press, 2006. 2 7/8 × 2 1/8. 14 pp. letterpress by Patrick Reagh. Gilt olive green cloth by Mariana Blau. Commonwealth of Dominica postage stamp of Bob Hope used as frontispiece. Decorative endpapers. 175 copies.

120

Hershey, The Man, The Company, The Candy

Weber, Francis J. Mission Hills, CA: El Camino Real Press, 2007. 2 7/8 × 2 1/8. 16 pp. letterpress by Patrick Reagh. Silver-stamped "chocolate brown" leatherette by Mariana Blau. Two USA postage stamps: a 1995, 32¢ stamp of Milton Hershey used as frontispiece; a 2001, 39¢ stamp from the "Love series" bearing a Hershey's Kiss on p. 15. Hershey candy wrapper on page 11. Decorative endpapers of Hershey's kisses. 150 copies.

121

Toward Equality In Our Schools. Mendoza vs Westminster

Weber, Francis J. Mission Hills, CA: El Camino Real Press, 2007. 2 7/8 × 2 1/8. 14 pp. letterpress by Patrick Reagh. 'Toward Equality" stamped in black on mustard yellow cloth cover and spine by Mariana Blau. USA 41¢ postage stamp as frontispiece; tipped-in photograph after page 14. Decorative endpapers. 150 copies.

122

The Space Needle

Weber, Francis J. Mission Hills, CA: El Camino Real Press, 2008. 2 15/16 × 2 1/8. 14 pp. letterpress by Patrick Reagh. Silver-stamped, silver leatherette by Mariana Blau. USA 4¢ postage stamp of Seattle World's Fair used as frontispiece. 150 copies.

123

A Memoir 1959–2009

Weber, Francis J. Mission Hills, CA: El Camino Real Press, 2009. 2 13/16 × 2 1/16. 13 pp. letterpress by Patrick Reagh. Gilt-stamped "Golden Jubilee" on cover and spine, taupe cloth boards by Mariana Blau. USA 3¢ postage stamp (50th Anniversary, Devil's Tower National Monument) as frontispiece. Grayish-green endpapers, (Note: Book issued to commemorate Weber's golden sacerdotal jubilee.) 300 copies.

124

Air Force One

Weber, Francis J. Mission Hills, CA: El Camino Real Press, 2009. 2 7/8 × 2 1/8. 13 pp. letterpress by Patrick Reagh. Silver-stamped blue cloth by Mariana Blau. USA postage stamp of Air Force One as frontispiece. Red endpapers. 50 copies.

125

Cesar Chavez

Weber, Francis J. Mission Hills, CA: El Camino Real Press, 2009. 2 13/16 × 2 1/16. 11 pp. letterpress by Patrick Reagh. Red stamped title on cover and spine, goldenrod cloth boards by Mariana Blau. USA 37¢ postage stamp of Chavez used as frontispiece. Decorative endpapers, 100 copies.

126

Benjamin Franklin

Weber, Francis J. Mission Hills, CA: El Camino Real Press, 2010. 2 7/8 × 2 1/8. 15 pp. letterpress by Patrick Reagh. Red stamped title on cover and spine, orange cloth by Mariana Blau. USA ½¢ postage stamp of Franklin used as frontispiece. Red decorative endpapers. 160 copies.

127

President Lincoln's Ten Cannot-Ments

Weber, Francis J. Mission Hills, CA: El Camino Real Press, 2013. 2 7/8 × 2 1/8. 18 pp. letterpress by Patrick Reagh. Gilt black leatherette by Mariana Blau. USA 3¢ postage stamp (75th anniversary, 13th Amendment to Constitution) used as frontispiece, "Brick red" endpapers. 150 copies.

128

Walter O'Malley and the "Blue Heaven on Earth"

Weber, Francis J. Mission Hills, CA: El Camino Real Press, 2013. 2 7/8 × 2 1/8. 12 pp. letterpress in two colors by Patrick Reagh. "Blue Heaven on Earth" stamped in silver on front cover. Gilt navy blue leatherette by Mariana Blau. Two postage stamps: a St. Vincent 60¢ stamp of Chris Gwynn and Jeff Hamilton (inside front cover); a USA 42¢ stamp "Take Me Out to the Ball Game" (Frontispiece). 162 copies.

129

Wonders of America, Land of Superlatives

Weber, Francis J. Mission Hills, CA: El Camino Real Press, 2013. 2 7/8 × 2 1/8. 20 pp. letterpress in two colors by Patrick Reagh. "Wonders of America" stamped in gilt on front cover. Gilt wine leatherette by Mariana Blau. USA 39¢ postage stamp of Grand Canyon used as frontispiece, 150 copies.

130. (2014) Comic Strip Classics
131. (2015) Memories of an Illustrator
132. (2015) The Inverted Jenny
133. (2015) Sr. Corita and the Love Stamp
134. (2016) The Feast of the Nativity
135. (2016) History's Great Popes
136. (2017) The Greatest Show On Earth
137. (2017) Gregory Peck
138. (2018) Cigar Bands
139. (2018) Theodore Hesburgh
140. (2018) God's Signature on Planet Earth
141. (2018) Whatever Happened to Valley Mills?

Miniature Book Overview

The following essay was delivered on numerous occasions, including to such groups as Los Compadres *at the Sherman Library and Gardens (February 12, 2000), and the American History Association (May 9, 1998).*

Welcome to the world of miniature books. I am here to give an overview of these little books – how they are made, where they are found and what they are about.

Miniature books date back to Johann Gutenberg and considerably beyond. In more recent times, the Empress Eugenie, wife of Napoleon III, owned a collection of miniature books that reportedly numbered about 2,000 titles. The literature about the subject began appearing in 1879 and the years that followed. In the past decade, the publication of miniature books has escalated and many of the more recent tomes have brought prominence to their authors, printers, binders and publishers.

For a book to qualify as a miniature, it should be no larger than three inches vertically or horizontally. The purists like them even smaller, but most collectors prefer books they can read without undue magnification.

There are exceptions to these and other general guidelines. Books up to four inches are often allowed, though most collectors would classify them as "oversize." There is some fudging, occasionally, since measurements can be calculated by either the size of the page or the cover.

Ideally, miniature books are printed from handset type, a feat that looks easier than it really is. Printers unfamiliar with miniatures have been known to despair before the challenge. Keeping the ink from splotching the paper separates the apprentices from the journeymen.

Over the years, miniature books have been issued in limited editions but relatively few have survived. Because of their diminutive size, the little books have often been neglected, forgotten, mislaid, lost or destroyed through accident or carelessness.

Like their grown-up counterparts, miniature books can be bound in a wide variety of materials and sizes. I know of one that is bound in snakeskin. By necessity, most binders do their work by hand, rather than by machine. In addition to gorgeous leather bindings, little books are sometimes bound in paper and then fitted into custom-made boxes. One prominent eastern collector fashioned attractive boxes for all her miniatures.

Msgr. Francis J. Weber
Miniature Book Collection
The Huntington Library
San Marino, California

Besides the vast number of Thumb Bibles and prayer books of every religious persuasion, the subject matter of miniature books ranges from *The Aeolian Harp* (1818) to *Zion's Bank* (1857). Rare indeed is the topic that has not been treated in a miniature book.

The question of how many miniature books there are must remain unanswered. One knowledgeable bibliographer enumerated 7,271 titles printed between 1470 and 1965. It would be reasonable to inflate that figure by another two thousand

The

Francis J. Weber

Miniature Book Collection

given to the

Huntington Library

San Marino, California

1991

There are three journals currently being published about miniature books and that number does not include several others treating the miniature world as a whole. Presently there is *The Microbibliophile,* the *Miniature Book News* and the *Miniature Book Society Quarterly,* each of which contributes mightily to the subject.

Rarely does one come across miniature tomes at Waldenbooks or Crown Books. Since they are a specialty item, miniature books are customarily reserved to a dozen or so dealerships around the country and world, like Bromers (Boston). And there are a number of shops that deal mostly by mail, such as Barbara Raheb (Agoura Hills), Diane Peterson (Atherton) and Michael Garbett (Almondsbury).

Older books often find their way into flea markets, rummage sales, thrift shops, antique salons and other similar places. The little gems are frequently available at antiquarian book fairs, trade shows and almost any other place which specializes in antiquarian books.

Miniature books are not less costly because of their smallness. The books currently being published sell for prices ranging from $15 to $35. Their value usually increases with age and, recently, a miniature psalter from the second half of the 13th century went on the market for a staggering $150,000. Condition, number of copies in circulation, craftsmanship, content matter and other considerations naturally figure into determining the value.

Miniature bookcases are not plentiful, except perhaps for the doll-house books which are not overly popular among mainline collectors. Clock cases, jewelry displays and shadow boxes can be accommodated to the purpose and carpenters can rather easily fashion small bookcases. It is generally inadvisable to store miniature books in shoeboxes or drawers because they are easily lost or misplaced. Why bother having the treasures that one cannot easily see, enjoy and show to others?

The camaraderie among miniature book collectors is among the greatest advantage of pursuing little books. Members of the Miniature Book Society hold annual gatherings called "conclaves" in different cities. The society circulates a quarterly newsletter which discusses all the pertinent aspects of collecting.

The number of miniature book collectors remains unknown, though about 350 have surfaced over the past decade. Of those who prefer to remain anonymous, a few have significant libraries. Presently, most of the major collections remain in private hands, though such institutions as the Huntington Library (San Marino), the Library of Congress (Washington,

D.C.), the New York Public Library (New York City) the Lilly Library (Bloomington) and San Diego State Library have formidable collections.

As to why anyone would want miniature books, I can only say that people collect all sorts of things. At different times in my own life, I have collected comic books, postage stamps, campaign buttons, autographs, toy soldiers, watches, coins, pewter automobiles, first-day covers and matchbooks, to name but a few.

I know others who have or are collecting ceramic dishes, prints, thimbles, camels (facsimiles), models of sailing ships, knives, Christmas tree ornaments, bells, baseball cards, bottles, beer cans, lapel pins, whistles, corkscrews and even classic cars.

Imelda Marcos collected shoes, Malcomb Ford purchased Faberge eggs and Henry VIII had many wives. I have one acquaintance who managed to amass sixty-four driving citations before being apprehended and reforming his life.

THE MICROBIBLIOPHILE

A Bimonthly Journal about Miniature Books and the Book Arts

Vol. XXXIV, Number 2, Issue 194   March, 2015

ASUSA PACIFIC UNIVERSITY,
The Weber Collection:

"Msgr. Francis J. Weber has given his personal collection of Weber miniatures to the Library at Azusa Pacific College. More miniature books have been written, edited, and/or compiled by Msgr. Weber than any other person, 130 by the latest count. Several more are in preparation, including one on the famous Sister Corita and her 'love' stamp issued by the United States Postal Service."

The release arrived with a glossy picture of this fine custom made cabinet to house the miniature books. Congradulations to Msgr. Weber on his many many achievments and his contributions to the world of miniature books over the years and this most recent contribution to the Azusa Pacific University. I am sure that the collection is a well appreciated additon to their Special Collections and will serve students well for all the years in the future. ☐🕮

Extensive studies have been made about the human tendency to acquire and/or hoard material possessions. Moral theologians generally regard acquisitiveness as a virtue or a vice, depending on one's point of view and ultimate purpose. An out-of-work psychologist could probably conjure up a whole new vista by matching personalities to specific collectibles.

Suppose we reflect, ever so briefly, on some of the reasons that motivate people to collect little books. At latest count, there are about 350 identifiable individuals who feel that miniature books are collectible. Here are fifteen reasons that motivate persons to expend their time, talent and treasure on assembling miniature libraries. There is no attempt to prioritize this enumeration.

    1. Miniature books are relatively scarce. Few publishers now or in the past have issued little volumes in any great numbers. With the exception of the works by Henry Frowde, few titles were printed

in press runs beyond a thousand, and most fell far below that number;

2. Miniature books do not demand great quantities of storage space or shelving. My own collection was easily accommodated in my fairly modest living quarters;

3. Miniature books represent the supreme effort and skill of printers. What is a relatively simple procedure for ordinary projects becomes a major challenge when one attempts to print with microscopic type without smearing the ink;

4. Miniature books must be bound by hand and that alone helps to account for their scarcity. Only the exceptionally talented and highly motivated binder will attempt to work on mini books;

5. Miniature books are probably as good an investment as any other of the leading hobbies. Though books of any size are not generally good investments, mini books easily surpass their larger brothers and sisters;

6. Miniature books are uncommon enough to attract attention, even from professionals. There are book dealers who have never heard of or seen one, and fewer still keep them in stock;

7. Miniature books are small enough to allow for mobility. Napoleon was one of the many great personages in history who possessed his own miniature traveling library;

8. Miniature books are interesting. Subject matter runs the gamut of human activity from *The Alphabetical Railway Guide* (1929) to *The Zodiacal Signs* (1979). Rare indeed are the topics that have eluded miniature authors and/or printers;

9. Miniature books are educational and usually worth reading. Most of the great classics have been reproduced in miniature form. Barbara Raheb has published hundreds of tiny volumes, including a considerable number of the "world's great books;"

10. Miniature books are relevant to the complexities of the contemporary scene. A copy of Robert Hutching Goddard's autobiography was flown to the moon and back in 1969;

11. Notable people have been associated with miniature books. Franklin Delano Roosevelt was a collector, John F. Kennedy was a subject and Stanley Marcus was an exhibitor. Miniature bookdom boasts some of the truly significant names in bibliophilic annals;

12. Miniature books have long and honorable pedigrees, predating as they do the invention of printing. The earliest miniatures were manuscripts originating in the 15th century. There is a Sumerian cuneiform clay tablet, measuring $1 \ 5/16 \times 4$ inches, that can be traced to 2060 B.C.;

13. Miniature books are fascinating conversation topics. I have spoken to crowds ranging from youngsters to spinsters. Audiences are

invariably fascinated with miniature books – what they are, where they originated and how they are produced;

14. Miniature books are usually not overly expensive, at least in relation to other modern collectibles. They even fit into the budget of an old country priest;

15. Finally, owners of miniature books are universally gracious and cordial people, as anyone who has attended one or another of the Grand Conclaves held annually since 1983 will readily testify.

The above reasons for collecting miniature books are mostly autobiographical, but I suspect enthusiasts will easily identify with most of these observations. All of which once again proves the "bigness" of collecting little books.

Sister Corita and the "Love Stamp"

(Published by El Camino Real Press, Mission Hills, CA, 2015, reviewed by Darleen Cordova.)

This is the 133rd miniature book written or edited by Monsignor Weber who became acquainted with Sister Corita when they were both teaching at Immaculate Heart College. As most collectors know, Msgr. Weber also collects postage stamps; his latest books have been related to postage stamps and usually contain a postage stamp as the frontispiece.

In the "Love Stamp," Msgr. Weber provides an interesting little history of Corita Kent, her work and the issuance of the 1985 "Love" stamp. Sister Corita taught at Immaculate Heart College from 1948 to 1968 and was *Time Magazine*'s "Woman of the Year" in 1966. Over 800 works of art, mainly serigraphs and watercolors related to love and peace, are attributed to Corita Kent, who left the Immaculate Heart of Mary Community in 1968 and moved to Boston.

Her largest copyrighted piece was originally on the side of the Boston Gas Company's natural gas tank. Probably her smallest work of art is her best known and one of the most popular commemorative stamps ever issued. On April 17, 1985, five years after submitting her design, the US Postal Service formally issued the 22-cent commemorative stamp in a ceremony on *The Love Boat* television show.

The rainbow-swash "Love" stamp had a press run of 619,050,000 and is probably the only such artwork credited to a Catholic nun. Corita, however, was dismayed that "her" stamp was associated with a television program and not the love that unites people everywhere. Unfortunately, she died of cancer in 1986.

by
Msgr. Francis J. Weber

Printed in a limited edition of 150 copies, this miniature book measures 2 7/8″ × 2 1/8″ and consists of eight numbered pages, letterpress in five colors (black, red, green, purple, and yellow) on Mohawk Superfine paper, by Patrick Reagh in Sebastopol, California. The typeface used for "display" is Pepita and the text is in 6 pt. Sabon. Patrick Reagh has done a beautiful job on the title page in complementing the rainbow-swash of the "Love" stamp frontispiece; he indicated this is the first time he has used so many colors on a miniature. Bound in an attractive sunshine or buttery yellow leatherette ("calf" finish) by Mariana Blau; "Sister Corita" and the *"Love Stamp"* is stamped in red on the front cover. One of the 22-cent USPS commemorative "Love" stamps is used as the frontispiece in each book. Overall, another delightful miniature from the Old Country Priest.

Rock Star and the Old Country Priest

(*Rock Star and the Old Country Priest*, by Marla Daily, published by El Camino Real Press, Mission Hills, CA, 2015. Reviewed by Darleen Cordova.)

This fascinating miniature book published by El Camino Real Press discusses the 25-year friendship of Msgr. Weber and Joe Walsh of the Eagles. Last January when I was talking to Msgr. Weber, he commented that he had celebrated his birthday (as usual) by having lunch and spending the afternoon with Joe Walsh.

Marla Daily was writing about Santa Cruz Island, for release on May 3, the Feast of the Holy Cross. Since Msgr. Weber had already published his own book about Santa Cruz Island, I was intrigued, especially about his friendship with a rock star. Then for Valentine's Day, I received two wonderful books from the Old Country Priest: *Corita's Love Stamp* and the *Rock Star and The Old Country Priest.*

Marla Daily, a friend of Joe Walsh, was personal assistant to Carey Stanton the Santa Cruz Island owner. In *Rock Star and the Old Country Priest,* Marla Daily provides a very interesting account of how Msgr. Francis Weber and Joe Walsh met through their mutual friend, Carey Stanton. Daily begins her story with a history of the island's owners starting in 1880. The Chapel of the Holy Cross was completed in 1891 but was not much used for almost thirty years.

However, in 1968, Carey Stanton wanted to have a Mass celebrated each year on May 3, and for half a century, Msgr. Weber volunteered his services. Daily also relates the stories of how Carey Stanton met Joe Walsh and how Walsh invited Stanton to the Eagles' "Hotel California Concert" in October 1976. Unfortunately, Stanton died suddenly on the island in 1987 and is buried near the Chapel. Msgr. Weber wanted to continue Stanton's annual Mass tradition and Joe Walsh volunteered to provide the musical accompaniment. From 1988 to 2016, the two men celebrated the Feast of the Holy Cross, and the sounds of Amazing Grace could be heard in the wind.

Printed in a limited edition of 200 copies, this miniature book measures 2 7/8" × 2 1/8" and consists of ten numbered pages, letterpress in two colors (black and green) on Mohawk Superfine paper, by Patrick Reagh at Sebastopol, California. The typeface used is 7 pt. Sabon. Bound in attractive gilt black leatherette ("calf" finish) by Mariana Blau, with the title gilt-stamped on the front cover. The frontispiece is unique: an official 49-cent stamp containing a photo of Weber and Walsh. Stamps.com, a partner with the U.S. Postal Service, was used to create this wonderful photo stamp.

Marla Dailey has provided a very entertaining story about these friendships. Although the press name is not indicated on the title page, Msgr. Weber's mission bell logo is on the colophon page. This is another delightful miniature from El Camino Real Press.

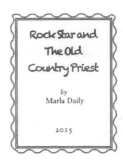

The Divine Comedy (1948)

While parents might profess to love all their children equally, they generally exhibit more affection for the youngest, especially when that offspring comes along late in their lives.

So it is with miniature book collectors. Some of my real "favorites" have been those most recently acquired. Of course, it goes without saying such affection in no way detracts or lessens one's love from the rest of the brood.

Into that category would go a precious little tome, *La Divina Commedia di Dante Alighieri,* which was published by G. Barbera at Florence in 1899. The 455-page book is printed on India paper and elegantly bound in red leather.

But what is most attractive about this book, part of the *"Vade Mecum"* edition, is its provenance. It belonged to the library of H. T. Sheringham and carries his personally inscribed *"ex libris,"* along with the date "Oct. 1900."

Hugh Tempest Sheringham (1876–1930) was one of the earliest bibliophiles to write about miniature books. The son of a clergyman, Sheringham was a Queen's scholar at Westminster and a graduate of Trinity College, Cambridge.

Recognized by his peers as a talented writer, this co-author of *The Court of Saccharissa* would surely have been a successful novelist had he not turned to journalism. An avid fisherman, he became angling editor of *The Field*, a position he held with distinction until his death. According to the *National Union Catalogue,* Sheringham wrote no fewer than nineteen books on the subject, some of which were regarded as "minor classics."

Sheringham was a serious book collector, especially of tiny volumes. In 1902, he wrote a lengthy essay about his own collection in which he offered "my hints on the formation of a miniature library." That his article was recognized for the quality of its composition and context is evident from its publication in *The Connoisseur* which was on an intellectual par with today's *New Yorker* magazine.

Superbly written and highly informative, the essay was reprinted at the Favil Press for the Java Head Bookshop at London in 1948. That 79-page book, entitled *A Library in Miniature*, was issued in a press run of 500 copies.

My copy of Dante's *Divine Comedy* is mentioned by Sheringham in his essay, when he wrote about "another little modern series" consisting "of three volumes of Italian poetry," among which was *Da Divina Commedia*. He went on to observe that "these tiny books are only 2½ in. in height and 1¾ in. in width, but they are so beautifully printed that they are quite legible."

To have one of Sheringham's own books, one which he esteemed enough to mention in his celebrated essay, is a privilege indeed, another confirmation of the old dictum, "what is old is better."

The Grabhorn Brothers (1958)

With the possible exception of John Henry Nash, Edwin and Robert Grabhorn are generally considered to have been the premier American printers of fine press books prior to the mid-1960s.

Opening their shop at San Francisco in 1919, the Grabhorns began printing books of incomparable quality and beauty. As early as 1930, they were considered by one English scholar to be "the greatest printers in the world today" and they clung to that distinction for another three decades.

While they brought to their books a freshness, a newness and a complete departure from any traditional school, Oscar Lewis could still say of the Grabhorns that their works had a "boldness of treatment that inevitably suggests the fifteenth century craftsmen."

For some unknown reason, neither Edwin or Robert ever attempted to print a miniature book. And that is surely a shame for they deprived bibliophiles of what certainly would have been a gorgeous mini tome.

There is, however, one Grabhorn publication which miniature enthusiasts highly covet, and it is H. C. Schulz's essay on *French Illuminated Manuscripts* which was printed by the Grabhorn Press for David Magee in 1958. In addition to a scene of the Coronation of the Virgin re-drawn and hand-colored by Mary Grabhorn, the book has a tipped-in 3½ × 2¼ inch original leaf from a *Book of Hours* illuminated at Paris in the first half of the fifteenth century.

The 30-page book, measuring 7¾ × 5¾ inches, is printed on English handmade paper and bound in orange and tan decorated boards. Published in a press run of 200 copies, the book now sells for upwards of $500.

As an aside, Schulz mentions in his masterful essay that the leaf was "representative of the diminutive-sized manuscript," and offered his view that "any manuscript with each of its dimensions less than ten centimeters is a bibliographical Lilliput."

One final "association item" that might be mentioned in this context is Harry Lyman Koopman's work on Miniature Books which Dawson's Book Shop published in 1968. Though it bears the Grabhorn-Hoyem imprint, the book was actually the last book designed by Bruce Rogers. It hadn't been printed at the time of his death and was resurrected a dozen years later by Andrew Hoyem.

While one can only fantasize what a true Grabhorn miniature book might have looked like, surely it would have been a treasured production. James D. Hart probably had the last word about the Grabhorns when he noted, in 1969, that "the Grabhorn name is honored the world around, wherever men and women appreciate finely made books. Behind it lies the character, the independence, the integrity, the art and craft that belong to the brothers Grabhorn."

10

Miscellaneous Articles from the Past

The Last Word (1989)

(This essay contains a series of reflections delivered to the Los Angeles Corral of the Westerners on February 8, 1989. In his introduction, Sheriff Siegfried G. Demke explained that "Our speaker tonight is an historian who paid his way through college and graduate school by working in the local funeral trade. During most of the 1950s he was an employee of Mark Pierce, owner and operator of Pierce Brothers Mortuaries. Msgr. Francis J. Weber has long been interested in the history of the funeral business. A logical outgrowth of that concern is his knowledge of cemeteries, both locally and nationally He will speak on an upbeat aspect of boothill that may fascinate our members.)

May I begin with the apocryphal story of an elderly lady who lived with her equally old cat deep in the bogs of Northern Ireland. She was, as they say, dirt poor and often at night she went to bed hungry.

One day, as she was sifting through some old containers, a genie popped out of a bottle. She was a lovely thing, complete with magical wand and earrings.

Looking at the elderly and bedraggled Irish lady, the genie said: "I have been instructed to grant you three wishes. Then I will disappear and you will never see me again."

"Well, first of all," the lady said: "I would like to be young again, this time pretty and with fine clothes." The genie agreed, waved her wand, and the lady became young, pretty and beautifully attired.

"Then the genie said: "Now what about the second wish?" The lady responded: I would like to be wealthy, draped with fine jewels and have a large bank account." With no hesitation, that wish was also granted.

There was one more wish. "Now what would you like as a final wish?" the genie asked. "Oh, my cat has been a faithful companion for all these years. Could you make him into a charming, handsome, young knight?"

The final wish was instantly granted. The genie left and the handsome young man walked over to her, grabbed her hand and said: "What a shame you had me neutered!"

It was kind of Sig Demke to ask me to speak to this distinguished assemblage. It occasionally happens that talks at gatherings like this get a little heavy, sometimes maybe even a little boring, so I thought it might be well to depart a little from the usual format in this presentation. As an historian, I surely identify with and applaud your interest in the development of the West.

Some of you may know that I financed my education by working in the funeral business here in Los Angeles. Between 1950 and 1957, my summers and other vacation periods were spent performing all the many chores involved in "putting people away."

After spending a few spare hours one afternoon at historic Rosedale Cemetery, looking at the tombstones of local pioneers, I became intrigued with the epitaphs of the high and mighty, the lowly and the insignificant. It was rather sobering to reflect that a person's whole earthly existence, accomplishments, successes, failures, whatever, is crammed into a few lines on one's tombstone. For the great majority of people, the inscription of his or her marker becomes the only lasting record of a lifetime.

Initially I collected rubbings, but that soon became too unwieldy for practicality, so I settled for making transcriptions of the more interesting stones, most of them chiseled on marble, many onto granite, and a goodly number in wood.

I discovered that these inscriptions had inspired the great philosophers, poets and writers of all ages. Dante and Shakespeare found in the graveyard the inspiration for their greatest genius, and some of the sublimest thoughts of the modern poets have been associated with the graveyard and the tomb.

There's a lot of history on headstones, and even a little dash of humor. This evening I'm going to share with you some of the ones I've seen and transcribed. In this particular presentation, we'll concentrate on the humorous.

The *rhymed* epitaphs are generally the most expressive, but I doubt if any could outdistance the one George Bernard Shaw composed for his stone: "I knew if I stayed around long enough, something like this would happen."

Western *aficionados* will appreciate recalling the Wells Fargo agent who unwisely insisted on collecting for a shipment in Tombstone, Arizona. On his marker are these words.

Here
Lies
Lester Moore
Four slugs
from a .44
No Les
No Moore

Then there is the granite slab, this one in Hatfield,
Massachusetts, which reads:

Beneath this stone, a lump of clay
Lies Arabella Young
Who on the 21st of May
Began to hold her tongue

Often quoted without details is this verse in Fairfield, Vermont:

O fatal gun why was it him
That you should kill so dead?
Why didn't you go off a little higher
And fire above his head?

Sometimes the gruesome details about a person's departure from
Planet Earth find their way into the decedent's epitaph. From Schenect-
ady, New York, is one which says:

He got a fish-bone in his throat
And then he sang an angel's note

A Colorado tombstone proclaims:

> He was young,
> He was fair,
> But the Injuns
> Raised his hair

And there is one found in Medway, Massachusetts, which reads:

> Under this stone, this piece of clay
> Lies Uncle Peter Daniels,
> Who too early in the month of May
> Took off his winter flannels

In the churchyard in Woolwich is a very beautifully carved marker which says:

> Sacred to the memory of Major James Brush,
> Royal Artillery, who was killed by the accidental discharge
> of a pistol by his orderly, 14th April, 1831.
> Well done, good and faithful servant.

At Cross Kirk, Shetland, is a tribute to Donald Robertson, which gives his birth and death date, followed by this reflection:

> He was a peaceable, quiet man, and to all appearance a sincere Christian. His death, very much regretted, was caused by the stupidity of Laurence Tulloch, of Clotherton, who sold him nitre instead of Epson Salt, by which he was killed in the space of three hours after taking a dose of it.

Occasionally, a person is remembered for his profession or vocation in life. Some examples might be….
For Henry Kirk, a key-fitter:

> A zealous locksmith died of late,
> And did not enter Heaven's gate
> But stood without and would not knock
> Because he meant to pick the lock.

For Harvey Peterson, a dentist:

> View this gravestone
> With profound gravity
> For he is filling his last cavity.

For Knute Knopp, a sky-diver:

> In mid-air
> Luckless Knute
> Learned that moths
> Had ate his chute

For Lance Figini, a swimmer:

> Saw five sharks
> Off the coast
> Four he missed
> One almost

For Ben Esterhazy, a novice farmer:

> Here lies uncle Ben
> Whose life was full
> Until he tried to
> Milk a bull

For Morris Meershaun, a printer:

> Stood too close to the press,
> Heaven is now his address.

For Darrel Meegan, a clerk:

> Here lies buried beneath these stones,
> The beard, the flesh, and all the bones
> Of the Parish Clerk – old David Jones.

The term *"Hic jacet,"* translated "here lies," is the most commonly used formula for epitaphs, at least in the United States. Here are some samples:

> Here lies Andrew MacPherson
> Who was a peculiar person;
> He stood six foot two
> Without his shoe,
> And he was slew,
> At Waterloo.

An epitaph on a great English statesman:

> Here lies the body of Robert Lowe
> Where he's gone to I don't know,

> If to the realms of peace and love,
> Farewell to happiness above!
> If to some lower level,
> I congratulate the Devil!

Another marker, this one in Lafayette, Indiana, reads:

> Here lie the bones of Lazy Fred,
> Who wasted precious time in bed
> Some plaster fell down on his head,
> And now old Freddie's dead.

And for Anne Hopewell, in Enosburg, Vermont:

> Here lies the body of beloved Anna
> Done to death by a fresh banana.
> It wasn't the fruit that laid her low,
> But the skin of the thing that made her go.

There are several versions of this one:

> Here I lie and no wonder I'm dead,
> I fell from a tree, down on my head.

From the churchyard at Aberdeen:

> Here lie the bones of Elizabeth Charlotte
> Born a virgin, died a harlot.
> She was a virgin at seventeen,
> A remarkable thing in Aberdeen.

In Carrolsport, Virginia, is this one:

> Here lies Johnny Cole
> Who died after eating a plentiful dinner
> While chewing his crust.
> He was turned into dust,
> With his crimes undigested – poor sinner

The epitaph for a money-lender in San Francisco reads thusly:

> Here lies old thirty-five per cent
> The more he made the more he lent,
> The more he got the more he craved;
> Great God! Can such a soul be saved.

On a tombstone in Saint Mary's churchyard, Burlington, New Jersey, is this stanza:

> Here lies the body of Mary Ann Lauder
> She burst while drinking a seidleitz powder
> Called from this world to her heavenly rest,
> She should have waited 'till it effervesced.

And these are some *hic jacets* from England:

> Here lies two children
> By water confounded
> One died of dropsy
> T'other was drownded.

At Kingsbridge, Devon, one can read this one:

> Here be I, by the chancel door,
> Here be I, because I'm poor,
> The further in the more you pay,
> Here lie I as warm as they.

And in Wolver Hampton, Staffordshire, is this memorial:

> Here lie the bones of Joseph Jones
> Who ate while he was able;
> But once over-fed, he dropt down dead,
> And fell beneath the table.

A final English epitaph, this one from St. Paul's:

> Here lies Bernard Lightfoot who was accidentally
> killed in the forty-fifth year of his age.
> Erected by his grateful family.

Then there are those whose manner of death elicited a fanciful remembrance.

For the victim of a mob killing, Edward Stark:

> Edward learned with dismay
> Loansharks mean what they say.

For an overly trusting dog fancier, Dudley Groon:

> No one told poor old Dudley
> Doberman-Pinschers just aren't cuddly!

For a heart attack victim, Dwight Flensch:

> Dwight pulled through, with stubborn will,
> Then, alas, came the bill.

For a careless motorist, Glen Schnurr:

> Tried to pass a trailer truck,
> Found out quick, what's a schmuck!

For an urban dweller, Ralph Hendricks:

> Ralph found out, sure as heck,
> That muggers wouldn't take a check!

Though wives normally bury their husbands and then live on to a great age, a few lucky fellows have managed to outlive their spouses. Here are some of the epitaphs they composed for their dearly departed. Patrick O'Leary of Belfast, Ireland wrote:

> Beneath this stone lies Katherine, my wife,
> In death my comfort, and my plague through life.
> Oh Liberty! I must not boast,
> Or she'll haunt me with her ghost.

Aubrey Cuenod had these words chiseled on his wife's tombstone:

> Here lies my wife; here let her lie:
> She's now at rest, and so am I.

On the stone of a troublesome spouse is this inscription:

> Here lies Cynthia, Steven's wife.
> She lived six years in calm and strife
> Death came at last and set her free.
> I was glad and so was she.

This inscription is seen on a stone in the Barlinine Cemetery:

> Here Beneath this Stone We Lie
> Back to Back my Wife and I,
> And when the Angels Trump shall Trill
> If She gets Up, then I'll lie still
> Some have children, some have none:
> Here lies the mother of twenty-one.

Among the just plain funny epitaphs are these:

> Erected to the memory of John Philips
> Accidentally shot as a mark of affection
> By his brother

Abraham Newland composed this epitaph for himself:

> Beneath this stone old Abraham lies,
> Nobody laughs and nobody cries.
> Where he has gone and how he fares,
> Nobody knows; and nobody cares.

In Lee, Massachusetts, is this one:

> In memory of
> Mrs. Alpha White
> Weight 309 pounds
> Open wide ye heavenly gates!

Epitaph for a two-week-old baby:

> Came in
> Looked about
> Didn't like it
> Rushed right out.

The memorial for Maybelle Hunter of Redford, Maine:

> She drank good ale,
> good punch, and wine,
> And lived to the age
> Of ninety-nine.

For the dis-edification of the legal profession:

> God does do wonders now and then
> Here lies a lawyer who was an honest man.

For a non-believer in Thurmont, Maryland:

> Here lies an atheist
> All dressed up and no place to go

And, finally, to end this monkey business – the two words that adorn the tombstone of Gerald Maginnis:

> *Finis – Maginnis*

Tribute to Dr. Doyce B. Nunis Jr. (1994)

I would like to welcome you here for this dinner honoring Doyce B. Nunis, Jr. on the occasion of his being invested as a Knight Commander of Saint Gregory the Great.

You may notice that Cantwell Hall has been freshly plastered and painted. This is the only room at San Fernando Mission that has been fixed since the January 17th earthquake. It was thoroughly trashed – to the extent of fifty wheelbarrows of broken plaster and other assorted debris.

This event is a combined tribute to Doyce – anticipating as it does his 70th birthday by only a few months. It is fitting that Doyce's knighthood comes relatively late in life – you'll recall that Our Lord saved the best wine until last.

There is no formal program this evening. We didn't want to make this just another testimonial – of which he has had many in his career. Nor did we want to make it a roast, because the knighthood is really a serious honor.

You have at your table an article that traces the Knighthood of Saint Gregory here in California. You will recall that, unlike other knighthoods, this one comes directly from the Holy Father and, in that sense, it is the most prestigious.

This honor was instituted by Pope Gregory XVI who created the Diocese of Both Californias in 1840. And I think its long history in California has many parallels with Doyce's lifework.

Someone asked me how one obtains this most distinctive honor. The general answer would be that it is bestowed for truly *outstanding* service to the Church.

In Doyce's case, I can tell you that he has been the longest and most consistent supporter of the Archival Center since way back in 1962 when it was formally established downtown.

He later organized the Friends of the Archival Center and has served as its president and driving force for the past ten years. Without hesitation, he has been available for advice and encouragement over all these thirty-two years – to an *extraordinary* way.

I cannot recall any archival project that Doyce has not supported over the years and there have been many. He once even traveled to Chicago's Newberry Library on our behalf and he has used his good offices in a multitude of other ways.

Now this isn't meant to be a eulogy, but I do want to stress that the Knighthood of Saint Gregory is indeed a most prestigious and rare honor – and this time it is being bestowed upon a worthy and deserving man.

Some years ago, when I was in Rome, I went to a flea market and was enamored by a medallion bearing the insignia of Saint Gregory the Great. For some unknown reason, I bought it.

I wanted to give it to Doyce as a lapel pin, but it had apparently been used earlier as a uniform button or a cuff link. I was finally able to find a jeweler who encapsulated it in a casing which allows for its use as a lapel pin. Surely Doyce will be the only one at the Cathedral tomorrow with such a treasure – which the jeweler told me was over a hundred years old.

Thank you for coming. Doyce compiled the guest list, so you know that all of you are very special to him.

Reflections on the Archival Center (1996)

(Delivered to the Staff at the Los Angeles Chancery Office)

Before launching into a survey of the Catholic Church in Los Angeles, let me reflect very briefly on the archives for the local church. Alzheimer's Disease is one of the most distressing illnesses that can befall a person, especially if that individual has led an active and productive life.

People having that disease in its advanced form have no memory of or interest in the past and pay minimal attention to the present. Otherwise healthy people, they can live long lives but they do so in an almost sub-human state.

Institutions can also have Alzheimer's Disease and it is manifested when employers and employees know nothing or, worse, care nothing about the history of their institution, when it was founded, by whom, for what, etc.

I once knew a lady who worked for thirty years in the employ of Arm and Hammer Baking Soda. She told me that the founder of her company was Armand Hammer, the industrialist and art collector. And, when I attempted to set her straight, she nodded and said – "who cares, as long as I get my check."

James Francis Cardinal McIntyre blesses the Chancery Archives

The local Church, too, can suffer from a form of Alzheimer's when its members and/or its employees exhibit no curiosity or interest in its purpose, its goals, its works or its organization.

I mention this only because last week, after working in this complex for thirty-four years, an employee asked me if I was Cardinal Manning. I didn't bother to explain that he went home to God seven years ago, but I was tempted to tell Human Resources that we had a forty-year-old brain-dead person on the payroll.

Fortunately, for the Church and other institutions, there is a cure for Alzheimer's Disease and it really doesn't involve all that much effort – just a little healthy motivation.

Increasingly, in recent decades, companies have been investing heavily in record management and archival programs. Invariably they are finding that it is a superb investment, which pays rich dividends, far outdistancing the cost.

Happily, the Catholic Church has long recognized the usefulness of archives. Since the Middle Ages, Rome has been a treasure trove of the past. So valuable were the Vatican Archives that Napoleon once stole them and moved them to Paris.

Thanks to the foresight of James Francis Cardinal McIntyre, the Archdiocese of Los Angeles has had a canonically constituted archives since 1962. In that context, this area of the Lord's vineyard was light-years ahead of most other American ecclesiastical jurisdictions.

Since 1981, the Archives have been located in a building adjacent to the San Fernando Mission which you are all invited to visit – and, more importantly, to support – by sending your retired and obsolete files.

Whenever you have something in that category, just call someone at Mission Hills and we will have it picked up. Or contact either Gerri Spray or Bob Harner, and they will arrange to have your materials delivered. We ask that you include an inventory of the materials you send, as well as carefully record the box number you leave off on if shipping multiple boxes, or starting a new collection, so we don't have duplicates. We also ask that you check your materials against the Record Retention Schedule in Chapter 17 of the Administrative Manual before sending them on. And all items entrusted to the Archival Center can be retrieved with a phone call.

Those wishing to define or describe the Archives for the Archdiocese of Los Angeles could say, in computer terminology, that the Archives are the "memory bank" for the Catholic Church in Southern California.

People whose memory bank is impeded or burned out have very little to think or talk about. So would it be with the Church. And, after all, we have a lot to tell the world – twenty centuries worth of heroic activities for the Lord.

Francis Bacon shrewdly observed that "there can be no history without documents." The Church, which means God's people, has a glorious history and it needs to be told. Countless numbers of people have been first attracted to Catholicism by reading about its unique and glorious track record. And that's very good.

Commercials on television and radio, and in newspapers and magazines, advertise their products most effectively by appealing to their performance ratings or endurance. Consumers are impressed when they hear, for example, that 65 percent of all the Mercedes-Benz automobiles ever built are still in operation, that Neutrogena hand lotion has been used since prehistoric times or that Ever Fresh water is melted from centuries-old glaciers.

Whatever our particular role or vocation in life, we all share the common obligation of telling the world about Christ – who He was, what He did and why we should subscribe to His blueprint for salvation.

The greatest story ever told could not have been related without the scriptures – which are nothing more or less than the footprints of Christ on Planet Earth.

We are to this century what the apostles were to theirs. We record what we do in documents – and we must, therefore, be aware of their importance and the need to properly house and care for them.

Because – without a past, we have no future. I have a brochure for the local Catholic Church, known officially as the Archdiocese of Los Angeles. Please read it over at your leisure.

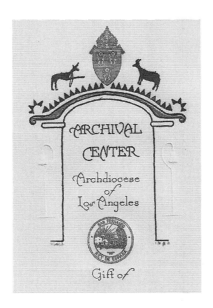

Reflections on Vatican Council II (2012)

I was present in Rome for the opening of Vatican Council II fifty years ago. These reflections on that event appeared in the magazine of Saint John's Seminary, the fall issue of 1962 of the *Evangelist*.

There was certainly much of the past evident in Rome on the 11th of October 1962, but much more of the present. Gone was the thunder of canons on the Aventine which greeted the 744 prelates at the First Vatican Council. Also missing were the Papal States, once thought an integral part of Church machinery. Rome itself had suffered a transformation beyond that of any other ancient center of religion.

And yet, as the bells of the city's churches pealed forth, the city seemed to possess that mysterious continuity which not even the lapse of time can interrupt, change or diminish.

From early morning, the six tribunes behind the tiers of Episcopal seats in Saint Peter's Basilica had been filled with theologians, canonists and a few fortunate observers. At precisely eight-thirty the throngs outside the Vatican Basilica glimpsed the first of the solemn procession as it moved slowly down the *Scala Regia*, through the *Portone di Bronzo*, onto the vast square of Saint Peter's.

In front walked the Sistine choir, followed by generals of religious orders, abbots, bishops, archbishops, metropolitans, patriarchs and cardinals, arrayed in shining silver copes and white linen miters. Finally came the eighty-one-year-old pontiff, John XXIII, led down the Bernini staircase from the Sistine Chapel by his attendants and surrounded by the picturesque Swiss guards.

When the Pope arrived at the papal altar, he intoned the *Vent Creator Spiritus*, and that ancient hymn was instantly taken up by the assembled prelates. On the altar, the four Gospels were opened, in keeping with the custom at all great synods from the earliest times.

In 1962 the governing body of the Church was far larger numerically than it was only ninety-two years earlier at Vatican Council I. The alignment of its members greatly differed from that of 1869. Roughly 37 percent of the Fathers at the Council represented Europe, about 33 percent represented the Americas, more than 11 percent came from Africa and 8 percent came from Asia and Oceania. Hence it can be seen that the center of influence had shifted from the European world.

The last century had witnessed an unprecedented expansion of the Church in English-speaking countries as well as the newly emerging nations of Africa, all of which has brought with it, in the words of President Kennedy, "staggering problems which, from the human point of view, seem at times to be almost insoluble." And yet, he continued, "it is very heartening to know that the Council ... will strive to deepen the fellowship and love which are the natural needs of man and are imposed on the Christian as rules for his relationship between man and man, and between people and people."

Vatican Council I was held in the right transept of Saint Peter's where tiers of thrones had converted the sixteenth-century basilica into a giant *aula concilians*. Elaborately surrounded with bright red carpets, gold brocades and pictures, the bishops formed eight rows along the two sides of the council chambers. The Papal throne was situated in the apse and the cardinals and patriarchs sat in a large semicircle on either side of the venerable Pius IX. A raised tribune, reserved for temporal princes, was occupied by such royal personages as the Grand Dukes of Tuscany and Parma.

Necessity demanded that Vatican Council II be held in a larger chamber. Hence seats were erected down the entire length of the basilica's nave, over 328 feet. The enclosure stopped short of the canopied altar of the confessional, which stood in the junction of nave and transepts, forming the basilica's giant Latin cross. An aisle eighteen feet wide separated the tiers of seats facing inward along each side of the aisle. All members with a deliberative vote had a seat, a desk and a prie-dieu.

The Council gathers in St. Peter's Basilica

The Papal Throne backed up to the confessional facing the entrance to the basilica and on the Holy Father's left were tables for the general secretariat. A pulpit to the right of the throne was used by those addressing the assembly. Near the fully-vested statue of Saint Peter was a movable altar which was wheeled into place for Holy Mass.

Historically speaking, the opening of the Second Vatican Council was the culmination of plans begun forty years earlier. In an encyclical letter of December 23, 1922, Pope Pius XI first set forth his hopes for re-convening the Vatican Council I but he was unable to carry out its planned activities because of the unsettled political condition of Europe.

Pius XI apparently wanted a council from his earliest days as supreme pontiff but, as he said, he never received the manifest sign for actually summoning the world's hierarchy into session. His council would have completed action on the projected schemata of the earlier council and would have devoted much of its attention to the subjects of unity and catholicity.

The industrious pontiff even worked out a doctrinal program which, in its teachings on the Church, the Pope, and the episcopate, continued that of the Vatican Council I, and in the Church's moral and social teaching, and subsequent papal pronouncements.

Soon after Achille Ratti's death in 1939, Msgr. Ernesto Ruffini, later the Cardinal Archbishop of Palermo, suggested that Pope Pius XII summon a Council to meet the changes in social conditions brought on by the advance of science and the need for re-emphasizing the religious and ethical principles of the twentieth century. Apparently the plea had some effect on the pontiff. One cardinal mentioned in his memoirs that Pius XII had made preparations for an Ecumenical Council "at which, according with his instructions, a select group of ecclesiastics were working for several years."

Pope John XXIII

Nonetheless, it remained for John XXIII to officially proclaim Vatican Council II "in obedience to an inspiration which we felt given in the humility of our heart as a sudden, unexpected motion ... the spontaneous flowering of an unexpected spring." Thus, for the second time in history, a General Council of the Church had been summoned. The earlier Council had been called in 1414 by the pseudo-pope, an action subsequently validated when the two other papal claimants endorsed the proposal.

Vatican Council II would not be "a magic and immediate remedy" for all the problems facing the Church, according to Giovanni Cardinal Montini, Archbishop of Milan. "We must guard against two illusions which could become disappointments for the future," he explains.

To expect "the council would decree radical and bewildering reforms in the present rules of the Church, to the extent of changing its century-old features and turning it into a completely new institution" would be no less wrong than hoping it "will remedy all defects, imperfections, and abuses which we find today in Catholic life."

As a matter of fact, Vatican Council I only produced two constitutions, both of them doctrinal in content after seven months of labor. But, with the greater preparation given to this Council, perhaps a larger volume of work could be expected.

In any event, the Catholic Church was certainly in a transitional period. And as this observer watched the precedent-shaking departure of the Pope on the Italian Government's presidential train for Loreto and Assisi, he could hardly deny that the Holy Father was leading the Church into a new era where tradition is the theory and progress is the practice.

Whatever be the Council's outcome, Pope John XXIII had long before adopted the attitude of John Henry Newman that "nothing would be done at all, if a man waited till he could do it so well that no one could find fault with it."

The Archdiocese of Los Angeles

Though already launched toward its tricentennial, there is still something fresh and exciting about the one-time *Pueblo de Nuestra Señora de los Angeles*. The story of its progress, from Hispanic colonial foundation to international center for learning, art and commerce is as much a work of imagination as it is of history.

Historians and others maintain that more than any other major city, Los Angeles has achieved its unique place in human annals because a handful of pioneers – from the Kings of Spain to the barons of land, rail and industry – dreamt and decreed that it would be so, and because thousands of others, working people from Sonora and Indiana, Shanghai and Odessa, bought and built accordingly.

Los Angeles is not perched aside the confluence of major waterways or along a vital commercial route; it is not blessed with a great natural harbor or outstanding physical location; neither was it built atop some ancient center of human habitation or upon a pre-existing religious cult. About all the city ever had and continues to have is an unequalled place in human imagination. But, alas, that's what really counts when all the chips are down.

If New York is identified on bumper stickers as the "Big Apple," and Chicago as "gangsters gulch," then Los Angeles must surely be the city of the giant dream, the grand illusion and the hard reality.

Unimpressed by its own past and certainly not intimidated by that of its sister cities, *El Pueblo de Nuestra Señora de los Angeles* is a place where everyone is entitled to a second, even a third chance.

Angelenos have never measured the cost nor considered the contradictions of their accomplishments. Their quest for water, to cite an outstanding example, is a monumental feat of human ingenuity and skill.

Or, again, when pressing demands of new immigrants and the financial interest of aggressive developers converged in postwar Los Angeles, the San Fernando and San Gabriel valleys blossomed forth with suburban housing tracts that defied demographers around the globe.

Probably no community in all of recorded history managed to house so many of its working-class and middle-income people so well, while continuing to provide them with amenities usually associated only with the wealthy. For the thousands who continue to pour into the area annually, Los Angeles is the community that invented itself. It remains the city of exceptions and exceptional "dreamers."

And why not? After all, was it not the "Dreamers of God" who began it all for *El Pueblo de Nuestra Señora de los Angeles?* Even those outside her fold must accord the Catholic Church a special "historical pre-eminence" in discussions about the earliest days of Los Angeles.

The "Catholic presence" in the area now comprising the City of Los Angeles actually pre-dates the city by a dozen years. The very name derives from the diary of Fray Juan Crespi, who introduced the Feast of the *Portiuncula* into California's vocabulary.

And it was a group of Catholics, most of them predominantly Negro in racial strain, who effected the actual foundation of *El Pueblo de Nuestra Señora de los Angeles,* in the fall of 1781.

Fray Junípero Serra, the *Presidente* of the California Missions, first walked the dusty pathways of the *pueblo* the following year. Interestingly enough, he and his Franciscan companions initially objected to the establishment, feeling that premature Spanish towns would infringe upon the Indian and mission prerogatives. And they did!

In any event, despite the reservations of the friars, the *pueblo* was borne, from the very outset the un-mistakable seraphic imprint of those dedicated pioneers who came to share their religion and civilization with an aboriginal people.

Los Angeles continued for some years to be a "Catholic" enclave, with most of its inhabitants worshipping, at least sporadically, at the Old Plaza Church. Oh, that's not to say that the *pueblo* was, by any means, a virtuous city. Unfortunately, the Catholic Church has always been blessed (or cursed) with more than its share of renegades.

On January 17, 1837, just a year and a half after Los Angeles had been raised to the status of a city, the *ayuntamiento*, or council, passed, without a dissenting voice, a resolution declaring that "the Roman Catholic apostolic religion shall prevail throughout this jurisdiction."

While there is no evidence that this expressed but never enforced "establishment of religion" benefited Catholics, it did provide adherents with a unique distinction in Western Americana's historical annals.

Plans were unveiled to open a Catholic school in the city in 1849 and two years later the institution opened its doors with twenty-six "scholars." Bishop Joseph Sadoc Alemany entrusted the administration of the school to the Picpus Fathers.

As late as 1853, Harris Newmark said that "nearly all the population was Catholic." Another creditable authority noted that "up to 1854, the only organization in Los Angeles upholding any standard of morality whatever was the Roman Catholic Church. It erected houses of worship, hospitals and schools; it was the pioneer of all good works."

And while it all changed following the onrush of the gold seekers, Los Angeles continued through the decades to be a unique haven for religious-minded peoples of all creeds.

In a survey of local history published in 1967, Christopher Rand observed "there are probably more religions in Los Angeles than in the whole previous history of mankind." And it all started with the Catholic Church, in 1781.

The geographical derivation of the 8,762 square miles presently comprising the Archdiocese of Los Angeles can be traced to April 27, 1840, when Pope Gregory XVI created the parent jurisdiction from the already established See of Sonora.

Boundaries for the gigantic Diocese of Both Californias were the Colorado River in the east, the 42nd degree of north latitude (Oregon line), the Pacific Ocean in the west and all of Baja California. The title was officially changed to Monterey in 1849.

Bishop Joseph Sadoc Alemany

The subsequent transfer of sovereignty in California made a further delineation of boundaries imperative. On

April 17, 1853, Bishop Joseph Sadoc Alemany received word that the Sacred Congregation of Propaganda Fide had removed Peninsular California from its attachment to the Diocese of Monterey.

Several months later, on July 29th, Pope Pius IX created a Metropolitan District at San Francisco. The southern parallel of the parish at San Jose was fixed as the demarcation between the new Archdiocese of San Francisco and the larger but suffragan Diocese of Monterey.

Bishop Thaddeus Amat

The Monterey jurisdiction, which encompassed all of Southern California, remained territorially intact for the next seven decades. On July 8, 1859, Bishop Thaddeus Amat was authorized to move his episcopal seat to Los Angeles. At that time he was also permitted to add that city's name to the diocesan title.

During the subsequent years, there were a number of proposals for dividing the large and unwieldy Diocese of Monterey-Los Angeles. As early as 1866, Bishop Amat confided to a friend that he expected, "within a few years," to see another bishopric formed in the Southland.

While no official action was taken by Amat, his successor, Bishop Francis Mora, petitioned the Holy See several times for a reduction of his jurisdiction. The proposal was shelved temporarily, in 1894, when Mora was given a coadjutor. Rumors of a division were revived after Bishop Thomas J. Conaty's death in 1915, and were sustained by the long interregnum that ensued before the appointment of John J. Cantwell.

Bishop John J. Cantwell

Early in 1922, Bishop Cantwell asked that the 90,000-square-mile Diocese of Monterey-Los Angeles be dismembered, with twelve counties formed into a separate jurisdiction. Pope Pius XI acquiesced and, in June, created the new Diocese of Monterey-Fresno. The larger area, known as the Diocese of Los Angeles-San Diego, embraced the remaining Southland counties stretching to the Mexican border.

The final major alteration in the Southland occurred on July 11, 1936, with the erection of a second Metropolitan District in California, at Los Angeles. Simultaneously, the four southernmost counties were fashioned into the Diocese of San Diego. Included in the newly formed Province of Los Angeles were the suffragan Sees of Monterey-Fresno, San Diego and Tucson.

In January 1948, the Apostolic Delegate informed officials at Los Angeles that in order to avoid confusion with the older Archdiocese of Puebla, in Mexico, the southland's jurisdiction would henceforth be known officially as the Archdiocese of Los Angeles in California.

The archdiocese retained its geographical integrity from 1936 until June 18, 1976, when Pope Paul VI created a new diocese for Orange County. Remaining in the parent See were the counties of Los Angeles, Ventura and Santa Barbara.

Historical commentators are quick to observe that almost everything in Southern California has been imported – plants, flowers, shrubs, trees, water and even religion!

More than three decades ago, the late Carey McWilliams pointed to the unprecedented influx of peoples – a factor that today accounts for the multi-ethnic nature of the onetime *Pueblo de Nuestra Señora de los Angeles.*

The Indians were the first to inhabit the area. And though they are mostly gone now, they left an indelible mark behind in such names as Cahuenga, Malibu, Mugu and Pacoima.

Then came the Catholic *pobladores* from Sonora who laid out the original *plaza* on a bluff above the river named by Fray Juan Crespi to honor Our Lady of the Angels.

For a while after the war with Mexico and the discovery of gold, Los Angeles remained a small and insignificant town. But that was soon to change.

Statehood came, in 1850, and then, following the Civil War, the railroads reached out to touch Los Angeles, bringing newcomers from the south and midwest, many of them lured westward by the well-publicized sunshine.

The roots of the Bible were solidly transplanted by the great midwestern migration. Los Angeles remains predominantly Protestant, though the importance of the Catholic faith was first attested, in 1953, when the Archbishop of Los Angeles became the first cardinal in the western United States.

Though the city is famous for its revivalists and cultists, they have probably drawn attention out of all proportion to their numbers. Studies indicate that the great majority of churchgoers belong to the traditional faiths.

The Chinese and Japanese arrived; French, Poles and German Jews also came and many of the beach areas became popular resort meccas for English tourists.

Early in this century, the Mexican population began rising again, this time forming the bulk of the migratory work force. The Blacks, who presently constitute 12.5 percent of the population, began their treks in 1900.

And the waves of immigration roll on. In the last decade, Vietnamese and Koreans, with their distinctive contributions, have flooded into Los Angeles to join dozens of other Asiatic groups, like the Samoans, more of whom live in Los Angeles than reside on the Island of American Samoa itself.

The people thronging to the area have generally been an adventurous and inventive lot. In Hollywood, for example, creative minds have entertained and informed the whole world, reflecting both America's manifold problems and its unique promise.

A major port city, the aircraft and electronics industries expanded to meet the challenges of World War II and then spun around to handle contemporary transportation and communication needs.

This largest of the world's cities dedicated to Our Lady provides a haven for its perpetual transplants. It amazes, amuses and eventually absorbs. New arrivals are confronted with culture shock – the climate, the freeways, the lifestyles and the ethnic mix.

But one can rest assured that new blood will keep Los Angeles alive, vigorous and growing as it inches toward its tricentennial.

There you have it – a thumbnail sketch of the Archdiocese of Los Angeles.

The Old Country Priest and Archbishop Jose Gomez

Twelve Italian "Apostles" in California (1998)

Apart from several early prominent Jesuits who began their missionary work in Peninsular California in 1697, the association of those born in what became the Kingdom of Italy with the area now comprising the State of California appears to be almost synonymous with the earliest European penetration.

Indeed, those wishing to equate the term "Italian" with the occupants of the Roman papacy can trace that connection back to 1774, when Pope Clement XIV first authorized Fray Junípero Serra to administer the Sacrament of Confirmation along *El Camino Real*.

In very few regions of the United States have Italian activities been so important and successful as on the west coast. From the very earliest explorations up to the present time, Italians as individuals and as a group have consistently shared in the work and sacrifices which made possible the constant growth of the Pacific Coast.

The first Italian to anchor in California waters was probably Captain **Allesandro Malaspina**, who in the years 1786–1788 made a controversial scientific voyage around the world in the service of Spain. A valiant navigator of Florentine origin, Malaspina (1754–1809) is given recognition for having explored the Pacific Coast in great detail. His reflections were published in 1885.

Malaspina and his crew visited San Carlos Borromeo Mission where, his biographer states, "they took delight in learned conversation with these soldiers of Christ." Members of the expedition portrayed Fray Fermin Francisco de Lasuen as enthusiastic about their collections of natural history. The friar dispatched neophytes to assist in gathering botanical specimens, collecting Indian artifacts and garnering information on a variety of subjects of interest to the visitors.

Malaspina vigorously defended the mission system, arguing that certain foreign authors had confused the system with its abuses and ignored its primary objectives, thereby painting it as horrible and oppressive. He pointed out that the Spaniards, without the slightest shedding of blood, had brought an end to local tribal wars that were destroying the native Americans and had provided them with the beginnings of a sound social life. They had taught them a pure and holy religion, provided them with safe and healthful food and fostered in them such respect that the friars could traverse all. After returning to Spain, Malaspina fell victim to a sinister political conspiracy. He was tried, convicted and sent to jail in 1796, where he lived until 1802 when he was released and banished from the empire. Officially, Malaspina became a non-person and the fruits of his scientific labors were nearly lost completely.

Captain Allesandro Malaspina

Fray Francesco Antonio a Farnesio was an Italian who arrived at Monterey on the *Concepcion* en route from China via the Philippines, in the later part of December 1804. The fifty-eight-year old Farnesio had labored for a number of years as a missionary in the Far East until he was forced, for reasons of health, to seek a milder climate. From Monterey, Farnesio proceeded to Mission *La Purisima Concepcion* where he was cordially welcomed and given permission to offer Holy Mass and perform limited other ecclesial functions.

Farnesio liked California and shortly after his arrival at La Purisima, he wrote to Fray Estevan Tapis, the *Presidente* of the missions, for authorization to remain in the jurisdiction on a permanent basis. On January 7, 1805, Tapis replied that he would gladly grant him the customary facilities if the matter were his to decide. However, the *Presidente* pointed out that only those sent to California by "our Catholic Spanish King" could be approved for the priestly ministry. Nonetheless, Tapis obligingly forwarded the request to the Guardian of the Apostolic College of San Fernando, in Mexico City. The decision of the Viceroy, acting in the name of the King, was negative, and on June 10, 1805, he notified Tapis that Farnesio should continue on to Italy.

The Franciscan *Presidente* informed Farnesio of the ruling, noting that his earlier appointment from the Sacred Congregation of Propaganda Fide, as a missionary to China, could not be interpreted as a license to pursue the ministry in California. Shortly after receiving the *Presidente's* reply, Farnesio made arrangements to leave for Europe. He departed from San Diego, on the *Princesa*, November 6, 1805.

Angelo Noce (1847–1922), an Italian-American from California, was the man chiefly instrumental in having a national holiday set aside each year to honor Christopher Columbus. Columbus was not much acclaimed in Anglo America prior to the eighteenth century. Gradually, the whole tenor began changing and Columbus, after George Washington, became the republic's "most exalted hero."

His popularity was evidenced by the number of towns, schools and places named in his honor, including the national capital, which was designated the District of Columbia. Columbus had provided a way of escape from Old World tyranny. Mythology found the perfect hero from a distant past, someone seemingly free of any taint from association with the European colonial powers.

Born in Genoa, Angelo Noce had come to the United States with his parents in 1850. After a brief sojourn in the east, his family journeyed to California with others interested in the gold discoveries. In 1863, Angelo entered Saint Mary's College and later moved on to Santa Clara. Upon graduation, he found employment as a typesetter. He later recalled that he had "worked on the principal journals of the west, both as journeyman and foreman."

In 1876, Noce inaugurated his campaign to have a national holiday each year in recognition of his hero, Christopher Columbus. [The movement became popular because it was a secular substitute for the religious *feste* of Italy.] Columbus represented an ethnic hero and a welcome surrogate for the others who had served to unify their communities in the New World while, at the same time, being a figure commanding respect from all Americans. Noce's fellow Italians were especially supportive of his efforts because the Genoese explorer symbolized the harmony existing between the Italian and American cultures.

Though he died before the holiday became nationally sanctioned, Noce saw it adopted as a state observance in thirty-five of the country's commonwealths. Others share in the credit for that development but Angelo Noce retains his title in the annals as "the Father of Columbus Day."

Though hardly a prototype Catholic missionary, Father **Louis Rossi** (1817–1871) wrote an exceedingly colorful account of life along the west coast of America in the 1880s. Born Abramo De Rossi, the young native of Ferrara was a convert from Judaism at the age of twenty-one. It was then that he adopted the name Luigi Angelo Maria Rossi.

In January 1838, Rossi entered the Passionist Order at Paliano. Though later expelled for being "choleric and impetuous," Rossi eventually re-entered the Order at Monte Argentario. He made his final religious profession on October 29, 1839, and, after further theological studies, was ordained priest in April 1843.

Rossi spent his early sacerdotal years teaching rhetoric, philosophy and theology at various Passionist houses in the Italian province and, during his stay in Rome, he wrote a biography of Saint John of the Cross. In 1853, he was instrumental in establishing a Passionist foundation at Bordeaux, France.

Rossi came to the United States in 1856, and spent the following six years along the west coast. Those were times of expansion and excitement and Rossi was confronted with great loneliness and isolation in the relatively unpopulated vastness of Western Washington and Northern California.

Upon his return to Europe in 1863 Rossi worked at writing his memoir, which was published at Paris and Brussels in 1863 (as *Six ans en Amerique Californie et Oregon*). It is a remarkable book that offers interesting insights to what was occurring in a considerable area of the west coast. He knew San Francisco, for example, as a burgeoning, post-gold-rush city.

An Italian with a solid overlay of French influence and discernible anglophobic tendencies, his admiration for the then infant American system is refreshingly devoid of the patronizing attitudes often present in European visitors of the time.

Even in these days of inflated monetary values, there were relatively few millionaires. The statistical charts indicate that in the 1990s only a small percentage of people could be classified in that distinctive category.

California once had a millionaire priest. In addition to his financial holdings, Monsignor **Egisto Tozzi** (1882–1961) was among the more colorful of San Francisco's early clerics, and all the while he wore his fortune well. Egisto was baptized in the parish church of Civitella d'Angliano, a suburb of the Eternal City. He was fond of recalling that his pastor predicted on the day of his baptism that he would one day be a priest.

The Tozzi family had close ties to Rome's so-called "Black Nobility." The youthful Egisto was enrolled at Bagnoregio Seminario, Vescovia. Ordained for the Diocese of Bagnoregio on June 18, 1905, Father Tozzi spent the earliest years of his priestly life devising methods of uplifting the disadvantaged people of his poverty-ridden parish.

Shortly after his ordination, Father Tozzi was befriended by one of Italy's leading bankers, Amadeo P. Giannini. While still in his twenties, Tozzi was advised to invest his family inheritance in shares of Giannini's Bank of Italy. It was probably the best advice of his life. The investment proved a shrewd one and the habit of playing the stock market stayed with Father Tozzi over the next half century. In time, the Bank of Italy became the influential Bank of America and Father Tozzi's original investment multiplied many times.

Tozzi came to San Francisco in late 1908 and, from that time onward, served in many capacities for Archbishops Patrick W. Riordan, Edward J. Hanna and John J. Mitty. After serving as Pastor of Saint Peter's parish in Cloverdale, Tossi served in pastorates at Saint Anthony's (Manteca), Saint Paul's (San Pablo) and All Souls (south San Francisco). In all of those places, Tozzi was known for his charitable benefactions and his willingness to share his financial expertise.

He lived on until October 11, 1961, when he was killed in an automobile accident. When an inventory of his assets was filed in San Mateo county superior court, Redwood City, it showed that the priest had left an estate of $1,123,139. The inventory disclosed that Monsignor Tozzi owned shares of forty-four blue chip stocks.

Luigi Brusatori

Luigi Brusatori (1885–1942), one of California's most outstanding (though unknown) artists, was the tenth of the children born to Santino and Savina Brusatori. In 1902, at the age of seventeen, Luigi painted his first fresco in the church of San Marcario near Milano. From that day until his death, he never felt that his work was completed or successful until the local priest blessed it.

Luigi married Ida Castellana in 1908. Within three years their children were born. The youthful artist found himself with a growing family and little means by which to support it.

Brusatori's great dream was to build a home for his family, and it was that goal that led him to seek employment in the United States. For the next decade he worked hard in California to achieve his dream.

Brusatori's paintings are in a number of churches in the Bay Area. One of the best examples of his work is in Our Lady of Guadalupe Church located over the Broadway Tunnel in San Francisco. Virtually the entire church is covered with his paintings, including the ceiling. One observer said that "the faces of the angels were modeled after members of the children's choir."

After finishing that commission, Brusatori painted Saint Francis of Assisi Church on Vallejo Street. Although many of his works have since been painted over, two remain, one on either side of the altar. One scene depicts Francis receiving the stigmata, while the other portrays his death.

Luigi's fame spread rapidly as he was called on to paint not only churches, but other buildings as well. At one time, his works could be found in the Old Palace Cafe on Ellis Street, a theatre in Watsonville, a mausoleum in San Pablo, as well as Sacred Heart Church in Red Bluff and Saint John in Fresno. What may have been his greatest work was done in the Church of Santa Clara in Oxnard. Unfortunately, it was covered over after a fire damaged the church in 1972.

Because of their accuracy of detail, the paintings of **Hector (Ettore) Serbaroli** (1881–1951) are today regarded equally as "historical landmarks" and pieces of art. His legacy of religious masterpieces is of great importance to the Church in California. Born in Rome, Hector Serbaroli's early life fell under the tutorial influence of Allessandro Ceccarini, a painter known throughout Italy for his ecclesial embellishments.

Later Hector was apprenticed to the famous Cesare Maccari. It was that Sienese muralist who took Serbaroli to Loretto where he played an important role in completing the interior of that city's great basilica. After several extensive courses at the Academia di San Lucca in Rome, Hector left for Mexico City, where he was assured of work in several of the public buildings then under construction or being repaired. The subsequent political unrest in Mexico motivated Hector and his bride to emigrate to the United States. They resided for a while in El Paso and then moved on to San Rafael. There the artist found several lucrative commissions for the California Building at the Panama Pacific International Exposition.

Serbaroli's most celebrated painting there was the huge (4 × 20 feet) panorama of Mount Tamalpais and its upland meadows. That painting was later moved to the San Francisco Ferry Building and then to the Mill Valley Bank where it hung from 1928 to 1947.

In 1922, Serbaroli met William Randolph Hearst, who asked the artist to do restorative work on some ceiling murals recently imported from Europe. Serbaroli, his wife and their four children lived at San Simeon for several years while he worked at the castle.

Through the auspices of Adela Rogers St. John, Serbaroli moved to Hollywood, where he worked for some years designing sets at the First National Studios (now Warner Brothers). His paintings of Tyrone Power, Darryl Zanuck, Bette Davis and H.B. Warner, to mention but a few, are classical renditions of Hollywood's greatest personalities.

A decade later, Serbaroli determined to spend the rest of his life at his real love, religious art. His murals adorn Holy Family Church (South Pasadena), the Rosary Chapel of Immaculate Conception Church (Los Angeles), Saint Ignatius (Highland Park) and Saint Monica's (Santa Monica). There are many others too.

Hector (Ettore) Serbaroli

The ceilings, walls and dome of the recently refurbished Saint Joseph's Cathedral in San Jose are elaborately adorned with murals and paintings designed and executed by Father **Luigi Sciocchetti** (1878–1962).

Luigi was born in Ripastransome, Italy. His early education embraced his two great loves – the priesthood and the palette. He seems to have integrated these interests in a most admirable way. When Archbishop Edward J. Hanna met Father Sciocchetti in Assisi, in 1922, he urged the young priest to affiliate himself with the Archdiocese of San Francisco, which was then preparing to celebrate the golden jubilee of Saint Joseph's Church in San Jose. Nephews and nieces of the priest acted as models for the various figures in the murals. Guido Sciocchetti, his brother, was himself an artisan and he was charged with providing and erecting the scaffolding for the project.

Father Sciocchetti spent about five months in his San Francisco studios working on the drawings. The most difficult part of the designs was executing the original sketches, for they had to be drawn on paper, then divided into small squares and, finally, transferred to canvases. The canvases were painted in an empty school building in back of Saint Joseph's church. Once the murals were finished, the artist spent another five months gluing them to the walls, ceiling and domes.

Interior of St. Joseph's Church, Oakland, CA

Newspapers of the time carefully recorded the artistic program and packages of clippings from the *San Francisco Chronicle* explain in great detail how the work advanced over a three-year period. In the *Chronicle*'s rotogravure pictorial section for August 27, 1933, Father Sciocchetti is also featured and applauded for his work in the Salesian Church of Saint Joseph in Oakland.

Sciocchetti's mural of Don Bosco as a peasant shepherd is one of his finest works. His murals can still be viewed at Immaculate Conception and at Saint Paul of the Shipwreck. Father Sciocchetti remained active in a host of pastoral activities over the years he spent in the Bay Area. He was a confessor of wide renown and his Sunday homilies were noted for their simplicity and sincerity.

Although there are few raisin or table grapes produced in Southern California, over a hundred tons of wine grapes are grown annually in the western part of San Bernardino County. Today some of the finest quality wines in all of California, along with champagnes, vermouths and brandies, originate in that "oldest wine-producing district" in the state.

It was the recognition that viniculture dates from provincial times that prompted **Secondo Guasti** to erect a modest little church in the midst of his vast vineyards as a memorial to "the many and glorious missions of California." The scenic edifice, with its thick walls and enchanting bells, is located at the foot of the Cucamonga Mountains, forty-three miles east of Los Angeles, in the center of 5,000 vine-covered acres of the Italian Vineyard Company.

Secondo Guasti, for many years one of the leading viticulturists in the states, built the attractive little edifice in 1924. He personally supervised the smallest parts of its construction and furnishing, including such objects as the five wrought-iron chandeliers that hang from the big wooden beams of the ceiling.

Built originally to provide for the spiritual needs of the employees of "the world's largest vineyard," the white-washed adobe church retains all the simplicity associated with an earlier generation in California. In design, the church was patterned after the one in Guasti's native Italian village dedicated to his patron saint, the protector of the Piedmontese, San Secondo d'Asti. The largely circular stained-glass window above the white marble altar depicts San Secondo arrayed in a purple mantle. In his right hand he holds the reins of a horse, while grasping a picture of the city of Asti to his heart with his left hand.

The origin of our national anthem, "Star Spangled Banner," vociferously disputed in the 1930s, was a controversy that received wide coverage in the southland's secular press. The basic melody was used in a dozen or so countries. Adapted from "God Save the King," it was claimed by the Irish, Germans, English and others.

In Los Angeles, Father **Giuseppe Tonello**, a "valiant defender of the rights of Italy," told a reporter for the *Los Angeles Examiner* that "the tune is Italian and originated with Giambattista Lulli," a Florentine who was often thought to be a Frenchman. Tonello, an acknowledged authority, was regarded as "one of the leading figures in the American music world." He had written a number of compositions which were played by the Los Angeles Philharmonic Orchestra.

The newspaper account referred to the priest as a "scholar" whose investigations on the subject of "America" carry weight. While admitting that the names of Handel, Carey, Anson and others were associated with "America," Tonello insisted that the sole credit belonged to Lulli.

Tonello (1851–1933) was himself a colorful person. He was a member of the Order of Charity (Rosemenians). Ordained on September 8, 1878, he was later sent to the United States to establish a college in Illinois. Tonello subsequently served as pastor in Galesburg, an area that was then predominantly Italian. In 1912, Father Tonello came to Los Angeles for health reasons. For many years the Italian-born priest administered to Catholics at Our Lady of Lourdes parish in Tujunga.

A story in the *Los Angeles Examiner* for January 30, 1923, told how the gentle priest has been awarded a Knight Chaplaincy in the Sacred Military Order of St. George, one of the rarest and highest honors given by the Vatican. Described in a newspaper account at "an intimate friend of Caruso and known affectionately by Pope Pius X," Father Tonello wrote a number of musical compositions, including the popular ballad "Souvenirs of Italy."

In order to further document his contention that Giambattista Lulli was responsible for "America," Father Tonello provided a biographical sketch of the composer for the local press. He concluded his interview by saying that "plainly, historical facts prove that Lulli was an Italian and that he composed the original tune, "Grand Lieu Suave le Rot," which became "America."

When word reached Los Angeles that Father Tonello had died at Turin, the conductor of the Los Angeles Philharmonic Orchestra announced that Chopin's Funeral March would be played in Tonello's memory during the following week's performances.

Like the original band of "apostles," the band of twelve here enumerated had its black sheep. Surely one of the most colorful and memorable clerics ever to function in California's southland was Father **Alexander Bucci** (1875–1959), who bears the distinction of being the only priest in California's religious annals to have been publicly reprimanded in the pages of the local Catholic newspaper.

Ordained on May 14, 1899, for service in the Italian Diocese of Larino, Bucci came to the United States in 1905. He served briefly at Saint Patrick's Cathedral in New York City and then journeyed west to Salt Lake City. Coming to the Diocese of Monterey-Los Angeles in March 1906, he was assigned to serve the local Italian community at Saint Peter's Parish in downtown Los Angeles. He officiated there for the following twelve years. In 1918, Father Bucci was transferred to Cayucas. Later that year, he was appointed to Tres Pinos, a community in Central California. It was there that Bucci's enthusiasm began getting him into trouble.

A resourceful man, he raised funds for his poverty-stricken parish by installing a distillery in the sacristy of the church. Those were prohibition times and because of the eighteenth amendment, the illicit manufacturing of alcohol was a federal crime. Though permission was obtainable for the production and use of altar wine, Bucci's activities went considerably beyond acceptable practices. On several occasions, he was warned by Chancery officials.

In the summer of 1922, Bucci was formally arrested for violation of the Volstead Act. Officials agreed not to prosecute if the Bishop of Monterey-Los Angeles would administer an appropriate penalty. Since there was some question about Bucci's canonical status, Bishop John J. Cantwell told the priest to return to his native diocese. By then an American citizen, Bucci adamantly refused on the grounds that the bishop had no right to punish a priest for violation of a public law.

It was then that Cantwell suspended the priest and had the following notice placed in *The Tidings:* "It is officially announced that a certain priest, by name Alexander Bucci, for many months past and at the present time, has not and does not enjoy the faculties of the Diocese of Los Angeles-San Diego."

Bucci never acknowledged or abided by the canonical decree or the revocation of his faculties. He took up residence in Burbank, performing baptisms, marriages and funerals, often from a makeshift chapel in his sister's home. In December 1933, Father Bucci asked the bishop for reinstatement. "There's nothing to reinstate," he was told. "Return to your diocese in Italy!" A subsequent letter for the Apostolic Delegate reaffirmed Cantwell's stance.

It was then that Bucci "went public." He began performing funerals and weddings at Forest Lawn Cemetery, something that especially annoyed Cantwell who expressly forbade his priests to officiate there. Bucci went a step further. On at least one documented occasion, he celebrated Mass in the funeral parlor of Godeau and Martinoni.

In May 1935, Father Bucci gained national notoriety by offering Holy Mass in the "Wee Kirk o' the Heather" chapel at Forest Lawn for Trent Durkin, a popular teenage film star who had been killed in an auto crash. The *Los Angeles Examiner* featured a photograph of "Father A. Bucci, retired Catholic priest of Burbank" leading a procession of mourners to the grave. Cantwell was livid.

Then, two months later, Bucci once again hit the headlines when the *Los Angeles Times* reported that he officiated at Forest Lawn for the funeral of Leland Deveraigne, known in Chicago's underworld as "Two Gun Louis" (Alterie). "Two Gun Louis" was killed when enemies fired twelve shotgun slugs into his body after he allegedly turned government informant on a bond case. Another story in the *Examiner* said that "Bucci, now resigned from an active pastorate, was a friend of Alterie."

Father Bucci had some rather shady relatives too. He was a brother-in-law of Nicola Pietrantonio, who was assassinated in a raid by federal agents looking for alcohol. Reports of that incident stated that "the Pietrantonio home served also as a private chapel for Father Alexander Bucci."

Bucci continued his unorthodox ministry until his health began to fail. In his later years he lived quietly in Burbank with a younger sister. He remained on close terms with Msgr. Martin Cody Keating and was reconciled to the Church prior to his death. He was the first priest interred in the "new" San Fernando Mission Cemetery in 1959.

Surely **Luigi Providenza** (1894–1981) deserves a place all his own among the Italians who walked along California's *El Camino Real.* Luigi was born in the small and ancient city of Chiavari, by the waters of the Gulf of Genoa. After spending his childhood among his native people, Luigi began a career working in the shipyards. An ardent follower of Luigi Sturzo, he became secretary of the local Partito Popolare.

Anxious to be away from the violent political strife and hatreds of postwar Italy, Luigi and his wife, Augusta, came to the United States in 1921. He first worked for *L'Unione,* an Italian Catholic newspaper published in San Francisco.

As the tall, upright and impressive Providenza moved around the Golden State, he was appalled by the fact that a staggering percentage of the Italian Catholic immigrants had abandoned their faith commitment. After many months of intensive soul searching and prayer, Luigi developed the idea of a Catholic apostolate aimed specifically at peoples of Italian origin.

In 1924, he established the Italian Catholic Federation, a group whose sole purpose was that of bringing Italian-Americans back to the active practice of their faith. The first meeting of the ICF took place in San Francisco's Church of the Immaculate Conception. Luigi was fond of recalling that there were twelve "disciples" at that inaugural gathering.

Because so many influential Italians refused to cooperate with his work, Luigi realized that the ICF would need a strong yet flexible structure. At that juncture, he enlisted the talented Father **Albert Bandini** to draft the organizational format. At first, the work was arduous but Luigi was persistent. He was a charismatic orator and along with Father Bandini, he traveled over the state spreading the message and forming new branches.

Luigi somehow managed to squeeze his other activities into his busy schedule. He became business manager for the *Central California Register* in 1937 and during his decade with that newspaper the circulation increased by 250 percent.

After 1948, Luigi devoted his whole time to the Italian Catholic Federation. By the time of his demise, the Federation numbered 28,000 members in California, Indiana, Illinois, Nevada and Wisconsin. At the time of his death, on February 7, 1981, Bishop John S. Cummins said that "what Luigi gave to his people was identity and pride of heritage, and he did it in such a way that it was astonishingly successful. . . We are grateful for what his life was among us."

Presumptuous indeed would be the historian who contended that his selection of outstanding Italians is definitive or complete. Among the other outstanding Italian pioneers who visited, colonized or otherwise influenced California would be Leonardo Barbieri, Leonetto Cipriani, Federico Biesta, Juan Bonifacio, Paolo Emilio Botta, Domingo Ghiradelli, William Ralston, Fathers Anthony Maraschi and John Nobili, Andrea Sbarbaro, Gaetano Merola and Simon Rodia. On and on the list could go.

Most knowledgeable Californians would endorse the words of President Calvin Coolidge that "Italians have immensely contributed and are still contributing with their skill, with their love for liberty, with their genius for science, arts and humanitarian deeds, to make this country what she is today."

San Buenaventura Mission (2013)

(The Tidings, December 20, 2013)

The Golden State's poet laureate, John Steven McGroarty, once wrote that "the story of the conception, foundation, the rise and fall of the Franciscan missionary establishments in California is at once the most unique, colorful and romantic of stories in the annals of human history, and one of the most important."

The mission named for San Buenaventura was among the earliest frontier outposts envisioned for *El Camino Real.* It was to be located near the entrance of the Santa Barbara Channel, which Fray Junípero Serra felt was better suited than San Diego, Santa Barbara or Monterey "or any other place we have so far discovered."

Just nine days after the inauguration of San Carlos Borromeo, the Franciscan *Presidente* spoke hopefully about the foundation earmarked to be the "third mission in New California." For a host of reasons, however, another dozen years passed before Serra's dreams could be realized.

Finally, on Easter Sunday, March 31, 1782, the mission dedicated to *el Glorioso Obispo-Cardenal Serafico de Iglesia, San Buenaventura,* was formally begun, at a place initially designated *as Asuncion de Nuestra Señora* or *La Assumpta.*

It was a fortunate location, indeed, for at that time the Santa Barbara Channel was the most densely populated coastal area south of San Francisco. Serra had earlier observed that the countryside was "dotted with great numbers of well-organized *pueblos.*"

The relationship between the friars and the neophytes was regulated by a decree issued in 1773, from Viceroy Antonio Maria Bucareli, which directed that "the government control and education of the baptized Indians should belong exclusively to the missionaries." The Bucareli directive further stipulated that the supervision was to be carried out "in all economic affairs as would a father of a family regarding the care of his household, and the education and correction of his children."

Hence it came about from the earliest days of European presence at San Buenaventura that the Christianized Indians and those preparing to embrace the Catholic faith were totally subject to the friars in all spiritualities and temporalities. In the exercise of their administrative duties, the friars received whatever aid and protection was needed from the military garrison attached to Santa Barbara Presidio.

The main objective of the friars at San Buenaventura and elsewhere was always the salvation of souls through Christian indoctrination and practice. They realized that however time-consuming and onerous the economic aspect of the missions were, such burdens were an absolutely vital part of their overall apostolate.

The Spanish government was quick to understand that the best means for the Indians to receive both a Christian and Hispanic social, political and economic training was one which encompassed all aspects of daily living. Thus the friars became, in effect, both apostles of the Church and agents of the state. The Christianized Indians, for their part, became practical Christians and useful citizens of the commonwealth.

San Buenaventura Mission

The first Baptism at San Buenaventura was administered by Fray Pedro Benito Cambon on April 27, 1782, to Jose Crescensio, the infant son of Eugenio Valdez and Sebastiana Josefa Quintexa. Nine months later, the sacrament was conferred upon the first native of the region, Domingo Jose, a ten-year-old boy from the *Rancheria de Valesque*. By the end of 1785, there were 133 entries recorded in the Baptismal Register. On August 30, 1782, Fray Francisco Dumetz performed the first marriage, uniting Alejandro de la Cruz and Maria Concepcion Monteil. Thirty-six adobe buildings were built at the mission in 1804, and another twenty-nine the following year. Other crude structures were added soon after, including a tannery and granary.

George Vancouver visited the ninth and last of Fray Junípero Serra's missionary outposts in 1793. The English navigator was impressed with its well-mannered Indians, the orchards of apples, peaches, plums and pomegranates, its vineyards, vegetables and herds of cattle.

In a report for 1806, the resident friar at San Buenaventura reported that "our flock continues to grow steadily. A few years ago there were only slightly more than 700 neophytes at the Mission; but at the close of 1805 they numbered 1,141. At present," he said, "eighty-four others are also under instruction."

Except for a three-month period after the disastrous earthquake of 1812, when the friars moved the neophyte population to safer regions, San Buenaventura Mission has been in constant use since its foundation.

The mission attained the pinnacle of its development in 1816, when the neophyte population reached 1,328 souls. In the years following 1820, a decline set in which continued without abatement until the baneful blight of secularization totally ruined the once-flourishing establishment.

On May 31, 1819, a small band of Mojave Indians arrived at the mission, much to the bewilderment of the local natives. A scuffle ensued and trigger-happy soldiers shot and killed ten of the visitors. Two soldiers and one neophyte from San Buenaventura were also fatally injured.

In a report for 1822, Fray Jose Señan enumerated the material holdings of the mission and noted that wheat, barley, maize and kidney beans had been planted. He pointed out that those crops, together with the weekly slaughter of forty or more head of cattle, was sufficient to sustain the Indians and whites attached to the mission.

Prior to 1834, there were 3,924 baptisms, 1,107 marriages and 3,216 deaths recorded in the register books. At the height of its service, there were 1,297 Indians living in or attached to San Buenaventura. From 1812 to 1823, the *Presidente* of the California Missions, Fray Jose Señan, made his residence at San Buenaventura.

Eugene Duflot de Mofras, a youthful attaché at the French Embassy in Mexico City, visited San Buenaventura in 1842. He described the mission's location as "very beautiful," but noted that the buildings were in "a rather bad condition," some of them occupied by local *rancheros*.

The initial episcopal visitation occurred in April 1843, when the Right Reverend Francisco Garcia Diego y Moreno, Bishop of Both Californias, confirmed 182 persons at San Buenaventura. In November of that year, the mission became the southland's first canonically established parish, with the appointment of Father Jose Maria Rosales as resident pastor.

The original mission lands were leased for nine years to Narciso Botello and Jose Arnaz on December 1, 1845. Pio Pico compounded that injustice the following June 8th, by selling the property to Arnaz, a sale that was invalidated by President Abraham Lincoln on May 23, 1862.

The widely travelled artist, Henry Miller, visited San Buenaventura in 1856, and found it "to be a quiet village of about seventy or eighty houses, inhabited principally by natives and Mexicans." An earthquake did considerable damage the next year by destroying the original roof of the church and totally leveling a number of the remaining structures.

Though only its historic church remains at present, San Buenaventura Mission continues to occupy a unique role in the historical annals of Ventura County. It is a living testimony to a spirit of devotion and sacrifice which can be understood only within the context of that divine vocation which called the friars to leave home and kindred on behalf of the aboriginal peoples confided to their spiritual care.

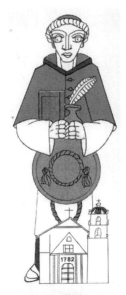

San Buenaventura

Memoir of a Papal Visit (2017)

If ever my diary or even parts of it are published, I suspect the most intriguing entry will be that made for September 16, 1987, the day Pope John Paul II dropped by for lunch.

At the outset, it should be pointed out that the Holy Father's presence at what *Time* magazine called "the lovely San Fernando Mission" was anything but a casual visit. A goodly portion of the preceding year was spent getting ready for what proved to be the most singular event in the almost two hundred year history of California's seventeenth missionary outpost.

And though one might fantasize that the Roman Pontiff came just to see "the best of the California missions" or "the finest of the nation's Catholic archives," the real reason was to meet with members of the National Conference of Catholic Bishops during Pope John Paul's second pastoral visit to the United States.

There were weekly and then daily briefings with members from the Papal Visit Office, the Secret Service, police and fire officials, traffic controllers, caterers, representatives from the United States Catholic Conference, media pools and other concerned agencies and individuals. San Fernando Mission became an integral part of the most elaborate and intensive preparations ever made for the visit of a foreign dignitary to the United States.

The already scheduled maintenance programs for the Old Mission were revised, updated and advanced in order to have the buildings, and grounds in top shape for the papal visit.

Las Damas Archivistas inaugurated plans for commemorating the event with appropriate splendor by commissioning the renowned artist, Isabel Piczek, to design and fabricate a giant tile portrayal of the Holy Father being welcomed to the Old Mission by Fray Junípero Serra. The ladies began raising the necessary funds by sponsoring bake sales, boutiques and other service-related projects. Theirs became the most visible and surely the most colorful of all the preparations and involved the largest number of people.

On the eve of the Holy Father's arrival, a gigantic "spit and shine" party was staged on the grounds. Forty-five volunteers brought brooms, rakes, dusters, clippers and bags to complete the final preparatory phase. Thousands of fallen leaves and flower buds were picked up, bagged and removed. By mid-afternoon, the five acres comprising San Fernando Mission resembled a giant Hollywood movie set, except that ours was real. We prayed long and hard for good weather, and the Lord answered our supplications favorably.

Pope John Paul II San Fernando Mission – East Garden Luncheon

A veritable army of Secret Service agents, police and fire personnel, Air Force bomb specialists, journalists, television crew and ecclesial officials began arriving at 2:00 a.m. on the targeted day of September 16th.

The entire area was "swept" by electronic sensors and then "snuffed out" by three specially trained canines. That the security net worked is confirmed by the fact that an "intruder" was indeed detected, discovered and placed in custody. The only mishap of the day occurred when an overly zealous policeman accidentally set fire to a dry area of the adjoining property. Happily, the local incendiary squad reacted promptly and successfully.

A contingency of *Las Damas Archivistas* was processed through the command post at 6:30 a.m. and they quickly set about to complete preparations for feeding the bishops. About an hour later, the first episcopal contingency arrived from the New Otani Hotel.

The seven other buses bringing the cardinals, archbishops and bishops from the LAX Hilton rolled in on schedule at 7:45 a.m. Each of the prelates was greeted and then escorted to a staging area, where a continental breakfast was served by the colorfully costumed ladies.

At 8:45, the 305 members of the hierarchy were ushered to the mission church. The simple house of worship, decorated tastefully but simply by yellow and white gladiolas and tuberose lilies, symbolized the roots of the Church along the Pacific Slope. Towering over the assembled prelates was the stately figure of *San Fernando, Rey de España,* the same statue that presided over the establishment of the mission in 1797.

Marine #1, the helicopter bringing the Holy Father from Saint Vibiana's Cathedral, arrived precisely at 9:05 a.m., landing on the field of Queen of Angels Seminary. Three additional khaki-colored helicopters transported the rest of the papal party.

After His Holiness had been officially welcomed to "Mission Hills International," he entered a limousine with Archbishop Roger Mahony for a short motorcade around the western perimeter of the seminary to the gate leading into the mission cemetery. During his short walk towards the Church, the Holy Father blessed the graves of the almost 1,200 Indians interred there between 1797 and 1840.

As he approached the church, the Holy Father glanced upward at the magnificent tile portrayal commemorating his visit. The smile that came across his face was likely inspired by the depiction of the little Sheltie doggie, smallPAXweber, which sits ever so quietly at the feet of Fray Junípero Serra.

Mural by Isabel and Edith Piczek
San Fernando Mission Church – North Wall

At the entrance to the church, the Holy Father was presented with an artistically embroidered stole. He blessed himself and his party with holy water and then entered the church where he was greeted by applause from the assemblage. *Lauds*, or Morning Prayer, was sung and recited by the Pontiff and the American hierarchy. In his homily, Pope John Paul II exhorted the bishops to "be examples to the flock," saying that "we shall be precisely that to the extent that our lives are centered on the person of Jesus Christ."

At the completion of *Lauds* Archbishop Mahony, acting on behalf of the local Catholic community, presented the Holy Father with a beautiful oil painting of the Old Mission, together with the historical concordance entrusted to Fray Junípero Serra by his Mallorcan confreres in 1749.

The Holy Father arrives for Lauds with the American Bishops

Afterwards, the Pontiff was led through the mission gardens to the seminary dining hall where he was officially welcomed by the cardinals, archbishops and bishops of the United States. In what *Time* magazine described as "an exceptionally cordial encounter," Pope John Paul II listened intently to several interventions by representatives of the episcopacy and then engaged in a dialogue that lasted well beyond the allotted time. Details of that meeting were divulged through official channels.

A moment in prayer

Following a short pause in the Old Mission's rectory, the Holy Father returned for a buffet luncheon in the garden area. About an hour later he rose, thanked the episcopal conference, and went back to the rectory for a brief rest. It was exactly 2:30 p.m. when "Marine # 1," lifted majestically into the sky.

Lunch with the American Bishops

As requested, the Holy Father left behind his signature in our guest book, on an autograph card and on a white zucchetto. In addition, he presented a chasuble and stole with a papal crest to the Historical Museum, together with a small box of rosaries and medals "for your dear friends."

It took several days for those of us here at San Fernando Mission to digest the happenings of those five and a half hours—to fully appreciate that Pope John Paul II had prayed in our church, lunched in our garden and rested in our quarters. Hereafter and forever, San Fernando will be the "papal mission," the first of those great frontier establishments along the Pacific Slope, visited by the Vicar of Christ.

Presentation of Gifts (2013)

On the day before the Pope John Paul II's arrival at San Fernando Mission, three sacerdotal "liturgists" on the staff of the National Conference of Catholic Bishops descended on the grounds for a last run-through of the ceremonies during which the Holy Father would recite Morning Prayers with the members of the American hierarchy.

The sanctuary furniture was rearranged again, as was the procedure of the services themselves. Elegant programs printed for the occasion were placed in the pews of the church.

Archbishop Roger Mahony had planned to present the Holy Father with two gifts on the occasion of his visit to Los Angeles, a *Concordance* to Holy Scripture used and signed by Fray Junípero Serra and a gorgeous painting of San Fernando Mission by the renowned artist Ben Abril. It had earlier been decided by the archbishop that the gifts would be given to the Holy Father at San Fernando Mission.

When I asked the liturgists at what time during the ceremonies the presentation would take place, Msgr. Alan Detscher became visibly agitated and growled that such a procedure was totally inappropriate. "The Holy Father is coming here for the sole purpose of meeting with the country's bishops and no such interruption will be tolerated."

That evening, I tried unsuccessfully to apprise the archbishop of what would be a major alteration in our plans. However, the more I thought about it, the less it bothered me. Liturgists tend to be imperialistic and insensitive to realities.

During the night, after putting the sanctuary furniture back in place (for the umpteenth time), I arranged an easel with the painting to one side of the sanctuary and veiled it with an artistic tapestry. The *Concordance* was placed in an unobtrusive end of the shrine of Our Lady.

Happily, when the liturgists arrived early the next morning, they totally overlooked the easel and the book. So excited were they that even the sanctuary furniture was left intact.

Everything proceeded on time. The Holy Father's helicopter arrived at precisely 9:05 a.m. He was driven around the north end of the seminary and approached the church through the mission cemetery.

The Old Country Priest and Pope John Paul II

My minimal role in the ceremonies involved handing the Holy Water to the Pope as he approached the side entrance of the church. Archbishop Mahony was walking at the side and a little behind the Pope. As the archbishop passed me, I slipped him a note, which read: "The painting and concordance are in place for the presentation."

Presentation of the Concordance

I had been instructed to remain at the entrance during the ceremonies and was unable to be anywhere near the archbishop. And, since he hadn't been informed that the presentation had been cancelled, he proceeded according to earlier plans.

I was able to see the agonizing expression on the face of Msgr. Detscher when the archbishop began the presentation. It was almost amusing and certainly satisfying to see how tastefully the archbishop integrated the presentation into the ceremonial.

After the Holy Father had departed for his meeting with the bishops, Detscher expressed his irritation by asking me, "Who does Mahony think he is?" I couldn't resist answering that "If there were an identity problem, it surely wasn't with the Archbishop of Los Angeles."

Walter O'Malley and the Blue Heaven (2014)

(Excerpted from The Friends of the Archival Center Newsletter, **#129,** *February 2014)*

In the annals of Southern California, Walter O'Malley easily ranks among the "founders" of modern-day Los Angeles.

Educated at the Universities of Pennsylvania, Columbia and Fordham, he studied law and went on to earn a doctorate of letters in his chosen field. On September 5, 1931, he married Katherine E. Hanson (1907–1979). Two years later, Therese O'Malley was born and, in 1937, Peter.

Walter's association with the Brooklyn Dodgers dates from his days as legal counsel for the team. These were the years that Jackie Robinson broke the color barrier in baseball.

From 1950 to 1979, O'Malley owned the Dodgers, and it was in that capacity he facilitated the movement of the team to Southern California. He was also influential in coordinating the relocation of the New York Giants to San Francisco.

O'Malley, tabbed the "Wizard of Baseball," brought fresh energy, unleashed rivalries, attracted new audiences and injected dynamics when baseball was losing followers to football. The bold move to Los Angeles startled the baseball world and brought the national pastime west. Southern California finally had its own major league team.

After coming west, the Dodgers played for several years in the Los Angeles Memorial Coliseum, made famous for its hosting of the 1932 Olympics. Chosen for their permanent home was Chavez Ravine, northeast of downtown Los Angeles, an area comprising a network of washes, gullies and gulches with lavish hills and twisting roads.

The artistic stadium, opened on April 10, 1962, was destined to become an essential fixture for Angelenos. Described as the "almost perfect Baseball Palace," the stadium seated 56,000 people with parking for 16,000 automobiles on a terraced lot adjacent to the stadium. An observer counted 3,400 trees adorning the 300-acre landscape.

Contractors moved more than eight million yards of earth to reshape the area. For the stadium itself, designers employed a multilevel theory, affording every seat in the column-free stadium a completely unobtrusive view of the symmetrical playing field.

One writer noted that time when "the patriarch Walter O'Malley began to build his own baseball field that it was an act of shrewd business sense, heightened by a genuine love for the game." When dedicated, Dodger Stadium became baseball's most popular and beautiful showplace.

When Kay O'Malley saw the Seal of the City of Los Angeles encircled with the Rosary, she suggested landscaping olive trees around the inner clockwise stadium road with ten smaller trees and one large tree spaced five times and planted as a living Rosary in honor of *Nuestra Señora de Los Angeles*, for whom Los Angeles was named.

Future historians will write the definitive story about the Dodgers in Los Angeles and therein Vince Scully, Tommy Lasorda, Walter Alston and a host of other baseball greats will share in the dream of Walter O'Malley.

Suffice it here to say that the Dodgers became an economic and artistic part of the warp and woof of the city. Another metropolis might have been embarrassed at having a team whose traditions, lore and personality seemed to belong to another town. Such wasn't the case in Los Angeles, a city full of people whose family traditions lay elsewhere. In a city already settled by new arrivals, the Dodgers fit right in with all the rest.

The spiritual highlight for the stadium occurred on September 16, 1987, when Pope John Paul II celebrated Holy Mass there. That grace-filled experience was described by one onlooker as the "pinnacle of the Holy Father's presence in the United States."

Walter O'Malley succumbed of congestive heart failure on August 9, 1979, at the Mayo Clinic. At the time of his burial at Holy Cross Cemetery in Los Angeles, one elderly lady was heard to say that "he was one of a kind too rarely found on old Planet Earth."

To Battle For The Truth (2015)

(Excerpt from *Catholic Directory Archdiocese of Los Angeles*, 2015)

On June 29, 1895, Patrick Croake trudged down Main Street from McElheney's Print Shop with a hefty mailbag on his back. He was on his way to the post office with 1,000 copies of *The Catholic Tidings* – Volume I, No. 1.

The issue date itself – on the Feast of Saints Peter and Paul, which celebrates the apostolic and persecuted founders of the Church – foreshadowed many of the challenges the newspaper would face.

Croake and his staff—retired sea captain James Connolly and type-setter Kate Murphy – were not the first to attempt a Catholic publication in Southern California.

Yet *The Tidings* became the longest continuously published Catholic newspaper on the West Coast of the United States.

The Tidings, which dropped "Catholic" from its masthead early on, defied the influence of the American Protective Association. Founders of the APA claimed their organization combated "attacks by the Catholic Church on the public schools and other American institutions." The APA also attempted to exclude Roman Catholics from positions in the government.

Anti-Catholicism was prevalent throughout the United States starting in the mid-nineteenth century due, in part, to the influx of immigrants.

Croake and the launching of the newspaper marked the beginning of the end for the APA in the Diocese of Monterey-Los Angeles.

From the beginning, *The Tidings* took a stance on contemporary issues, questioning wars and advocating for the rights of Native Americans, especially with respect to Indian schools and reservations.

Under Bishop Thomas J. Conaty, *The Tidings* became the official publication of the Diocese of Monterey-Los Angeles on Oct. 7, 1904. Bishop Conaty gave *The Tidings* its motto: "To battle for the truth."

The Tidings has had 20 different editors in 120 years, including seven priests (six monsignors and one bishop), 12 laymen and one laywoman – Alice Stevens, who served as editor from July 15, 1908 to October 15, 1913. Stevens, a convert, started *"El Rodeo,"* the newspaper's editorial column, which ran off and on for decades. She also helped establish the Catholic Press Association in 1911.

In the June 28, 1966 *"El Rodeo,"* Msgr. Patrick Roche wrote that he hoped *The Tidings* would be in "every Catholic home of the archdiocese." Msgr. Roche served as editor from 1957 to 1973.

"One of the basic functions of a Catholic newspaper, the popes tell us, is to act as a channel of communication which conveys, in their completeness and clarity, the messages of the Holy Father and the bishops of the nation to mankind," according to Msgr. Roche.

The years following Vatican Council II demonstrated the need for the paper, he wrote, to distinguish "fact from rumor and balance," genuine authority against the voice of transient opinion."

The Tidings chronicled the creation of the archdiocese in 1936 its Centennial in 1940 and the appointment of Archbishop J, Francis A. McIntyre to the College of Cardinals in 1953. The paper reported on the visit of St. John Paul II to Los Angeles in 1987 and Pope Francis' visit to the Holy Land in 2014. The paper has consistently chronicled the growth of Catholic parishes, schools, agencies and departments.

"Somewhere there are people, both lay and religious, who are living lives of quiet and heroic devotion," Msgr. Roche wrote in *"El Rodeo."* "They seek no chronicle to sing their praises, but the Catholic newspaper should strive to keep their presence warm among us."

In the 1950s, Catholic high school teachers used *The Tidings* for classroom projects. On June 29, 1955, the California State Legislature recognized *The Tidings* for "significant contributions made in the field of journalism which brings honor and credit to the State of California." By 1964, the paper had a circulation of 125,000 to serve the 1.5 million Catholics in the archdiocese.

Alphonse "Al" Antczak – son of Polish and Mexican immigrants – served as the fifteenth editor of *The Tidings* (1973–1989). He first started writing for the paper in 1947 after graduating from Loyola University.

Over the years, Antczak interviewed John Kennedy, President of the Philippines Ramon Magsaysay, King Hussein, Prime Minister Itzakh Rabin and Cardinal Karol Wojtyla.

"Pilgrims walking together today on the road to salvation should not walk as strangers," he wrote in his first editorial about the disciples on the road to Emmaus. "In the breaking of the Bread, all in the family of faith should recognize each other as *hermanos – brothers – que los somos* (we are brothers)."

Msgr. Francis J. Weber, a historian and longtime archivist for the archdiocese, also wrote "California's Catholic Heritage," a column that ran for more than thirty-two years. He served as interim editor from May 18 to August 24, 1990, and while in that post, he wrote:

"The Catholic press has an obligation to inform its readers about everything that touches upon the Church or its mission in the world.... But we do endeavor, to the best of our ability, to report such events within the context of their occurrence. This is all the more necessary because the secular press often exaggerates or otherwise distorts events that involve religious personages or policies."

The publication's mission began reaching Spanish-speaking readers with the inaugural issue of *The Tidings'* sister publication, *Vida Nueva*, on April 10, 1991. The award-winning publication is the largest circulated Catholic Spanish-language newspaper that faces similar challenges – both in terms of religious liberty as well as financial struggles.

Yet the mission articulated by Bishop Conaty and long-serving editors Msgr. Roche and Antczak remains the same: to chronicle the life of the Church in Los Angeles and "to battle for the truth." The Grand Old Lady of the Catholic Press is striving to meet the changing needs of the community it serves.

The final issue of the paper was published on June 24, 2016.

11
Obiter Dicta

T.A.N. (1907–1983)

On the Feast of Our Lady's Visitation, a memorial Mass was offered at San Fernando Mission for Thomas Atwill Neal (1907–1983), one of Southern California's most respected booksellers.

A graduate of Loyola University, Tom entered the trade in 1925 as an employee of C. C. Parker, the then acknowledged "Dean of American booksellers."

He later hung his shingle at the Hollywood Book Store and, finally, on Saint Valentine's Day in 1933, Tom joined the staff of Dawson's Book Shop, where he became a revered fixture for the next half century.

Probably no other person in the area's history appraised, priced or sold a greater quantity of books. The tiny, penciled code letters T.A.N. indicated that numerous volumes passed through his hands a half dozen times or more.

Thomas Atwill Neal was a rarity among booksellers – in that he read what he sold. Very few scholars (and surely no dealers!) in the south-land were better read in the classics. Tom was rightly regarded as a walking concordance.

He was a practitioner of the written word, too. One of Tom's most elusive books is the one he wrote about *Saint Vibiana's Los Angeles Cathedral 1876–1950* of which only fifty copies were printed by William Cheney.

A goodly number of the almost five hundred catalogues issued by Dawson's were compiled (and often illustrated) by T.A.N. Tom also authored six outstanding miniature books, including *Sixth & Figueroa,* his reflections of four decades among the bookstalls.

One day in the late 1930s, San Francisco's Archbishop Edward J. Hanna paid one of his visits to Dawson's. Always enamored by Tom's knowledge of books, the archbishop suggested that he write a column for *The Tidings*.

Not so long afterwards, Tom received a deadline schedule from the editor of the Catholic weekly. That marked the beginning of "Books and

Backgrounds," wherein Tom attempted "to showcase the facts about some of the forgotten classics."

An accomplished "pop artist" (those are his words), Tom frequently added his own illustrations to letters, bills of sale, paper sacks and broadsides. He was equally gifted as a versifier and his poetic observations found their way into a wide variety of publications.

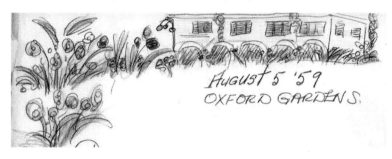

Just a few weeks before his death at Saint Vincent's Hospital, Tom's autobiography appeared as Volume XIV in the *Los Angeles Miscellany* series. Entitled *Farewell My Book*, it is a delightful portrayal of a well-spent lifetime in Los Angeles.

Tom noted how his appreciation for books had ripened into an intense letterpress love. He pointed out that "the effects of the miracle of Johann Gutenberg are still with us, and are as deep and clear as the impressions of his editions."

If so many of his patrons and friends loved Tom, it was because he lived what he preached, said what he felt and read what he sold.

Proud of his faith, he rarely missed daily Mass at Saint Basil's or other neighboring churches. If he was proud of anything, it was that he had a cousin who was a priest (Msgr. William Atwill).

The *liber vitae* or Book of Life for Tom is impressive. His routine was simple and plain, hardly the kind historians are accustomed to write about. And yet, there are likely few among his contemporaries who were not spiritually uplifted by their having known Thomas Atwill Neal.

A Visit to Yosemite (1914)

Of all the country's national parks, Yosemite is easily the most popular. Each year, visitors throng to the area in record numbers. The quantity of literature about Yosemite is extensive enough to fill two large bibliographies.

One of the early reflections about Yosemite was written by Roger Baudier, a teacher at Watsonville's Saint Francis Orphan Asylum, after his visit in 1914. It is here excerpted from a neatly written, four-page journal in the archives for the Archdiocese of New Orleans.

On July 7th, Baudier, a seminarian from Santa Barbara, and a forty-two-year-old Frenchman set out for their trek. An aging horse accompanied the trio that Baudier purchased in Santa Cruz and renamed Hannibal. The trip was a rugged, outdoor adventure for the two young men and their older companion. They traveled just over 500 miles in thirty-one days, mostly on foot. They camped out under mulberry trees, along rivers, and in abandoned houses.

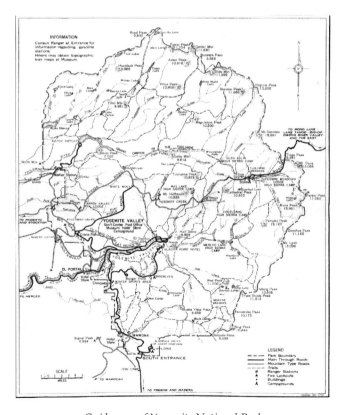

Guide map of Yosemite National Park

The travelers passed through several scattered small towns on the way to and from Yosemite. Merced was "a fine little town with tree-shaded, paved streets, a fine courthouse, park and busy business quarters" as well as a railroad depot.

Coulterville, on the other hand, was a "dying town" that had suffered three fires, which helped reduce the population from 3,000 to 250. San Felipe consisted of one barroom, one barn and two houses, while Los Banos was "a thriving, ambitious little center."

Baudier jotted down his impressions of the rugged scenery: the "dry, parched, brown hills" around Mountain House; the "miserable, flat, swampy country" at the San Joaquin River; the "fine mountain scenery" and abandoned gold mine on the approach to Coulterville; the "rough, steep, zigzagging trail" to the summit of Yosemite Falls; and the "splendid panorama" from Glacier Point.

He noted that the old road from Hazel Green to Bower's Cove was the same one that Indians and oxen had used in the 1850s. Handler's box camera captured some of the rugged beauty described in the journal.

The trio met a few travelers on the way to and from Yosemite; a hostile Dane at San Luis Ranch who "growled because our horse was hitched in front of his domicile," two strangers at Hazel Green who shared a pan of fried potatoes and Father Jerome Enright who preached a good "simple sermon" to the small tourist community at Yosemite Village.

The return trip from Yosemite to Watsonville was agonizing. The travelers came down with malaria and had to allow Hannibal to pull them in the rickety wagon. On July 31, Baudier wrote: "so tired and out of spirit that Edward Poetzl and I ate out of the same bowl to avoid washing dishes and work." They tried to avoid the intense heat by walking through the San Joaquin Valley at night.

When the exhausted pilgrims reached Los Banos the following day, they made a "bee-line" for the nearest saloon "and feebly asked for something to drink." The weary travelers finally marched into Watsonville on the afternoon of August 6th. Baudier and Castell both needed a doctor while Hannibal was so worn out that he had to be shot.

Each night during the trip, Baudier sat by candlelight and recorded the day's main events and his own impressions: the number
of miles traveled; impressions of towns, people and mountain scenery; personal weariness, discomfort and delight; and the newspaper
accounts of the ominous outbreak of war in Europe. He even noted
his dream of tarantulas after one "spooked" the trio by crossing their
outdoor table.

Saint Brendan Parish

(A Personal Memoir)

While young people fantasize about the future, their elders often take
comfort in recalling the past. One of my favorite memories reverberates
around the vibrant spiritual life in the Los Angeles parish of Saint Brendan and its indefatigable pastor, Father Thomas F. Fogarty (1902–1966),
in the 1940s. The Catholic density of that mid-Wilshire district exceeded

by far that of other parts of the city, mostly because Fogarty kept abreast of available houses to buy and apartments to rent. A remarkable percentage of the parishioners had come to this second smallest parish in the archdiocese of Los Angeles at his personal behest. Realtors and pastor worked hand-in-hand and, if there were a commission or finder's fee, Fogarty would enter it as the initial offering on the census cards he meticulously kept in three neatly organized wooden boxes in his tiny rectory office.

Fogarty, himself, could have walked out of a Charles Dickens' novel. Irish-born, he always claimed Chicago as his birthplace because he felt that people wanted a native-born clergy. He was a perpetual-motion machine whose turtleback Buick moved up and down the streets of Hancock Park with the regularity of the Wilshire bus. He knew every one of his people (and all the kids in the school) by their first names.

A workaholic, his masterfully prepared sermons anticipated many aspects of the post–Vatican II Church. Punctuality was one of his hallmarks and people could set their watches by the beginning of his services. He parceled out jobs to practically everyone on the parochial list and Saint Brendan parish had the politest ushers, the most enthusiastic greeters and the best-trained altar servers in the west.

RT. REV. MSGR. THOMAS F. FOGARTY
1903 – 1966

In those days, there were six crowded Masses on Sundays at 7, 8, 9, 10, 11 and 12 o'clock. People expected and received well-conducted liturgies, theologically sound homilies and professionally trained choral accompaniment. On Saturday afternoons and evenings there were long lines at all three confessionals. Evening services were scheduled on Sundays (Rosary), Mondays (Miraculous Medal novena), Wednesdays (Holy Hour) and Fridays (Sorrowful Mother novena) at 7:45 p.m. There were annual missions, solemn novenas and Stations of the Cross twice on the Fridays of Lent. Each of the services was concluded by Benediction of the Blessed Sacrament. Truly the parish offered a wide variety of experiences for every level of the spiritual spectrum.

Most all the parishioners belonged to one or another of such parochial organizations as the Altar and Rosary Society, the Third Order of Saint Francis and the Holy Name Society. Each of those groups had a monthly Mass and breakfast at which their respective banners were unfurled in their colorful splendor.

Father Fogarty was bigger than life in every way. An example would be the radio Mass broadcast on Sunday mornings at 10 o'clock to all parts of Southern California. The broadcast, the first of its kind in the west, was financed wholly by the parish and featured the talented commentaries of Pedro de Cordoba and the spirited musical renditions of Bob Mitchell and his internationally known Boy Choir. The unsolicited letters that flowed into the rectory from hundreds of shut-ins was motivation enough to keep the program on the air, even in times of financial distress.

The two full-time, able-bodied assistants (now called associate priests) attached to Saint Brendan parish spent the majority of their time teaching catechetics in the school, bringing Holy Communion to the ill and infirm, conducting Pre-Cana and convert classes and taking door-to-door census. The single car for both curates was used primarily for making pastoral calls to parishioners in neighboring hospitals. Dinner was a time for exchanging daily experiences, keeping one another updated on the spiritual and physical well-being of the parishioners and strategizing on expansionary plans for the future. The younger of the priests looked after training the altar servers who abounded in numbers and excelled in service. Annual investiture in the Knights of the Altar was a public event anxiously anticipated by the boys.

Interior of St. Brendan's Church

Living conditions in the two-story rectory at 311 South Wilton Place were cramped. There was no air conditioning, precious little heat and a plumbing service that barely worked. Three priests, an occasional clerical visitor, housekeeper, cook and secretary all lived in the ramshackle duplex, which dated from the early years of the century. The sextant lived in a tiny apartment behind the garage.

The school was the apple of the pastor's eye. His "kids" ran away with a host of sports trophies and literary awards. Conducted by eight Sisters of Charity of the Blessed Virgin Mary from Dubuque, the school's convent was small and inadequate, with two ends of the upstairs hallway cordoned off for bedrooms. The schoolhouse was antiquated, but neat and clean. A live-in custodial couple kept the classrooms and campus in good order. There was no food service for the 375 youngsters jammed into an area that had earlier served as both church and school for the parish. The nuns were outfitted in full-length habits and no one had ever seen one out of uniform. Often, their afternoons were occupied visiting the homes of sick children. Though funds were scarce, the nuns always managed to leave behind a piece of candy or a cute little toy. They walked two-by-two in those days before they were allowed to drive.

There was even a parochial choir school located on an adjacent parcel of land on Manhattan Place. A priest director came each day for classes in music and, for many years, the Saint Brendan Boy Choir provided chant for several of the Sunday Masses.

Saint Brendan parish was affectionately known as a "priest factory" and for good reason. Each September, the pastor and school principal began measuring up candidates for priesthood and sisterhood. Rarely did a graduation pass that didn't find Fogarty announcing that one or another youngster was entering the seminary or convent. Between 1938 and 1960, there were nine ordinations to the archdiocesan priesthood and six to the Jesuits.

When Fogarty was handed his appointment as pastor, the archbishop also entrusted him with an indebtedness of 1.2 million dollars, a phenomenal amount of money in those depression years. Yet, by the time of his demise, the debt was paid, the shell of the church had been completed and consecrated, the convent was renovated and later completely rebuilt, the schoolhouse was first modernized and then replaced and the rectory was relocated and built anew.

There are few today who remember the priest once referred to by the Los Angeles *Times* as a "three ring clerical circus." There's only one priest in the parish and a single nun in a school with 313 enrollees from a Catholic populace slightly exceeding that of fifty years earlier. There are five weekend Masses, one of them in Korean.

As to whether the post conciliar parish of Saint Brendan can or will rebound after sixty years is a question beyond the competence of this observer. Today the mix is eschewed, the rules have changed and the goals are different. But as long as the young can dream, maybe history will repeat itself. After all, anything is possible with God's grace.

The Old Country Priest Graduate of
St. Brendan's School

How to Find One's Roots (1995)

(While The Archival Center has only a limited collection of resources, people almost daily call or appear with requests for familial information. As an aid to such amateur researchers, I compiled a guide or "How to Find One's Roots" which was first published in *The Branding Iron* for the Los Angeles Corral of Westerners (#200 Summer, 1995). Because of its popularity, the article is here reproduced.)

Ever wonder about your ancestors – who they were, where they came from, what they were like or how they got here? In recent times, the study of genealogy has become almost a national pastime. Perhaps the following guidelines will be useful for those interested in pursuing their familial "roots."

It is wise, for practical purposes, to restrict the search to only one of the ancestral lines. Probably the one bearing the family name will be the most appealing.

First of all, search the attic, basement and other areas in the family homestead. Look for names, dates and places. Earlier generations often recorded such information in Bibles or prayer books.

Interview elderly relatives. Find out where they originated and when they moved to this country, state, or city. Carefully write down marriage and birth dates. Do not presume that memory will serve you infallibly.

Check out cemeteries. In previous times, families tended to prefer "cluster" graves. Very likely a dozen or so relatives would be buried in the same section. Their tombstones usually disclose dates and even birthplaces. Inscriptions are also useful. The character of a deceased person may be reflected in the epitaph. The simplicity or grandeur of the headstone can provide an insight into the decedent's character.

School and college records may also provide useful information. Fraternities keep membership rosters which are often helpful. School magazines and newspapers are invaluable sources.

 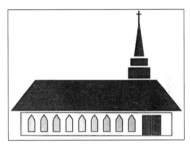

Churches are especially useful to genealogists because of their sacramental records. When writing, give name, approximate dates, along with your relationship. (These records are private and access is often restricted to relatives.) Always include a stamped, self-addressed envelope.

Libraries often have information in their local history department. One of the finest genealogical departments in the nation is housed in the Los Angeles Public Library, at Fifth and Grand. Neighborhood and county newspapers and advertisers often have "morgues" which are exceedingly useful to genealogists.

Do not overlook the National Archives (General; Services Administration, Washington, D.C., 20408). Records of every census since 1790 are filed there. They reveal the names of everyone in a given household, the year of their immigration, country of origin and occasionally religious background. The National Archives can also provide pension records and military information for those who served in the armed forces prior to 1917.

The names of immigrants who arrived in the United States after 1820 are often listed in the passenger arrival lists of ships (Form GSA-711 available from the National Archives, is an official request for passenger lists).

The Immigration Office is another excellent source for naturalized citizens. Further information about an ancestor's country can be obtained from writing that nation's embassy in Washington, D.C. Often they will give addresses of foreign record offices. The world's largest collection of genealogical data is on file in the central library of the Mormon Church, in Salt Lake City. They have there the names and data on people who immigrated to America (1538–1885) from over forty countries.

For a minimal charge, the United States Government Printing Office (write to The Superintendent of Documents, Washington, D.C., 20402) will send booklets on how best to locate certificates of birth, marriage, divorce or death.

There are professional genealogists who research these materials for a modest fee, but for a satisfying, stimulating experience, try on your own. The rewards of a successful search are worth the effort.

War On Books

Those who share my utter frustration that so many libraries have trashed their card files will surely want to read a new book by Nicholas Baker that further describes what is happening in some of the world's major libraries.

The book in question, *Double Fold: Libraries and the Assault on Paper,* is published by Random House. This 288-page tome has been aptly described as a "brilliant, bitter, fabulously knowledgeable expose" of what is going on behind the scenes in much of our modern-day library system. It tells about those institutions that for the past decades have been microfilming books and newspapers and then trashing the originals. The author knows that aspect of this story. Some years ago, he mortgaged himself into penury to purchase and rescue 6,400 bound volumes of American newspapers about to be jettisoned by the British Library.

Over the years, word had gone out that libraries would have to double their shelf space every sixteen years (which he denies); that books were crumbling into dust (which they weren't) and that microfilm would save endangered materials (which it doesn't). As a matter of fact, microfilm is expensive, unreliable and perishable.

The title for his book refers to the practice whereby any book with pages whose edges break off when folded back and forth (three or four times) is classified as "brittle" and in need of replacement. At that juncture, the book is "guillotined," with its binding chopped off so that it can be laid flat, photographed and then pulped.

Some of my friends who are librarians might secretly agree with Baker's observations. He quotes the director at the Library of Congress as saying that when he learned about his institution's war on books, he was utterly "shocked."

The author has four modest suggestions:

1) Publicly funded libraries should have to publish lists of what they discard;

2) The Library of Congress should warehouse (in call-number order) everything it doesn't want or can't retain on site;

3) Libraries in the United States should keep all current newspapers in bound form; and

4) The National Endowment for Humanities should fund only non-destructive microfilming and digital scanning.

A Gold Chalice

Most priests ordained in the 1950s would say that their most valu-able, cherished and sentimental possession is the chalice used each day at Holy Mass. It's the one thing that never perishes or changes over the years.

My own chalice was made by the Gorham Jewelry Company of New York. It was initially owned by Father James Collins (1852–1926) and could have been acquired by him as early as 1887. It later came into the possession of Msgr. Thomas F. Fogarty (1903–1966), longtime pastor of Saint Brendan's Parish in the Wilshire district of Los Angeles. He used it daily from 1927, until he was given a new one by the Santa Fe Studios of New Mexico. When Msgr. Fogarty said I could have anything in his possession as a gift for my ordination, I had the gall to ask for his chalice. Happily he acquiesced.

Peter L. Lesch (1901–1981), a local chalice maker, engraved an elaborate ring around the cup, along with Msgr. Fogarty's name on the base. To this day, it, along with my dog, are the only possessions I wouldn't want to do without on my earthly sojourn.

But there was a time when the chalice almost slipped away and it's a story that is interesting to recount, although, at the time, it caused me a great deal of anxiety.

In 1979, the chalice needed plating. I called Mr. Lesch and he came by the Old Mission at San Buenaventura to fetch it. When no phone calls or letters came telling me it was ready, I dropped by his house in Studio City.

When he opened the front door, I immediately sensed that something was wrong. Then in the early stages of Alzheimer's disease, Mr. Lesch had no recollection of the chalice, nor could the two of us find it in his backyard workshop.

After further prodding, he recalled that on the day he had picked it up, he had been involved in an automobile crash. His car had been totaled and towed away to the junk yard, with the chalice locked in the trunk. There was a different car in the driveway, so the story made some sense. A neighbor lady corroborated the fact of the accident.

A few days later, I recounted the story to a friend who had also left things with Mr. Lesch for plating. That evening, he went for a visit and found that his items were also missing.

My friend, a physician, easily identified Lesch's behavioral pattern. Figuring that he might have hidden the materials in a "safe" place, he went to his sleeping quarters, looked under the bed and found my disassembled chalice along with some of his own items.

He called me and suggested that I retrieve the chalice at the earliest opportunity. It was several days before that became feasible and, when I did appear at the front door of 4028 Alcove Avenue, there was a replay of our earlier encounter, accident and all. With utmost discretion, I asked if I could look under his bed.

By this time, however, there was no chalice there — only several pairs of old shoes and lots of dust balls. Nor was the chalice beneath any other of the beds in the house. I recall feeling very silly crawling around on his floors.

Then I remembered that my dear mother always hid her "cold cash" and other valuables in the freezing compartment of the refrigerator. So I ventured into the kitchen, opened the upper door of his antiquated icebox and, there, behind the frozen cauliflower, were the three parts of my beloved chalice. Unhappily and to my chagrin, the paten was never located.

I put the chalice into its box, which was located behind the fourth row of his bookcase and, in a gesture of gratitude to Saint Anthony, took the poor old man to dinner at the Tick Tock Restaurant in nearby Toluca Lake.

No one who looks at my chalice could ever imagine the fascinating six-month scenario that almost spelled the earthly demise of the historic cup. When Mr. Lesch died on January 20, 1981, I attended his funeral and prayed that he and his memory would be reunited in heaven.

Worst Books Ever Written

The Archival Center at Mission Hills is a facility that endeavors to make available to scholars of the American West all the extant evidence, irrespective of its quality. While discerning readers can generously make their own decisions about the worth of this or that volume, this writer has singled out a number of titles which would surely fall into last place in any serious competition:

1. Perhaps it was a *"felix culpa"* when fire ravaged A. L. Bancroft & Company in 1886, thus destroying most of the copies of Father William Gleeson's *History of the Catholic Church in California* (1871–1872). Today, that two-volume set, reproducing lectures given at Saint Mary's College, is more coveted for its scarcity than for its

contents. Unhappily, the work's inaccuracies and generalities detract considerably from its usefulness. The Center also has Gleeson's two volumes on *The Trials of the Church* (1880) and his book on *The Common School Question* (1883).

2. Joseph Sadoc Alemany deserved a better biography than he got when John B. McGloin's treatise on *California's First Archbishop* hit the bookstalls in 1996. Because of the careless and imprecise scholarship, this book could be effectively used to exemplify all the major pitfalls of historiography. Practically unmentioned are the Pious Fund and Vatican Council I, both of which events occupied a major portion of Alemany's time.

3. Father Andrew Greeley's "sociological interpretation of the American Church" was published in 1967 by Doubleday & Company under the title *The Catholic Experience.* The author's limited familiarity with historical sources led him to conclusions that further reading may have tempered or altered altogether, and his tendency to generalize made many of his observations indefensible. One reviewer suggested that Greeley "stick to sociology and novels, fields in which he excels."

4. Edith B. Waterhouse's book on Serra, *California's Conquistador,* published at Los Angeles in 1968 by Parker & Son, purports to be a "narrative history" written for children. Actually the entire book, often told in the manufactured words of Juan Evangelista, is a fanciful account which a reviewer for the *Los Angeles Times* said must "have been written while lying in a worn-out sleeping bag on the north bank of the Ventura River."

5. To paraphrase Saint Paul, "certain books would better be left unwritten," or at least unpublished. A primary example would be Merlin J. Guilfoyle's book, *The Little O,* which was released by William House of Stockton in 1972. This sixth book by the one-time Auxiliary Bishop of San Francisco contains thirty-three chapters of poetry, candid wit, and erudite impressions that earlier appeared in the prelate's weekly column for *The Monitor.*

6. In Stephen Birmingham's scurrilous book, *California Rich* (New York, 1980), is a jacket blurb admitting that the author "has made a specialty of combining history and anecdote." The most offensive chapters are 13 and 14, wherein the author makes a pitiful attempt to retry the complicated legal suits against Edward L. Doheny and Albert B. Fall, a narrative which reads like an excerpt from a sensational tabloid. *Sic caveat lector!* This cleverly written, attractively bound volume has no place alongside the creditable tomes on the subject.

7. Rupert and Jeanette Gosto are American Indians and founders of the American Indian Historical Society. In 1981, they published their 233-page diatribe on *The Missions of California: A Legacy of Genocide.*

In this collection of essays, oral accounts and other related materials, the authors violate historical methodology by equating folklore with fact, legend with truth, and oral history with evidential history.

8. If one were looking for a book that breaches practically every historical canon, a prime candidate would be Mike Davis' *City of Quartz* (New York, 1990). The author has compiled a history of Los Angeles as he would have liked it to have unfolded, not as it did. His factual inaccuracies and judgmental statements fade into insignificance when measured against the invented or fantasized scenarios, many of which have little, if any, relationship to reality.

9. There is little to recommend in *California Catholicism*, the first volume in The Religious Contours of California series, which was published by the Fithian Press of Santa Barbara in 1993. In addition to suffering from an exorbitant number of factual errors, the text is riddled with imaginary happenings, all of which prove the old dictum that "bad history is worse than no history."

10. Finally, in 1995, Robert H. Jackson and Edward Castillo co-authored a book on the *Indians, Franciscans, and Spanish Colonization and the Impact of the Mission System on California Indians*. Published by the University of New Mexico Press, this volume shows how evidence can be abused, misused and distorted. It is a classic example of "pyramiding," whereby the writers make dubious, misleading and otherwise unsubstantiated statements, and then later quote themselves – a fairly common occurrence in this book.

Incidentally, there need not be any direct relationship between the quality of a book and its success in book stores. Years ago, Father Joseph Brusher wrote a book on the *Popes Through the Ages*, which was panned unmercifully by the reviewers. When asked whether he was upset by the negative reaction, Brusher said that it only ran through his mind once each month when he went to the bank with his handsome royalty check.

12

My Last Hurrah

Several times over the past few years, people have asked me "Where would you like to travel if you had the opportunity?" The answer was easy: "To Eternal Rome, my favorite place in the whole world."

Well, the opportunity came in April when Andrew Walther conveyed the invitation by Carl Anderson, the Supreme Knight of the Knights of Columbus, to attend and speak at a seminar in Rome on Fray Junípero Serra. Even though the cobblestones there are not "user friendly" to the elderly, I happily agreed to go. It would be my last great "hurrah." I spent several feverish weeks preparing an essay on "Serra the Evangelizer," which would be part of a presentation to the world's media gathering on April 30th.

The long journey began with my departure from San Fernando Mission via US Airways on a trip that would cover a total of 35,995 miles. The giant plane achieved an average speed of 538 mph at an altitude of thirty-four thousand feet. "This old priest was truly flying high." We journeyed from Los Angeles to Philadelphia and then changed to an American Airlines "Airbus Bus" for the remainder of the flight to Europe. It was early morning when we arrived at the Voi Cicerone Hotel in downtown Rome.

The next morning, those scheduled to speak on the opening day of the seminar graciously accompanied the Old Country Priest to Saint Peter's Basilica to celebrate the 56th anniversary of my priestly ordination. While in the basilica I pointed out that the only stained-glass window there, atop the "chair," was fabricated by the firm who made the windows in the crypt of the Cathedral of Our Lady of the Angels.

Our seminar began at one o'clock on the afternoon of April 30th at the Augustinianum, adjacent to Saint Peter's Square. Present were representatives from all the major television and radio outlets, most of whom also interviewed the speakers personally either before or following the actual addresses. The printed program read as follows:

Panel of California Scholars to Discuss
Junípero Serra's Life and Legacy

Msgr. Francis J. Weber, Ph.D. is the author of more than 100 titles, many focused on aspects of California's Catholic history. His books include *The Life and Times of Junípero Serra, The Missions of California,* and the *Encyclopedia of California's Catholic Heritage (1769 to 1999).* He served for five decades as Archivist of the Archdiocese of Los Angeles. Msgr. Weber has also taught history at Queen of Angels Seminary in Los Angeles and served as president of the Association of Catholic Diocesan Archivists. He studied Church History under the legendary John Tracy Ellis at The Catholic University of America.

The Old Country Priest, Rose Marie Bebbe and Robert Senkewicz

Ruben Mendoza, Ph.D. is a Professor in the Archaeology Program, Division of Social, Behavioral and Global Studies at California State University, Monterey Bay, at which he was a founding faculty member. Professor Mendoza has directed major archaeological investigations and conservation projects at missions San Juan Bautista, San Carlos Borromeo de Carmelo, and Nuestra Señora de la Soledad, among others, and at the Royal Presidio of Monterey which recently resulted in the tandem discovery of the earliest Serra era Christian houses of worship in California dated to 1770 and 1772. His recent publications include the *California Missions Source Book* (with David McLaughlin), and his research interests and previous publications include works devoted to the ethics of anthropological research in American Indian communities, and on Native American art, culture, and technology in North and Latin America.

Robert Senkewicz, Ph.D. is a Professor of History at Santa Clara University in California. He is co-author of the just released 500+ page biography *Junípero Serra: California, Indians, and the Transformation of a Missionary* (University of Oklahoma Press, 2015). Prof. Senkewicz earned his Ph.D. at Stanford University, and has written extensively on Serra as well as on California history, including the Spanish, Mexican and Gold Rush periods.

Rose Marie Beebe, Ph.D. is a Professor of Spanish Literature at Santa Clara University. She earned her Ph.D. at Stanford University and is co-author, with Prof. Senkewicz, of the new biography of Junípero Serra. She is also the translator of Serra's letters and homilies, and her research interests include California during the Spanish and Mexican periods.

It was agreed that my address would lead off the discussion. Here is a *verbatim* copy of the presentation:

Serra – the Evangelizer

Among the evidence used by contemporary people for properly understanding and evaluating Fray Junípero Serra for canonization, none is more important than defining his role as an evangelizer.

When Our Lord bestowed His commission on the apostles and their successors, He thereby authorized them to assume a dual role of teacher and dispenser of the sacraments in that order. Every priest is, by ordination, both a catechist and conveyer of the Sacraments. This double role has been synonymous with the Church's function since apostolic times.

Those in the position of deciding whether Fray Junípero Serra is worthy of canonization spent seventy-two years sifting through the historical and verbal evidence bearing upon the evangelical practices of the Mallorcan-born follower of Saint Francis.

That they determined in his favor is further proof of what the people of his and later times have concluded over the years since Serra's death in 1784.

Even though five nations concluded that Serra was worthy of a postage stamp, a distinction and honor as rare as canonization, we emphasize here his role as evangelizer – mainly because that role tells onlookers what our candidate did in his priestly role – and that's vitally important because conferral of the sacraments provide the ordinary means used by Christians as they pass through this life en route to heaven.

Fray Junípero Serra began his teaching career in 1740. Fortunately one of his students kept a carefully written transcript of Serra's lectures which is still extant. It numbers no fewer than 868 pages. He was named to the chair of Scotistic Theology at the Lellulian University in Palma de Mallorca.

Not alone the holder of the prestigious chair of Scotistic theology, Serra was active as a preacher in the local cathedral and neighboring churches on the isle of Mallorca. Late in 1748, after much prayer and deliberation, the friar wrote to the Commissary General for the Indies asking permission to become a missionary in the New World.

The panel

That letter, referred to by one writer as the *"magna carta* of Serra's apostolate," reveals the friar at life's crossroads, a man who in strength of character, assisted by grace, made the irrevocable decision to leave aging parents, beloved homeland, associations of youth, cloister and community, books and university and possible future renown for a spiritual motive based on the Gospel.

By reflecting on the message of that letter, one can portray the Junípero of the future. Historians like to read other people's mail. Often letters can explain much of how a person thinks.

For example, Serra wrote to the parish priest at Petra, asking him to tell his parents about the "great joy" that filled his heart at becoming a missionary. Knowing that, "surely they would always encourage me to go forward and never to turn back, let them remember that the office of an apostolic preacher, especially in its actual exercise, is the greatest calling to which they could wish me to be chosen.

"Since they are advanced in years, let them recall that life is uncertain and, in fact, may be very brief.... Since this is true, it will be very much to the point and most conformable to the holy will of God if they will not emphasize the very little help that I could give them with regard to the needs of this life. Rather they should strive to merit from God, our Lord, that if we see each other no more in this life, we may be joined forever in future glory.

"Let them rejoice that they have a son who is a priest, though an unworthy one and a sinner, who daily in the holy sacrifice of the Mass prays for them with all the fervor of his soul and on many days applies the Mass for them alone, so that the Lord may aid them.... If I, by the grace of God, succeed in becoming a good religious, my prayers will become more efficacious, and they in consequence will be the gainers."

For Serra, *El Camino Real* began at Vera Cruz in the New World, a trail that would eventually culminate in Alta California. At Tepeyac, Serra visited the Shrine of Our Lady of Guadalupe where he entrusted what was left of his earthly sojourn to the Blessed Mother.

After a rewarding apostolate in the *Sierra Gorda* region of Mexico, during which time he translated the body of Church doctrine and a number of traditional prayers into Pame, he became reasonably proficient in teaching and preaching in the local dialects – winning over many to a more advanced form of life. Always he was practicing and teaching, preaching and dispensing the sacraments.

Serra was especially adept at motivating the Indians to worship God by providing for them the splendor of the liturgy. He saw to it that the major feasts were solemnized with ceremonies and devotions. Christmas was celebrated in the Franciscan fashion by a mystery play similar to those of his native Petra, enacted by the native American children themselves. And so on throughout the various liturgical seasons.

With this flock, Serra realized that visual expression of religion in dramatic form was of prime importance. If such expression was of significance in Mallorca after nearly a thousand years of Christianity, it

Fray Junípero Serra

was still more important in the *Sierra Gorda* where the faith was only taking root.

What Serra did in *Sierra Gorda* he did in an even grander scale in the years after 1769 when he arrived in Alta California as the *Presidente* of the missions, nine of which were established during his tenure.

Everywhere Fray Junípero Serra was the evangelizer *par excellence*. With his handful of Franciscan brethren, the exemplary role of evangelizer – teaching, motivating and baptizing the native Californians was a primary objective.

Others will relate the details of Serra's years in Alta California. Here we are concerned chiefly with the *President's* role as an evangelizer. Like Our Lord Himself, Serra generally used the effective device of parables in his preaching. Parables are basically stories and the most effective preachers are storytellers. We know no greater example than Our Lord Himself. Indeed Fray Junípero Serra recognized and utilized the story telling device to perfection.

Sanctity is obviously a necessary requirement for anyone being proposed for sainthood. In the case of Fray Junípero Serra, one is impressed by the almost universal testimony of those who knew and worked alongside the friar.

The notion of Serra's sanctity is not a modern one. Shortly after his death, for example, his superior at San Fernando College, in Mexico City, wrote to the Franciscan provincial of Mallorca.

> We have just received the sad news of the death of our beloved countryman, Fray Junípero Serra. He died a saint's death, and under such extraordinary circumstances, that all those present were highly edified. They all hold the firm conviction that his soul went joyfully to meet its account, and that it was carried across Purgatory without any scorching of its flames, straight to heaven.

He went on to observe that "all say he was a saint, and that his actions have always been those of an apostle. This is the opinion held by all, since he arrived in this kingdom of New Spain, and has continued without interruption and grown stronger up to his much lamented, irreparable death."

When Serra died, the Mission Indians adorned "the body of their deceased Venerable Padre," as they mourned the loss of their "*Padre Santo*."

After hearing of Serra's demise, Fray Pablo Mugartegui wrote from San Juan Capistrano that "in these past four months we have baptized more than in the past three years. We attribute these conversions to the intercession of our Venerable Fray Junípero, who is asking this from God, just as he ceaselessly asked it during life; and we piously believe that he is enjoying God, and that with greater fervor he will ask that favor from the Lord."

Serra's fame for sanctity endured too. On October 2, 1851, Father Jose Villarasa, one of California's pioneer Dominicans, wrote to friends, noting that "I am the chaplain for the convent in Monterey, and for the church of Carmel." The latter "was founded by Fray Junípero Serra a Franciscan of Mallorca, who died in the odor of sanctity."

Over a century ago, Fray Junípero Serra's death was commemorated at Carmel. Archbishop Joseph Sadoc Alemany and Bishop Eugene O'Connell attended. Father Joachim Adam, Vicar General for the Diocese of Monterey-Los Angeles concluded the homily with the hope that

Serra would soon be canonized and placed on the Church's calendar as St. Junípero.

More than 150 years after Serra's death, the late Maynard Geiger conducted a series of oral interviews in the 1940s with the descendants of Mission Indians who had known Serra. Even then, several generations after Serra's death, they still referred to him as "*el santo*," – the saint.

Charles Chapman, an outstanding California historian of an earlier era, said that Serra's "legendary fame attracted Californians to the story of the past.... The real Serra was indeed a remarkable man. Already at an advanced age when he came to Alta California, he nevertheless possessed the traits which were most needed in a pioneer.

"He was an enthusiastic, battling, almost quarrelsome, fearless, keen-witted, fervidly devout, unselfish, single-minded missionary. He subordinated everything, and himself most of all, to the demands of his evangelical task." Withal, his administration as Father President was so sound and his grasp of the needs of the province so clear that he was able to exercise a greater authority than ordinarily would have been permitted.

Though he fought with local governors, he won the confidence of Bucareli, who preferred his judgment to that of Fages or Rivera. Thus he was able in a measure to attain his ends, in the face of gubernatorial opposition, and so too must be given credit for much that was done because it was at his advice that many projects were undertaken.

Christ tells us that the greatest commandment is to love the Lord with all one's heart, soul and mind, and to love one's neighbor as one's self. Before He ascended into heaven He also instructed his Disciples to "go and make disciples of all nations, baptizing them in the name of the Father and of the Son and of the Holy Spirit."

Serra devoted his life to obeying these commandments to the fullest. Filled with an all-encompassing love for God, he gave up his beloved homeland and family for a life devoted to loving those neighbors farthest away from him, so that they could come to know God too.

Sanctity, in the end, is not a question of being a good administrator or of being a good builder of enterprises – although Serra was both of these. It is how well one responded to the call to love by loving God and loving man to the fullest capacity. Serra did this in a way that went far beyond the average person. He traveled to the periphery of the world to share this love of God with the Native Americans, whom he also deeply loved.

This devotion to God and neighbor is Serra's most lasting witness. That is the reason why we celebrate him today as a saint.

Following the actual presentation there were questions for the panel members about various aspects of Fray Junípero Serra's life and legacy. A concluding luncheon was staged and afterwards several of us set out to visit various historical attractions of Eternal Rome.

May 1st, the Feast of Saint Joseph the Worker, a holiday in Rome, is modeled on our own Labor Day. I was invited to dine with Archbishop Jose Gomez at the Milia Hotel. Carl Anderson and Andrew Walther of the Knights of Columbus joined us.

The second session of the seminar was scheduled at 8:30 a.m. for May 2nd at the Pontifical North American College. The program was as follows.

Chair: Card. Marc Ouellet
President of the Pontifical Commission for Latin America.

08:30
Msgr. James Checchio,
Rector of the Pontifical North American College.
Welcome and introduction, in anticipation of the Holy Father's upcoming apostolic visit to the United States.

08:45
R.P. Vincenzo Criscuolo, OFM Cap.,
General Relator of the Congregation for the Causes of Saints.
Bibliographical Notes on Junípero Serra:
The Path to Holiness

09:30
Most Rev. José H. Gómez,
Archbishop of Los Angeles.
The Religious Origins of America

10:30 Break

10:45
Prof. Guzman Carriquiry,
Secretary in charge of the Vice-Presidency of the Pontifical Commission for Latin America.
The Canonization of Fray Junípero Serra in Light of
"Ecclesia in America"

11:45
Carl Anderson,
Supreme Knight of the Knights of Columbus.
Our Lady of Guadalupe, Mother and Guide of
Fray Junípero Serra, Patron of America

12:15
**HOLY MASS,
OFFICIATED BY THE HOLY FATHER,
POPE FRANCIS.**

13:15
Lunch at the Pontifical North American College

The various presentations were succinct and precise, with the possible exception of Fray Vincenzio Criscuolo, Postulator General for the Cause of Saints, who spoke for forty minutes in Italian.

Especially interesting and relevant were the comments of Archbishop Jose Gomez of Los Angeles and Grand Knight Carl Anderson, both of whom discussed Fray Junípero Serra's devotion to Our Lady of Guadalupe. Their remarks are available in the published accounts of the seminar.

The high point of the day was the arrival of His Holiness, Pope Francis, who came to celebrate Holy Mass for the panel members and students of the Pontifical North American College. His homily is here presented in full:

"I have set you to be a light for the Gentiles, that you may bring salvation to the ends of the earth." These words of the Lord, in the passage from the Acts of the Apostles heard show us the missionary nature of the Church, sent by Jesus to go out and proclaim the Gospel.

The disciples experienced this from the first moment when, after the persecution broke out, they left Jerusalem (cf. Acts 8: 1-3). This was true also for the many missionaries who brought the Gospel to the New World and, at the same time, defended the *indigenous peoples* against abuses by the *colonizers*. Among these missionaries was Friar Junípero; his work of evangelization reminds us of the first "12 Franciscan apostles" who were pioneers of the Christian faith in Mexico. He ushered in a new springtime of evangelization in those immense territories, extending from Florida to California, which, in the previous two hundred years, had been reached by missionaries from Spain. This was long before the pilgrims of the Mayflower reached the North Atlantic coast.

There are three key aspects to the life and example of Fray Junípero: his missionary zeal, His Marian devotion and his witness of holiness. First of all, he was a tireless missionary. What made Friar Junípero leave his home and country, his family, university chair and Franciscan community in Mallorca to go to the ends of the earth? Certainly, it was the desire to proclaim the Gospel *ad gentes,* that heartfelt impulse which seeks to share with those farthest away the gift of encountering Christ: a gift that he had first received and experienced in all its truth and beauty. Like Paul and Barnabas, like the disciples in Antioch and in all of Judea, he was filled with joy and the Holy Spirit in spreading the word of the Lord. Such zeal excites us, it challenges us! These missionary disciples who have encountered Jesus, the Son of God, who have come to know him through his merciful Father, moved by the grace of the Holy Spirit, went out to all the geographical, social and existential peripheries, to bear witness to charity. They challenge us! Sometimes we stop and thoughtfully examine their strengths and, above all, their weaknesses and their shortcomings.

But I wonder if today we are able to respond with the same generosity and courage to the call of God, who invites us to leave everything in order to worship Him, to follow Him, to rediscover Him in the face of the poor, to proclaim Him to those who have not known Christ and, therefore, have not experienced the embrace of His mercy. Fray Junípero's witness calls upon us to get involved, personally, in the mission to the whole continent, which finds its roots in *Evangelii Gaudium.*

Secondly, Fray Junípero entrusted his missionary activity to the Blessed Virgin Mary. We know that before leaving for California, he wanted to consecrate his life to Our Lady of Guadalupe and to ask her for the grace to open the hearts of the colonizers and indigenous peoples, for the mission he was about to begin. In this prayer we can still see this humble friar kneeling in front of the "Mother of the true God," who brought her Son to the New World. The image of Our Lady of Guadalupe was and has been present in the nine missions that Fray Junípero founded along the coast of California. Since then, Our Lady of Guadalupe has become, in fact, the Patroness of the whole American continent. You cannot separate her from the hearts of the American people. She represents our shared roots in this land. Indeed, today's mission to the continent is entrusted to her, the first, holy missionary disciple, a constant presence and companion, our source of comfort and hope. For she always hears and protects her American children.

Thirdly, brothers and sisters, let us contemplate the witness of holiness given by Fray Junípero. He was one of the founding fathers of the United States, a saintly example of the Church's universality and special patron of the Hispanic people of the country. In this way may all Americans rediscover their own dignity, and unite themselves ever more closely to Christ and his Church.

With the universal communion of saints and, in particular, with the assembly of American saints, may Fray Junípero Serra accompany us and intercede for us, along with the many other holy men and women who have distinguished themselves through their various charisms:

- contemplatives like Rose of Lima, Mariana of Quito and Teresita de los Andes;
- pastors who bear the scent of Christ and of his sheep, such as Toribio de Mogrovejo, Francois de Laval, and Rafael Guizar Valencia;
- humble workers in the vineyard of the Lord, like Juan Diego and Kateri Tekakwitha;
- servants of the suffering and the marginalized, like Peter Claver, Martin de Porres, Damian of Molokai, Alberto Hurtado and Rose Philippine Duchesne;

- founders of communities consecrated to the service of God and of the poorest, like Frances Cabrini, Elizabeth Ann Seton and Katharine Drexel;
- tireless missionaries, such as Friar Francisco Solano, Jose de Anchieta, Alonso de Barzana, Maria Antonia de Paz y Figueroa and Jose Gabriel del Rosario Brochero;
- martyrs like Roque Gonzalez, Miguel Pro and Oscar Arnulfo Romero;
- and so many other saints and martyrs, whom I do not mention here, but who pray before the Lord for their brothers and sisters who are still pilgrims in those lands.

May a powerful gust of holiness sweep through all the Americas during the coming Extraordinary Jubilee of Mercy! Confident in Jesus' promise, which we heard today in the Gospel, we ask God for this special outpouring of the Holy Spirit.

We ask the Risen Jesus, Lord of all ages, that the life of our American continent may be rooted ever more deeply in the Gospel it has received; that Christ may be ever more present in the lives of the individuals, families, peoples and nations, for the greater glory of God. We pray too that this glory may be manifested in the culture of life, brotherhood, solidarity, peace and justice, with a preferential and concrete love for the poor, through the witness of Christians of various confessions and communities, together with believers of other religious traditions, and people of upright conscience and good will. Lord Jesus, we are merely your missionary disciples, your humble co-workers so that your Kingdom may come!

With this heartfelt prayer, I ask Our Lady of Guadalupe, Fray Junípero and all the American saints to lead me and guide me during my approaching apostolic journeys to South America and North America. I ask all of you to keep this intention in your prayers, and to continue to pray for me. Amen.

With the conclusion of the Holy Father's Mass, our seminar was completed. What a glorious event for the holy man we have all loved and emulated over the years since he walked, prayed and evangelized on old Planet Earth.

13

Several years ago, I was asked to write my own obituary, a chore which everyone should be required to do.

OBITUARY
MSGR. FRANCIS J. WEBER

WEBER, Msgr. Francis J. Weber, Director of San Fernando Mission, longtime Archivist for the Archdiocese of Los Angeles (since 1962), author, historian, bibliographer, editor, columnist, professor and former pastor, fell asleep in the Lord on _____.

Born at 7:40 a.m. on January 22, 1933, in the Methodist Hospital, Indianapolis, Indiana, the son of Frank J. and Katherine Emaliene (Thompson) Weber; established residence in mid-town Los Angeles (1945) as a member of Saint Brendan's Parish (1945–1959).

Graduated from Los Angeles College (1953), Saint John's College (1955) and Saint John's Seminary in Camarillo (1959); ordained Priest by James Francis Cardinal McIntyre at Saint Vibiana Cathedral (April 30, 1959); appointed Curate of Saint Victor's Church in West Hollywood and Associate Director for the Legion of Decency.

Graduate studies in Ecclesial History at The Catholic University of America under Msgr. John Tracy Ellis (1961–1962) and in Archivology at the American University in Washington, D.C. (Certificated 1962).

Served as Professor of History at Queen of Angels' Seminary (1962–1972), visiting Professor of Western Americana studies at Immaculate Heart College (1963–1965), Mount Saint Mary's College (1966–1973) and the University of Southern California (1971).

St. John's Seminary – Camarillo, CA

Chaplain at Saint Catherine's Military School (1972–1975), Administrator and later Pastor at San Buenaventura Mission (1975–1981), Director of San Fernando Mission (1981 onwards) and Chaplain for Santa Cruz and the northernmost of the Channel Islands (1976 onwards).

Member of the Board of Consultors (1970–1975) and Priests' Senate (1978–1979) for the Archdiocese of Los Angeles; Director of the Borromeo Guild (1984–1987), member of the Ecumenical Commission (1975–1989), the San Buenaventura Mission Council 2498, Knights of Columbus (1980), the Awards Committee for the Archdiocese of Los Angeles (1989–1994) and the Advisory Board for the Cathedral of Our Lady of Angels (1995 onward).

Named Chaplain to His Holiness by Pope Paul VI (1974) and Prelate of Honor by Pope John Paul II (1988); hosted the Holy Father at San Fernando Mission in September 1987.

Member of the Board of Directors of Trustees for the Historical Society of Southern California (mid–1960s), the Santa Barbara Mission Archives (1979–1983), the Association of Catholic Diocesan Archivists (1989–1992), the Advisory Board of the Santa Cruz Island Foundation (1987–2000), *The Tidings* (1986–1995), Rosedale Cemetery (1990–1994), the California Missions Foundation (2000 onwards) and the Board of Directors, Santa Cruz Island Foundation (2000 onwards).

Served on the California History Planning Committee (1970); named member of Advisory Board, American Bibliographical Society (1973–1981); named editorial consultant, California Historical Society (1980); served on the Executive Council of the American Catholic Historical Association (1980–1982); acted as editorial consultant for the *Western State Jewish History* (1979 onwards) and *California History* (1980–1983); and member of the Historical Review Commission, Diocese of Monterey (1996).

Acted as consultant for the Chancery Archives, Archdiocese of Port-of-Spain, Trinidad and Tobago (1970), the Archdiocese of Denver (1979), the Archdiocese of New York (1980), the Archdiocese of Saint Louis (1998) and several other jurisdictions. Supervised the movement of the Chancery Archives, Archdiocese of San Francisco, to Colma (1977–1978).

Catalogued and rehabilitated two historically significant libraries, the *Biblioteca Montereyensis-Angelorum Dioceseos* (1967–1969) and the *Biblioteca Sancti Francisci Archdioceseos* (1968).

Member of the Los Angeles Corral of Westerners (1968 onward), the Book Club of California (1969 onward), the Board of Editors for the *Records of the American Catholic Historical Society* (1976–1986), the *Microbibliophile* (1987–1995) and the Fellowship of Catholic Scholars (1996).

Elected to the Executive Council of the American Catholic Historical Association (1979–1981); member of the Advisory Board, American Bibliographical Society (1973–1981); Founding Member and later President (1985–1986) of the Miniature Book Society of America; longtime member of the Zamorano Club (since 1969) and its President (1991–1993); and Consultant, Center for the Study of the Miniature Book (1990–1995).

Served as Secretary for the Serra Bicentennial Commission (1982–1984); Editor of *Hoja Volante* (1984–1995); Editorial Consultant for *Apostol y Civilizador* (1985 onwards); Founder of the Archconfraternity of Blessed Junípero Serra (1988); Charter Member of the Academy of Certified Archivists (1989) and Editor of *The Tidings* (1990). Vice President and President of the Association of Catholic Diocesan Archivists (1993–1997), Sheriff of the Los Angeles Corral of Westerners (1995), Second Vice-President of the American Catholic Historical Association (1996–1999) and Editor of the Miniature Book Society Quarterly (1995–1997).

The Zamorano Club

Certificate of Appreciation

presented to

Msgr. Francis J. Weber

for sponsoring the publication of
Essays by an Old Country Priest: Monsignor Francis J. Weber
2016

President

Recipient of commendations from *El Pueblo de Los Angeles State Historic Park* (1970), the Los Angeles County Board of Supervisors (1972) and the Los Angeles City Council (1981); received Awards of Merit from the California Historical Society (1972 and 1983) and the Rounce and Coffin Club for books on western themes (1960), (1971-2 awards), (1975), (1977), (1979-2 awards), (1980), (1984), (1985-2 awards), (1986), (1988), (1992-2 awards), (1993-2 awards), (1994-2 awards), (1995-2 awards), (1996), and (1997), and (1999); named a "Fellow" of the California Historical Society (1991); named a "Fellow" of the Historical Society of Southern California (1992); cited by the Zamorano Club "for his many services" (1993); commended by the Los Angeles County Board of Supervisors for "dedicated service to the affairs of the community" (1992); named a Recipient of the Grand Cross of *Isabel la Catolica* by King Juan Carlos (bestowed on Columbus Day, 1993); inducted to the Knighthood of The Holy Sepulchre (1994), the Military and Hospitaller Order of Saint Lazarus of Jerusalem (1998) and presented with the Archivist Award of Excellence by The California Heritage Preservation Commission (California State Archives Foundation 1995); named a Distinguished Benefactor of the Huntington Library (1995); advanced to the rank of Knight Commander, Equestrian Order of The Holy Sepulchre of Jerusalem (1997) and cited for Outstanding Achievement in the field of Historic Preservation by the California Preservation Foundation (1998); honored with an historic Preservation Award of Excellence by the Mayor and the Los Angeles Cultural Heritage Commission (1999) and given the Oscar Lewis Award for Outstanding Contributions in the Field of Western History (2000). Entrusted with publication grants from the American Association for State and Local History, the Dan Murphy Foundation, the Thomas and Dorothy Leavey Foundation, the Carrie Estelle Doheny Foundation, the Sourisseau Academy at San Jose State College, the Fred and Mary Meier Foundation, the Haynes Foundation, the California Catholic Conference, the Ernest Chagnon Estate, the Cardinal McIntyre Fund for Charity and the William and Virginia Hayden Foundation. Established the Francis J. Weber Research Fellowship in Roman Catholic History at the Huntington Library.

Supervised the exhumation and removal of the Right Reverend Francis Mora (1962), the Right Reverend Thaddeus Amat, C.M. (1962), the Most Reverend Joseph Sadoc Alemany, O.P. (1965), the Right Reverend Richard Pius Miles, O.P. (1969), the Right Reverend Eugene O'Connell (1982) and the Right Reverend Ramon Mestres (1984).

Author, editor and compiler of 286 volumes, 137 miniature books and scores of essays, articles and book reviews for encyclopedias, learned and popular academic journals; listed in *Who's Who for Religious* (1975), *International Author's* and *Writer's Who's Who* (1978) and the *American Catholic Who's Who* (1976); and a weekly columnist for *The Tidings* (1963–1995). Three of his books were selected by the Division for the Blind and Physically Handicapped of the Library of Congress for distribution in Braille.

Described by a writer in *Arizona and the West* (1971) as "one of the best known narrators of California history" and "Dean of California Catholic Historians" by Kevin Starr, State Librarian for California (1996).

Survived by a sister, Mary Alice Castagna of Monterey, California.

In Remembrance of

Msgr. Francis J. Weber

+

Born - Indianapolis, Indiana
January 22, 1933

Ordained Priest-Archdiocese of Los Angeles
April 30, 1959

Graduate Studies Catholic University of America
1961-1962

Professor - Queen of Angels Seminary
1962-1972

Certified as Archivist - American University
1962

Attended - Opening Session of Vatican Council II
1962

Archivist - Archdiocese of Los Angeles
1962-2011

Columnist for The Tidings
1963-1995

Pastor - San Buenaventura Mission
1975-1981

Member - later President
The Zamorano Club
1969 onwards

Member - later Sheriff
Los Angeles Corral of Westerners
1969 onwards

Chaplain - California's Northern Channel Islands
1976 onwards

Director - San Fernando, Rey de España, Mission
1981-2011

Director - Borromeo Guild Bookshop
1984-1987

Founding Member - later President of
American Catholic Diocesan Archivists
1982

Charter Member
Academy of Certified Archivists
1989

Awarded Grand Cross of Isabela la Catolica
King Juan Carlos I
1993

Honorary Doctorate of Humane Letters
Azusa Pacific University
2010

Funeral Homily

My longtime friend, Father Donald McNeil, C.M, was a fellow professor at Queen of Angels Seminary. Don spent several evenings a week attending Rosaries recited for his number of friends, and, by the time of his own demise, there were hardly any friends left – he had buried most of them.

The following homily will be available in case there's no one left to eulogize this Old Country Priest.

Dear Friends,

Inasmuch as most of my closest priest friends have preceded me to eternal life, I thought it might be appropriate to say a few last words myself. I am not sure whether my faculties in the archdiocese apply, for this procedure, but maybe no one will notice that nicety.

William Shakespeare classified ingratitude as the "black sin," for he claimed that it proceeded from a loveless heart, one best characterized by the color "black." Gratitude, the theme of these remarks, can be looked upon in three ways: as a vaccine, an antitoxin and an antiseptic.

It is a *vaccine* insofar as it protects against breeches of faith, hope and charity; it is an *antitoxin* inasmuch as it counteracts temptations against poverty, chastity and obedience; and it is an *antiseptic* that destroys the poisoning effects of sin and human weakness.

The ultimate test of a person's character, in my humble opinion, is the amount and evidence of one's gratitude.

Should a person not be grateful to God for the ability to see, rather than complain about the sun being too bright? Should one not thank God for the faculty to hear, rather than fuss about a sound being too loud? And so on.

This whole notion is plainly spelled out in Sacred Scripture. The first canticles which the Gospel presents are cries of gratitude – the *Benedictus*, the *Magnificat* and the *Nunc Dimittis*.

Therein we bless God for all His benefits, for His creation, His providence and, above all, for the mission of His Son.

So, may I go on record as being grateful to Almighty God for my very existence, my loving parents and sister; this great nation in which I have worked out my salvation; for my friends, benefactors and family who have supported me in my life and ministry; for my vocation to the priesthood; for my parishioners at San Buenaventura and San Fernando Missions; for three cardinals I have served; for my priest confreres; for my collaborators in academia and the book world; and for all who have prayed or otherwise assisted me along California's *El Camino Real*.

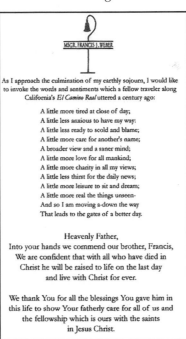

MSGR. FRANCIS J. WEBER

As I approach the culmination of my earthly sojourn, I would like to invoke the words and sentiments which a fellow traveler along California's *El Camino Real* uttered a century ago:

A little more tired at close of day;
A little less anxious to have my way;
A little less ready to scold and blame;
A little more care for another's name;
A broader view and a saner mind;
A little more love for all mankind;
A little more charity in all my views;
A little less thirst for the daily news;
A little more leisure to sit and dream;
A little more real the things unseen-
And so I am moving a-down the way
That leads to the gates of a better day.

Heavenly Father,
Into your hands we commend our brother, Francis,
We are confident that with all who have died in
Christ he will be raised to life on the last day
and live with Christ for ever.

We thank You for all the blessings You gave him in
this life to show Your fatherly care for all of us and
the fellowship which is ours with the saints
in Jesus Christ.

Saint Thomas was patient with every kind of human weakness except ingratitude. He once felt obliged to point out that it "is sinful to withhold the proper signs of appreciation."

So, in conclusion, may this grateful Old Country Priest quote a man I have long respected for his preaching ability, the late Rev. Robert Schuler, of the Crystal Cathedral, who frequently reminded his friends that "God loves you and so do I."

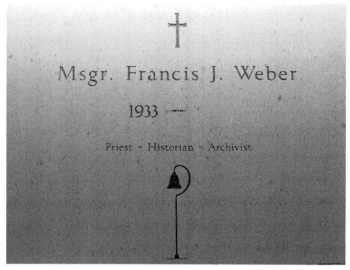

Crypt inscription at the Cathedral of Our Lady of the Angels

The Old Country Priest with one of his eight successive shelties.

Appendix I

Chronological List of Books Written, Edited, Translated, Compiled and/or Published by Msgr. Francis J. Weber, 2001–2018

156. (2001) Books, Books, Books

157. (2001) A Remarkable Legacy

158. (2003) A Tradition of Outreach

159. (2003) A Legacy of Healing

160. (2003) *Santa Margarita de Cortina Asistencia*

161. (2003) *Requiescant in Pace*

162. (2004) Unity in Diversity

163. (2004) Cathedral of Our Lady of the Angels

164. (2005) The California Missions

165. (2005) *Las Misiones de California*

166. (2006) A History of the Archdiocese of Los Angeles

167. (2006) *Una Historia de la Arquidiocesis de Los Angeles y sus jurisdicciones Presursoras en el sur de California*

168. (2007) Catholic Heroes in Southern California

169. (2007) *San Fernando, Rey de España Mission*

170. (2008) Blessed Fray Junípero Serra

171. (2009) History of the Newman Club of Los Angeles

172. (2011) More Memories of An Old Country Priest

173. (2013) Some Memories of the Catholic Hierarchy

174. (2013) Characters from the Gospels

175. (2014) Heroes and Heroines

176. (2016) Moments In Time at San Fernando Mission

177. (2016) Essays by An Old Country Priest

178. (2016) Sunday and Feastday Homilies

179. (2017) The Life and Times of Saint Junípero Serra

180. (2018) Final Memories of An Old Country Priest

181. (2018) Faith in the Southland

182. (2018) *Fe en la Tierra del Sur*

Appendix II

Retirement Schedule

Everyone needs a rigid daily schedule that finds and/or allows time for touching all the bases. Otherwise little is accomplished. Here is the one that I have utilized in recent years. There are 1440 minutes in every day and that is more than adequate time for accomplishing what is really necessary, even in old age.

2:30–3:00 a.m. – Arise, shower and shave

3:00–4:00 a.m. Plan for day – correspondence

4:00–5:30 a.m. – Breviary, Holy Hour and Rosary

5:30–6:15 a.m. – Write

6:15–8:00 a.m. – Prayers and Mass

8:00–10:30 a.m. – Archival Center

10:30–12:00 p.m. – Lunch – Newspaper

12:00–1:30 p.m. – Archival Center

1:30–2:00 p.m. – Errands

(market, pharmacy, barbershop, etc.)

2:00–2:45 p.m. – Feed and walk the dog

2:45–3:00 p.m. – Compline

3:00–4:00 p.m. – TV news – Bret Baier

4:00–5:15 p.m. – Holy Hour and Rosary

5: 15–6:30 pm – Sunday Homily – revise/expand

6:30–7:30 p.m. – Write

8:00 p.m. – Retire

Appendix III

A Living Legend

Living Legend #60
Monsignor Francis J. Weber

Los Angeles Corral of Westerners Living Legend Nomination

Monsignor Francis J. Weber

Monsignor Francis J. Weber is one of the most active of all members of the Los Angeles Corral of Westerners. He was first persuaded to come to corral roundups by the archaeologist and historian Mark Raymond Harrington in 1962, the same year he became the Archivist for the Catholic Archdiocese of Los Angeles. Weber became a member of the Los Angeles Corral in 1969, and presented his first invited lecture to it in 1970. His most recent of more than a dozen presentations came forty-six years later, in 2016. Monsignor Weber threw open the gates of San Fernando Mission to the Corral in 1973, for that year's annual *Fandango*. He has contributed more than a dozen articles to the *Branding Iron*, the Los Angeles Corral Quarterly, and was the editor of the *Los Angeles Corral Brand Book No. 21* (1999), an amazing collection of no fewer than 73 contributions by members, friends, and other local historians. Weber served as the Los Angeles Corral Sheriff in 1995, and his leadership is remembered fondly by all members, especially its female ones, for finally making the corral co-ed.

Francis J. Weber was educated at the Catholic University of America and is the recipient of the only Honorary Doctorate ever granted to a priest by Azusa Pacific University. He has taught at many different ecclesiastical and secular institutions, including Immaculate Heart College, Mount St. Mary's College, and the University of Southern California. Monsignor Weber has always been devoted to local history, and has encouraged many others, Westerners and non-Westerners alike, to take the plunge and get involved in research, writing, and publication. Foremost amongst such success stories is that of fellow Los Angeles Corral members Ken and Carol Pauley, who, after twenty-five years of research, published their magnificent historical volume (2005) on the California Mission most closely associated with Msgr. Weber: *San Fernando, Rey de España*. Weber, if not the only member of Westerners International to also be a priest, is certainly the only monsignor.

Father Weber has for more than half a century effortlessly navigated through both sacred and secular waters, offering guidance, leadership, and good fellowship to his diverse flocks, be they fellow historians or parishioners. Monsignor Weber is known to his many friends and admirers as "the Old Country Priest." He is Archivist Emeritus of the Archdiocese of Los Angeles, and by common accord the most knowledgeable living scholar of California's ecclesiastical history. Ordained in 1959, since that time he has celebrated Mass at a great many California locations, including Santa Cruz Island, and has been a tireless and effective spiritual and intellectual leader at San Fernando Mission. Msgr. Weber, in addition to his many local duties, serves as an Honorary Chaplain to His Holiness Pope Francis. Few historians ever get to see a major research archive built to their own specifications, much less one with their own personal, built-in "research cave," but for Francis J. Weber, this dream came true for him at Mission San Fernando, Rey de España, in 1980. He is still there at the Archival Center, thirty-six years

later, accompanied by his faithful dog (Shelty No. 7) *Wild Bill Cody*, just slightly younger (in dog years) than the Monsignor himself.

Weber is widely published on Spanish Colonial history, ecclesiastical history, and the history of California and the West. His books include: *The California Missions as Others Saw Them, 1786-1842* (1972), *A Select Bibliography of California Catholic Literature, 1856-1974* (1974), *The Life and Times of Fray Junípero Serra* (1987), *The Mission in the Valley: A Documentary History of San Fernando, Rey de España* (1987), *Century of Fulfillment: The Roman Catholic Church in Southern California 1840-1947* (1990), *Prominent Visitors to the California Missions, 1746-1842* (1991), *Memories of an Old Mission: San Fernando, Rey de España* (1997), *The Literary High Spots of Mission Hills, California* (1998), *Cathedral of Our Lady of the Angels* (2004), *The California Missions* (2005), *Catholic Heroes of Southern California* (2007), *Blessed Fray Junípero Serra: An Outstanding California Hero* (2008) and *More Memories of an Old Country Priest* (2011), to name just a few. Monsignor Weber is such a prolific writer that his 30+ years of newspaper columns were updated and republished in the year 2000 in an 1148-page volume (*Encyclopedia of California's Catholic Heritage, 1769-1999*), and the complete listing of his early publications, the 1995 hard-cover book *A Bibliographical Gathering: The Writings of Msgr. Francis J. Weber, 1953-1993* extends to a whopping 270 pages. In order to accommodate the 23 years of publishing since, a second volume is obviously indicated. Weber's present writing task is the third volume in his *Memories of an Old Country Priest* series.

The Los Angeles Corral of Westerners is proud to claim many outstanding members who have made their mark in educational, literary, and bibliographical contexts, above and beyond their service to our organization. Nevertheless, a very few illustrious members stand head and shoulders above the rest of us. Monsignor Francis J. Weber is just such a Westerner, and we hereby resolve, in the 70th year of our existence, that his name should join the ranks of our *"Living Legends."*

Brian Dervin Dillon, Ph.D.

Deputy Sheriff,

Los Angeles Corral of Westerners

October 29, 2016

Locations of Westerners Corrals

୨୦ ଏଏ

A FIVE-FOOT SHELF OF WESTERNERS

Prominent Historians

of the

Los Angeles Corral

of

The Westeners

Published as Keepsake #45
for the members of the
Los Angeles Corral
2017

Appendix IV

A Five-Foot Shelf of Westerners

**Prominent Historians
of the
Los Angeles Corral**
Based on a talk by *Phil Brigandi*
Presented September 14, 2016

In 2016, The Los Angeles Corral Of The Westerners celebrated its 70th anniversary. Seventy years is a long time, but I think sometimes we don't appreciate what seventy years means going in the other direction, backwards to 1946.

Think about this – we had members in the 1940s and '50s who could remember the Civil War. We had members who worked with Edward S. Curtis. We had members who met Chief Joseph, and John C. Fremont. And we've had many, many members who were prominent historians.

The key word here is "prominent." These are historians who were not just known among their peers, but recognized by readers for their knowledge and contributions. I suspect you all have some of their books on the shelf at home – and if you don't, you need to get crackin'!

I've selected just two dozen of them to highlight here (or this list could go on forever). Each entry includes a few biographical notes and a sampling of some of their books. There are also references to published biographies, bibliographies, and book reviews from the Corral's own publication, *The Branding Iron*.

FRANCIS J. WEBER (1933 –)

He is, as he likes to say, just an old country priest. He was also archivist for Archdiocese of Los Angeles for decades and administrator of Mission San Fernando. It's a good thing Msgr. Weber is also a bibliographer, because no one else could have kept track of all the books and articles he's published over more than half a century. Naturally, the California Missions and our local Catholic history fill much of that shelf, which includes biographies of California's early Bishops and his documentary history of the California Missions. And that's not even counting more than 130 miniature books he's written and his 33 years as a columnist for *The Tidings*. He served as our Sheriff in 1995 and as editor of Brand Book #21.

A Biographical Sketch of Right Reverend Francisco Garcia Diego y Moreno, First Bishop of the Californias, 1785–1846 (Los Angeles: The Borromeo Guild, 1961)

California's Reluctant Prelate: The Life and Times of Right Reverend Thaddeus Amat, CM. (1811–1878) (Los Angeles: Dawson's Book Shop, 1964) Based on his Master's thesis for the Catholic University of America.

Documents of California Catholic History (1784–1963) (Los Angeles: Dawson's Book Shop, 1965)

Readings in California Catholic History (Los Angeles: Westernlore Press, 1967) A collection of Weber's columns from *The Tidings;* it has been followed by (as of 1994) by a dozen subsequent collections.

The Missions and Missionaries of Baja California (Los Angeles: Dawson's Book shop, 1968) Baja California Travel Series, Vol. 11

Documentary History ... of the California Missions (compiler) (N.p.: Francis J. Weber, 1975–96) Collections of historical accounts of each of the California Missions, plus volumes on their Asistencias and Estancias, the Presidio Chapels, and a bibliography – twenty-five volumes in all.

Prominent Visitors to the California Missions (Los Angeles: McNally & Loftin Publishers, 1991) Review: Spring 1992 Twenty-four eyewitness accounts from 1786 to 1842.

A Centennial History of The Tidings (Mission Hills: Saint Francis Historical Society, 1995) Review: Fall 1998

Encyclopedia of California's Catholic Heritage, 1769-1999
(Mission Hills and Spokane: St. Francis Historical Society
and The Arthur H. Clark, 2001)
Review: Spring 2002
A thousand-plus pages of entries on the people, events, and
institutions that make up the history of the Roman Catholic
Church in our State.

Cathedral of Our Lady of the Angels
(Mission Hills: Saint Francis Historical Society, 2004)

A History of the Archdiocese of Los Angeles
(with Hermine Lees and Sister Joanne Wittenburg SND)
(Strasbourg: Editions du Signe, 2006)
A Spanish language translation has also been published.

Sunday and Feastday Homilies – Years A-B-C
(Strasbourg: Editions du Signe, 2016)

See Also:
Memories of an Old Country Priest
(Mission Hills: Saint Francis Historical Society, 2000),

More Memories of an Old Country Priest
(Mission Hills: Saint Francis Historical Society, 2011), and

Final Memories of An old Country Priest
(Mission Hills: Saint Francis Historical Society, 2017)

*A Bibliographical Gathering: The Writings of Msgr. Francis J.
Weber, 1953–1993*
(Mission Hills: Saint Francis Historical Society, 1995)

The Branding Iron
Spring 2006 – 2018
Memories of his first 35 years with The Westerners.

Appendix V

New Year Spectacle

The New Year of 2018 had a rocky beginning here at San Fernando Mission. I had just returned from breakfast with a few of our daily Mass crowd when the gardener, John De Fino, told me that he had discovered smoke coming from the *convento* building.

The Fire Department and I arrived about the same time to see billows of smoke rolling out of the entrance way to the Wine Cellar. Quick attention by the firemen saved one of Southern California's famed historical landmarks. Though the damage was substantial, the 200+ year old building remains intact for yet another generation of visitors.

There was other damage. At least five sprinkler devices had been torn apart and rendered useless. Some statuary was broken beyond repair and numerous floral containers trashed – all evidence of a concerted effort to severely damage the structures and contents of California's seventeenth mission.

Fortunately, the culprit was caught on film. She (Jenny Marie Sugar) was a relatively young lady who had climbed over a retaining wall into the lawn area in front of the Guard House.

Her many destructive activities were recorded on one or the other of the areas covered by the mission's 24-hour film system. She had arrived about 9 o'clock on New Year's Eve, gradually working her way up and down the far western grounds of the mission for the next 12 hours.

In addition to trashing the area, the unexpected guest seems to have had a fascination with fire. She is shown on film trying unsuccessfully to ignite the doorposts of the wine cellar.

Unfortunately, she was successful igniting a small conflagration from items pushed into the cellar area. Several chairs were burned almost beyond recognition and the doorposts smoldered for several hours.

The arsonist remained here until the Fire Department arrived. Somehow she managed to walk through their midst and across the street to Brand Park where she eluded the police who were following her.

Happily the Fire Department was able to extinguish the fire, leaving only black marks on the outside of the *convento* and a very unpleasant odor inside.

When nightfall came, I suggested that we needed someone on the grounds should the arsonist return. Those who commit crimes are known to return to the scene of their transgression.

Don Towell and his faithful "policedog" spent the night here and, once again, the little lady appeared, this time, looking for "something she had left behind on her last visit."

Knowing who she was, Mr. Towell let her into the garden and called the police. Arriving within minutes, the police quickly took her into custody. Two days later she was arraigned on a multitude of charges.

Fortunately the facilities at San Fernando Mission are well insured. Within a few hours agents were here appraising the smoke and fire damage. A crew was busy at work for the rest of month.

Once again, the *convento* was spared. It has survived two major earthquakes, and a myriad of mishaps bruised but intact. Thank you Lord for watching over us.

The Police Report reads as follows:

> **The suspect is Jenny Marie Sugar, white female, 5′6″, 200 lbs, age 30. She currently is in jail custody with no bail granted. Sugar has been charged with arson (Penal Code 451 (c); vandalism**
>
> **(PC 594) (a); and malicious mischief (PC 594.3 (a) under court case PA090166 in San Fernando Superior Court.**
>
> **Her next court dates are January 16th for an early disposition Hearing, and January 18th for a preliminary hearing.**

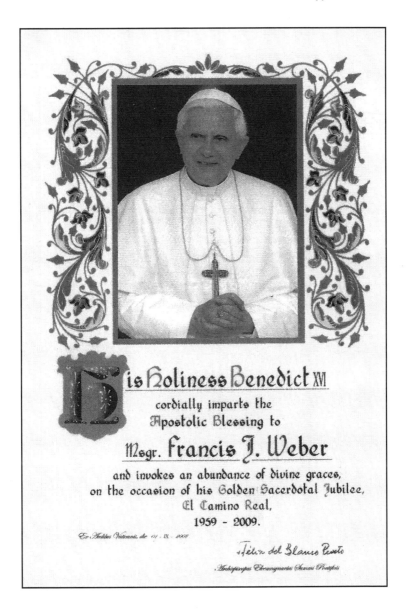

His Holiness Benedict XVI

cordially imparts the
Apostolic Blessing to

Msgr. Francis J. Weber

and invokes an abundance of divine graces,
on the occasion of his Golden Sacerdotal Jubilee,
El Camino Real,
1959 - 2009.

Ex Archivio Vaticanis, die 04 . IX . 2008

Felix del Blanco Prieto
Archiepiscopus Chronographus Sancti Pontificis

Appendix VI

Gratitude

I successfully wiggled out of receiving this distinction ten years ago. But this time I couldn't help but see a strange, maybe even spiritual relationship to each of the other recipients that occupy center stage today. All of which changes or at least updates my perspective.

First of all, Sister **Mary Elizabeth Galt** and I are both graduates of Saint Brendan's school in Hancock Park as well as disciples of that dynamic priestly giant, Msgr. Thomas Fogarty. She has been my canonical boss for many of my fifty-plus years as archivist for the archdiocese.

Then there is Msgr. **Richard Krekelberg** whom I taught in the minor seminary back in the Middle Ages. His brother, William, is archivist emeritus for the Diocese of Orange. The three of us traveled to the District of Columbia for the canonization of Fray Junípero Serra by Pope Francis in 2015.

Finally there is **Deacon Robert Seidler** who has served many years in the Regional office for San Fernando Valley as an associate to Bishop Joseph Brennan. He is part of the O'Malley clan who brought the Dodgers to Los Angeles.

I am among that vanishing species of clergy in this archdiocese known as a "lifer," one who has experienced the entire gamut of seminary training from high school to ordination.

It was 72 years ago, almost to the day, that I entered Los Angeles College, then the minor seminary, located at 241 South Detroit Street. Twelve years later I was ordained and then came more years of graduate study. Finally, just to round out my clerical education, and probably as a penance for my sins, I was sent to Queen of Angels Seminary where I taught history for another decade.

I left my footprints on local seminary history by writing two chapters on the seminary as I experienced it in my autobiography-but fret not that publication has not appeared yet on the *New York Times* best seller list.

Now, after almost sixty years of service to the People of God in the archdiocese, I am anticipating the day of my appearance before the Big Man in heaven.

When this old country priest is finally interred here at the Cathedral of Our Lady of Angels, I would unhesitantly say, for all the world to hear, **I would happily do it all over again. Seminary and all.**

Msgr. Francis J. Weber

Index

The Index was compiled by the printers of this book and does not follow the format used in the earlier volumes of *Memories*.